# Tom Crabtree on Teenagers

# Tom Crabtree on Teenagers

'I would there were no age between ten and three and twenty, or that youth would sleep out the rest; for there is nothing in between but getting wenches with child, wronging the ancientry, stealing, fighting.'
— The Shepherd in *The Winter's Tale* (III, iii)

Elm Tree Books
LONDON

First published in Great Britain 1980
by Elm Tree Books/Hamish Hamilton Ltd
Garden House 57-59 Long Acre London WC2E 9JZ

Copyright © 1980 by Tom Crabtree

British Library Cataloguing in Publication Data
Crabtree, Tom
    Tom Crabtree on teenagers.
    1. Adolescence
    301.43'15    HQ796
    ISBN 0-241-10398-3

Filmset by Pioneer
Printed and bound in Great Britain by
Redwood Burn Ltd, Trowbridge and Esher

Dedicated to the Crabtree family,
and its many colourful branches

# Contents

*Introduction*                                                    ix

1   Teenagers — What Do They Need?                                1
2   Growing Up and Reaching Out                                  12
3   Common Mistakes Parents Make                                 26
4   Parents Have Needs As Well                                   40
5   Reward and Punishment                                        50
6   Maladjusted Teenagers                                        64
7   Violence and Vandalism                                       71
8   Sex, Love and Relationships                                  86
9   The Pop Culture: Fashion, Music and Rebellion               102
10  The Education of Teenagers                                  118
11  Teenagers With Special Needs                                137
12  The Problem Page                                            152
13  Where's Father?                                             169
14  Conversations with Teenagers                                183

# Introduction

What is this book about?

It is about the youngsters of today, your teenagers and mine, trying to find their way into the adult world, bombarded by criticism from grown-ups.

Adults, believe me, have always been critical of young people. Aristotle, an ancient Greek philosopher, wrote of them: 'The young are permanently in a state resembling intoxication; for youth is sweet and they are growing.'

Plutarch, an ancient Roman, was dubious about them: 'The ripeness of adolescence,' he wrote, 'is prodigal in pleasures, skittish, and in need of a bridle.'

What about this, as a comment with an all-too-familiar ring?

You never see the old austerity,
That was the essence of civility,
Young people hereabouts, unbridled, now,
Just want.

Those words were written by Molière, a French playwright, in 1661.

I don't intend to add to this chorus of criticism. We hear plenty about youngsters who have 'gone off the rails'. This book discusses some of their problems. It also addresses itself to those thousands of youngsters who never make the headlines, never become delinquent, but get on with the difficult journey over that no-man's land between childhood and adulthood.

This book is about adolescents — young people not yet adult. Throughout, I refer to them as teenagers to emphasize that they are a product of our culture (and their own subculture) in our time. They are not the adolescents who lived in Greece before Christ; they are not living in the Victorian era; nor in the time when my father was alive. They are of now.

This is extremely important. The problems they face have never been faced before. The answers they come up with to life's difficulties must be new answers. We live in a time of accelerated change. Old values have died; new values must take their place, where necessary. It is today's teenagers who are at the forefront of that search for new (and, I hope, better) standards by which to live.

We have a tremendous duty towards them, the young in our midst. They are the next generation of parents. How *we* adults behave towards them will greatly influence how *they* (teenagers) will act out their future role as parents.

This book, then, is about a wide variety of young people: the good and the bad, the able and the less able, those who succeed, and those who fail.

They, today's teenagers, live in a complex world. They will find their way through it if we, adults, parents, teachers, members of the caring professions, are determined to help them and willing to understand them, as best we can.

It isn't easy; we can but try. Most important of all we can remember to enjoy ourselves whilst we're doing it. Teenagers have a great deal to offer us. We can learn a lot from them.

*Chapter One*

# Teenagers — What Do They Need?

Talking to a group of teenage schoolgirls recently I asked them: 'What do you need?' Immediately, their hands shot up in the air.

'Ten pounds, desperately,' said one. She didn't say what for.

'A new pair of jeans,' said another.

'A rest from homework,' said a third. I've noticed the same thing with other youngsters. If you ask teenage boys what they need, they tend to say a motorbike, some new clothes, money. One teenager told me that what he needed more than anything else was a girl to go out with.

With those schoolgirls there was a misunderstanding, and the fault was entirely mine. I really wanted to discuss basic needs rather than to ask them what they wanted at that particular moment.

What do I mean by basic needs? I would maintain that there is a list of things human beings cannot do without, and that list is very much the same whether you are a young child, a teenager, or an adult.

Let's consider the simple ones first. Everybody, I think we can agree, needs air, water, food, and a certain amount of physical comfort in order to survive. These are all physiological necessities and keep our bodies alive.

Besides those, we have safety needs. Like every other living creature, we try to avoid pain and discomfort. With human beings, who are more aware (thoughtful) than other animals, there is a need to live out our lives without being the victims of chronic anxiety or fear. We need to feel able to cope with life, and secure enough to deal with the troubles that will inevitably occur.

We all know people who worry too much. Thought, claimed Sigmund Freud, is a rehearsal for action. What we need to do is to think about a problem as clearly as we can, and then act. If we are too anxious, full of fear, we may expend all our energy on worrying about something and fail to take the right kind of action when the moment comes. Self-confidence, a feeling of safety, is vital to making the right decisions.

Besides the basic needs we have a large number of so-called secondary needs. These are mainly emotional and I think that they are just as important to human beings as physical needs. People, admittedly, can die through lack of air, food, or water; they can also die of a broken heart or loneliness.

Amongst our emotional needs is the need to belong: to be part of a group and to be accepted within that group. There are a very few human beings who are 'loners', who travel their own road, who do not seem to be dependent upon the approval and affection of others. Most adults, and nearly all teenagers, need the support which comes from being with others.

The first human group is the family and it is in the family that we first learn to be confident or fearful, to trust people or mistrust them, to love or to hate, to fight or be peaceful. If a child lives with love, he learns to love; if he or she lives with aggression, or malice or neglect he or she will learn to be aggressive, or malicious or neglectful. Our early experiences within the family can have a lasting effect on our outlook on life, on the roles we play in subsequent groups, and on our expectations of other people.

Having dealt with our primary (physical) needs and our 'secondary' (emotional) needs — like the need to belong and to feel safe — we can turn our attention to a whole variety of other human needs.

These have been called by the American psychologist Abraham Maslow *self-actualization* needs. What this means is that they are more to do with happiness than survival. They concern our self-image, our self-respect, and our efforts to make sense of the world, and a good job of being ourselves.

In a way, those jeans, new clothes, a rest from homework, a motorbike (and even Action man or a new doll for younger children) are all to do with self-actualization and the quality of life that youngsters lead, or want to lead. Those jeans are a symbol, possibly, of the sort of person that schoolgirl wanted to be: the image of herself she wanted to project to the world.

So it is when we buy new clothes (and many other things). I see myself as a pencil-slim, rather handsome, youngish man who is sartorially elegant. The mirror in my tailor's is no respecter of my self-image. The mirror reflects a golf-ball shaped individual, far from good-looking, middle-aged, and rather scruffy. No matter, throughout our lives we strive to be what we imagine to be our ideal selves. We struggle to achieve a part on Life's stage which we consider to be worthy of our potential.

Maslow was not really concerned with clothes. What he was concerned with was the individual's ability to be spontaneous, real, not 'phoney', and to be able to accept other people for what they

2

are, rather than shaping them into our own image. A self-actualized person is not cruel, or hypocritical, or selfish. He or she has some morals, thinks of others, has a sense of humour. Most of all, the self-actualized person is in the process of finding the very best person he or she is capable of being.

Anybody who is interested in reading Maslow should consult *The Farther Reaches of Human Nature* (Pelican Books) where his theories on achieving our best possibilities as human beings are set out. Suffice it to say here that *everybody wants to count for something* though what we count for, or want to count for, will differ from person to person.

Rather than think of human nature as static it is useful to see it as developing, growing. Our needs, when we begin life's journey, are very different from the needs we have at adolescence, or when we're adults, or when we're old. Our conflicts are different, our ambitions are different, our picture of ourselves is different. Yet, having said that, there are certain basic needs that (if we are able to satisfy them) make the journey through life a great deal more pleasant and enjoyable. Every child, in my opinion, requires:

1  To love, and be loved
2  To belong
3  To receive praise for his or her achievements
4  Some rules (a rough idea as to what is right and wrong)
5  Some pleasant experiences
6  Friends
7  Responsibility for someone or something
8  Self-respect
9  An identity of some sort
10  A certain amount of privacy from adults

'But,' you object, 'some of these needs are no different from the needs of adults. We all need to love and to be loved; we all need an identity; we all need privacy from time to time.' That's true; the yearnings, frustrations and hopes of teenagers are nurtured in the same common soil of humanity as our own. What is different about them, as teenagers, is the way they go about fulfilling their needs.

An example should help to make the point clear. I recently visited a disco to collect my teenage daughter. It was held in a large hall in which nearly 1,000 youngsters were dancing to a (very loud) hit record. The noise was deafening. Nobody could hear what anybody else was saying, and nobody seemed to care. Dazzling red, green, blue and yellow stroboscopic lights flashed on and off and the heat and hub-bub were overwhelming. I retreated hastily to the door marked 'Exit'. I'd been foolish enough to step into the teenage world and it was too much for me. I was glad to get outside, into the fresh air, and the peace and quiet.

After ten minutes my daughter emerged, smiling and not at all tired. She'd enjoyed it all, responding to the rituals and symbols of the current teenage world, the 'in' dances, the music, the mono-syllabic conversation. I felt an outsider and, of course, I was. It was not my scene.

'Pretty hot in there,' I said to my daughter, as she emerged. I didn't mention the questions that were really in my mind: how on earth do you find out what anybody looks like without dragging them under the purple light to see if they have spots? And another: how in heaven's name can anybody make out what anybody else is saying?

'It's different than it was in your day,' said my daughter. That put me in my place. In her search for identity, in her bids to foist off boredom, in her efforts to find a group to which she belonged, she wanted to do it her way, to make her own judgements, her own mistakes. I'm sure that if I had said that the disco appeared to me to be a terribly noisy, meaningless way of spending an evening, she would have been even more keen on it.

Who am I? This is the crucial question in the mind of the teenager and, to find the answer to the question, they have to experiment, to explore, and to 'try on for size' different person-alities, and different social groups. That disco visit, short though it was, had given me a glimpse of the PRIVATE — NO ADULTS world of the teenager.

In experimenting with personality, in trying to find appreciation, a place in a group, and status, the teenager may make choices which appear to adults to be quite alarming. A mother came to see me and told me that her son, aged seventeen, a shy and retiring lad, had recently joined a gang of Hell's Angels. What should she do about it?

She had, apparently, been sitting on the beach with her husband (they lived in a seaside town) when the Hell's Angels group roared up on their motorbikes, parked them on the promenade, and sat on the beach amongst the holiday crowds. There they all were, the Hell's Angels, dressed in studded, black leather jackets with clusters of metal badges on the lapels, or in torn denim jackets with stick-on cloth badges and crude slogans written on their backs with felt-tip pens. Their motorbike helmets, insignia and leather boots frightened the mother: she considered the Hell's Angels to be anti-social, sometimes violent, a group apart. To her horror she then saw her son sitting in the middle of the group, wearing a greasy T-shirt, a red-and-white polka-dotted sweat scarf and the regulation leather jacket, jeans, and long leather boots.

'It's really awful how he's changed,' his mother told me tearfully. I agreed he'd changed (I'd known the boy some time); however, I felt that the lad had changed for the better in some ways. Whereas, before, he's been excruciatingly withdrawn, he was now, in my view, much more outgoing and confident of himself. I think — in his own mind — he'd found some of the status and recognition he'd been seeking.

It's difficult to tell a mother like that what to do. Let's face it, that seventeen-year-old *did* get something out of belonging to that particular group. The motorbikes symbolize power, virility, autonomy ('doing your own thing'). The group had a strict code of behaviour which was enforced (though not necessarily a code of which adults would approve) and its rituals and symbols gave this lad a feeling of belonging. Symbolism and ritual are vitally important and deeply comforting to human beings: for this teenager the Hell's Angels were the people who provided him with both.

I'm not singing a hymn of praise to Hell's Angels or any other particular group. I'm pointing out an obvious truth: if we adults don't provide youngsters with action and excitement then they'll find action and excitement of their own. It had never occurred to this particular mother that his newly-found friends provided her son with both a role and a challenge: two essential ingredients in the mixture by which teenagers (and adults) concoct for themselves a little self-respect.

With teenagers, there is the space in which *they* live, there is the space in which we adults live, and there is the space we share — occupy together. How can we build a bridge towards that river-bank on which they live without intruding too much into their space?

The first thing is very simple to suggest, slightly harder to put into practice. It is: ENCOURAGE THEM TO DEVELOP THEMSELVES AS PERSONS. We can do this by giving them something to do, something which will enhance and build up their skills, and praise them when they do well at it.

A nation-wide project which is aimed at building up the character and resourcefulness of young people is the Duke of Edinburgh Award Scheme. There are three Awards — bronze, silver and gold — and they may be attempted, respectively, after the fourteenth, fifteenth and sixteenth birthday. The main sections of each Award are *Service, Expeditions, Interests* and *Design For Living* (girls) or *Physical Activity* (boys).

From activities such as care of animals, child care, coastguard service, community service and cycling proficiency, to expeditions carried out by small groups of young people on their own for example, camping and exploring in unknown country, the scheme

5

provides young people with challenge and excitement. In my opinion we need more schemes of this type, starting at an earlier age, which will give youngsters a chance to meet real challenges and learn to overcome them. The bored youngster is, as we all know, the youngster who is most likely to get into mischief or to end up on the wrong side of the law.

Let us now get down to the home situation and try and find out what it is that teenagers require from the family. I asked one mother what she thought her teenage children needed from her. 'Mainly money,' she said. 'They use the house as a hotel, and the only time they ever really talk to me is to complain about something or ask for something.' A not-very-inspiring picture. Is there an obligation on the part of teenagers to take some responsibility in the home?

I think there is. Teenagers are a part of the basic human group, the family. They should contribute something to that group: they should give as well as take, and I'm not thinking about family finances.

In our family we have an institution known as 'Day of Hell'. On that day, one member of the family is responsible for cooking and serving breakfast, tidying the house, and preparing and serving the evening meal. This system started when my youngest daughter was ten years old. When I suggested that she could be excused from it, she was most indignant. 'My scrambled eggs are the best in the house,' she said.

We've stuck with this system through the years (admittedly we have three children and this makes it mathematically easier since it only applies to the five days from Monday to Friday, inclusive. At weekends we have a more flexible approach since most members of the family want to do their own thing). It is surprising how active participation in the running of the home quickly disabuses youngsters of the notion that the home is a holiday inn, which supplies meals on demand.

I must admit, too, that there were arguments when the scheme first started. Somebody would leave dishes unwashed, and the person on duty the next day would (quite justifiably) grumble about his or her not doing the job properly. Now the scheme works well. Everybody has learned to cook, and to do housework. There has been participation by everybody. The alternative, as I see it, is an unfair work-load on one member of the family, or, worse, a chaotic, resentful, argumentative atmosphere in which nothing gets done at all.

The role of parents with regard to teenagers is quite different from their role with infants. In his novel, *East of Eden*, John Steinbeck says: 'The greatest terror a child can have is that he is not loved, and rejection is the hell he fears.' As children grow into adolescence they still need, from their parents, expressions of love and affection. But most of all they need friendship, and they want that friendship to be expressed in practical ways.

The notion of friendship is critical in dealing with teenagers. Infant children need, above all, a stern kindness (or kind sternness), based on love, and such children expect, and need, to be told what to do. There are many occasions on which it is essential to tell teenagers what to do; at other times it may be necessary to negotiate with them. I believe, strongly, that with the teenage child we must learn to *negotiate rather than dominate*. As in all negotiations between human beings, it is useful to start off on a basis of friendship rather than distrust, or dislike.

Consider the thorny question of teenage parties. A teenage girl asks her mother if she may have an all-night party. The mother will not allow it, and there are three reasons for her decision: 1. the parents do not want to go away for the weekend — the party is to be on a Saturday night, and they object to not being allowed to have a good night's rest; 2. the neighbours might object to the noise; 3. dishes and glasses, or furniture, might get broken by the late-night revellers. The mother says 'No'. We cannot quarrel with that. The mother has thought about it; parents *do* have the right to say no and that is the mother's decision.

Other parents vary in their attitude to teenage parties. Some lay down the law and forbid them, whatever the circumstances. Others take themselves off to friends or relatives, and leave the teenagers to it. I think that both of these (extreme) attitudes do not bear in mind that this is an issue that needs some thought, and open discussion.

My own view of teenage parties is that they have to take place after negotiation as to what is acceptable, and what isn't. There have to be some rules, some limits, and whatever rules are negotiated (the fewer the better) they have to be adhered to.

Every group of human beings, whether large or small, needs a set of rules in order to survive. I do not think that families get very far unless they have some rules: mainly to do with courtesy and consideration for others. Parties are a good instance of situations in which adults have to make clear (beforehand) what they think the limits of behaviour must be.

In my own family we allow teenage parties. Both parents go out until midnight; we then mingle with the guests, after that we go to bed. Any glasses or crockery broken must be paid for. If there is any damage to furniture or house fittings there are no more parties. In fact, most of these social occasions have been great fun, and the teenagers have enjoyed them without doing any damage to themselves, or others, or our property. Alcohol is not banned; most of the guests are eighteen so it is up to them not to drink too much and disgrace themselves.

This may appear lax. It is not meant to be another instance of Do As You Like: I think *that* reveals a lack of real concern. On the other hand we cannot watch over teenagers twenty-four hours a day, and we have to learn to trust them. 'What happens if a girl gets pregnant because of drinking too much alcohol at a party?' is a question I am often asked. My answer to that is if a teenage girl wishes to get pregnant she will do so whether there is alcohol about or not; if she has a real sense of responsibility to others, and respect for her parents, she is unlikely to become so drunk as to lose her self-control.

I should add that my own children's parties finish when they want them to finish but we, the parents, are on the premises, just in case of trouble. I would not ban teenage parties, but I think I have a right to know what they will entail and how much they are likely to inconvenience me. Parents must make their own decision and, whatever the answer, give good reasons for their decision.

Another word about rules. When my children were infants we used to have an attractive Dutch au pair named Cecille. (It was surprising how many young doctors came to the house to ask my advice when Cecille lived with us. I did notice, though, that after a few minutes each would ask the same question: 'Is Cecille in?'.)

Cecille was eighteen, and I had told her that she was to be home by 11 p.m. on weekdays, and midnight on Saturday. Was she resentful about these rules?

Cecille is now married with children of her own. When I saw her recently she told me: 'I liked those rules telling me what time I had to be back from a night out. It showed you cared about me.'

When we, as parents, let youngsters do as they like is it because we don't have any real care, any respect, for them? Or is it because we are afraid of our own children? Negotiation is better than domination but, however liberal and understanding you are, there will be times when you will have to put your foot down. When these times come, when you feel strongly about something, the only advice I can give you is to have the courage to put your foor down very firmly!

A sixteen-year-old boy is told by his parents that he cannot, especially during term-time, stay out until the early hours of the morning. He has to be back at home at a reasonable time if he is to cope with homework, school and forthcoming examinations.

What is a reasonable time? There is no rule of thumb on this. That is for each and every family to decide, having *listened* to the teenagers' points of view. Once a rule is made it should be stuck to;

all rules are meant to do is to help people to live together more easily.

Listening to youngsters is terribly important. I wish I had a pound note for every teenager who has said to me: 'My parents never listen to a word I say.' These youngsters are not idiots; they often have fresh, original and interesting opinions on various issues. Like adults, they are not always right. Right or wrong, they will certainly respect us more if we have the courtesy to listen, rather than talk.

With teenagers, as with our adult friends, it is important to act naturally, to be open and honest, and to try to be ourselves, warts and all. The teenager who has Florence Nightingale for a mother and Sigmund Freud for a father is being cheated out of real parents.

When we are honest, when we are able to admit our faults to our own children, we give them a chance to be honest back: to be real, rather than pretend to be the person we have concocted for them. In their search for identity, teenagers do not wish to be confronted with parents who are perfect, who have no defects. This would not only be a tremendous burden to them: it would also give them very little practice in relating to the majority of the human race (who are far from perfect). In a good relationship there should never be any need to pretend.

Having said that, I don't think that we should try to understand completely each and every facet of the teenager's personality. We can be friendly without trying to be amateur psychoanalysts. Curiously enough, teenagers have a need to be *mis*-understood. They don't want their every thought, action and motivation chewed over by anxious or over-analytical parents. No human being completely understands another and it is part of life that there will be areas of the characters of our friends, and our children, that will remain something of a mystery to us. Why should this be so awful? We cannot understand everything, and it makes people more interesting if we do not know everything about them.

Teenagers need privacy, and a chance to work things out for themselves. Being told about something is no substitute for first-hand experience. Even when they go wrong, and are hurt in a relationship, teenagers will not automatically wish to discuss the matter with their parents. (They may prefer to talk it over with friends of their own age group.) Should we, then, stand by and watch them being hurt?

Sometimes we may have to, especially in affairs of the heart. It is in their emotional relationships that teenagers are most vulnerable; and it is in this area of their lives that they often insist on privacy. If they don't want to take us into their confidence, if they have a

KEEP OUT sign up, there is nothing we can do other than respect their wishes, and be ready to give sympathy or advice only if asked.

It is one of the hardest things to do to be passive if one can see a son or daughter being hurt emotionally, but most teenagers want to live their own love-life and they will learn about emotional pain as we learned: the hard way. This is not an area in which parents can be too dogmatic or interfere too readily. Because of the teenager's natural tendency to rebel against parents, too much interference may well result in their doing precisely the opposite of their parents' wishes.

This is what I call the Iron Filings Law: if we go north they go south. If we are well-dressed, they are scruffy. If we are tidy, they are untidy. When I let my hair grow long I noticed that my son had his cut very short! On this basis, there is a certain amount of psychology needed in getting youngsters to behave in certain ways. For example, when my wife and I took to swearing during mealtime conversations I noticed that all three of our children forsook swearing and have never sworn since.

I cannot advocate that, in order to persuade our children to be well-dressed, we should go about like tramps. I merely think it is useful to observe this law of opposites: the tendency towards polarization.

Thus it becomes obvious why it is unwise, for instance, to tell a daughter that her boyfriend is highly unsuitable. This may be exactly the comment she needs to persuade her to forego her usual commonsense criteria and to take the relationship further. If nothing is said, she will find out herself whether he is suitable or not. She will judge him by her own standards, and her own emotional needs: the issue of defiance, doing the opposite of what you're told, will not enter into it. Similarly, these parents who identify too much with their teenage children's friendships may find that, to pay them for their excess of curiosity, the teenagers begin to choose the most bizarre friends merely to shock the parents. The parents then react, the teenager brings home even worse friends and a massive barrier is erected between parents and youngster.

In Ancient Greece, Socrates was put to death for corrupting the young. He was made to drink the fatal dose of hemlock because he had had the temerity to suggest that young people should think for themselves.

I think Socrates was right. Today, when youngsters have so much freedom, so many choices to make, it is vital that they learn to take a measure of responsibility for themselves, and are encouraged to act in ways which will not damage themselves or others. Parents, in helping teenagers to prepare for adult life, should adopt a socratic rather than an autocratic attitude towards them. Adult dogmatism, arbitary rules and regulations, stand a fair chance of being rejected. Adult sympathy, a willingness to listen and to give advice and practical help when asked, stands a much better chance of being accepted.

Verbal advice, telling people what to do, has its limitations. It is much better to find out about life for oneself, with appropriate guidance from not-too-intense adults. I suspect that one good club joined, or a new friend, is more useful to a teenager than hours spent discussing emotional problems with parents. There is now a whole network of community facilities available to teenagers, youth clubs, sports centres, leisure centres, the Youth Hostel Association, rambling clubs, motorbike clubs, evening classes, church groups, motorbike groups, cycling clubs and many associations and schemes. Helping others (young children in playgroups, or the elderly, or the mentally or physically handicapped) is a very good way for teenagers to get their own personal problems into some kind of wider perspective. Our job, as parents, is to get the youngster into social settings where he or she is happy and achieving something. It is not to over-advise, not to reduce the teenager to a patient on the couch. Action, for them, will always count more than our words.

*Chapter Two*

# Growing Up and Reaching Out

Alison and Mark are two teenagers. They have relatives who live abroad in Australia. The aunt and uncle haven't seen their niece or nephew for five years. When they come over to this country, on a visit, they are both amazed at the changes that have taken place in the two children.

Alison, for instance (now sixteen, she was aged eleven when her relatives last saw her), is five feet nine inches tall, takes size eight shoes (the same as her mother) and has the figure of a mature woman. Her face has changed, her voice is softer and deeper, and she wears the latest fashions. 'We didn't recognize her,' say her relatives.

Hardly surprising, since the last time they both set eyes on her she was a tubby little girl with a squeaky voice and an abiding interest in her bicycle, her hamsters and her guinea pigs.

Mark has changed equally dramatically. He was a skinny, freckle-faced twelve-year-old when his relatives last saw him: a boy obsessed by his model aeroplane and electric train set. He is now, at seventeen, six feet tall; a handsome young man with a passion for motorbikes and rock music. Mark is, to an outside observer, a fully-grown adult. 'Isn't he good looking?' comments his aunt to his uncle.

What has happened to Alison and Mark during those five years? They have been on a journey called adolescence; many changes have taken place in them on the way; their destination is sexual and emotional maturity.

I want to take a look at a sketch map of this journey and to point out some of the *physical, intellectual, emotional* and *social* changes that take place in young people along the way. These are the four main aspects of the youngsters' development.

First of all, physical development. The years from twelve to eighteen are usually thought of as the years of puberty (which simply means that a person becomes capable of procreation). Girls, on average, reach puberty eighteen months to two years earlier than boys, though there are enormous individual differences.

A girl may have her first period as early as nine or ten, or as late as seventeen or eighteen. Some boys at fourteen are sexually mature; others do not reach sexual maturity until the age of eighteen or nineteen.

During puberty, the pituitary gland — situated at the base of the brain — stimulates the endocrine glands to pour various chemical substances, hormones, into the bloodstream. The pituitary gland is the leader of the endocrine orchestra and co-ordinates the pattern of hormonal activity. This pattern determines the young person's physical growth.

In girls, the ovaries secrete oestrogen: this leads to development of the breasts and initiates the menstrual cycle; in boys, the testes secrete testosterone which causes growth of the pubic hair, and of the penis.

Since the testes, like the ovaries, develop considerably during puberty, the amount of testosterone produced causes marked changes in a boy's physical appearance. It stimulates growth of facial and axillary (i.e. armpit) hair, plus the growth of bones and muscles. The extra growth in height of boys during puberty is due to the secretion of testosterone.

The same is true of muscular strength. Girls have a small increase of muscle growth at puberty, caused (like the growth of their pubic and axillary hair) by hormones secreted by the adrenal glands. The increase in strength is nothing like that of boys who, for example, increase the power of their arms two and a half times during this period of development.

In early puberty, or pubescence, growth is centred on the extremities of the body: the neck, the arms and the legs, rather than the trunk. This explains the awkward, gangling, 'coltish' look so characteristic of young teenagers. At this stage, the boy's shoulders broaden and the girl's pelvis becomes larger and her hips become rounder.

There are changes in proportion of both the face and the body. The nose and chin become more pronounced. Girls develop a layer of subcutaneous fat which softens the contours of the face and the body. With boys, and their greater development of muscle and bone, there may be a leaner, more angular look but (with the hands, feet and nose all rather large in proportion to the rest of the body) there is still an odd appearance about the youngster.

The endocrine glands, the thyroid, the adrenals and the gonads (i.e. the sex glands), the testes in males and the ovaries in females all secrete hormones which have profound effects on the nervous system. So, in addition to marked bodily changes, the young adolescent may have to cope with disturbed emotions and rapid changes in mood. There is, with many adolescents, a feeling of unrest as the major adjustments take place within his or her body.

Let us chart the changes that have taken place in Alison over the last five years. Three weeks after her twelfth birthday she had her first menstruation (for which she had been prepared by her parents. I shall have more to say on this subject when we discuss Sex, Love and Relationships in Chapter 8). Her breasts have rounded, causing her some slight discomfort. She has axillary and pubic hair and the internal organs of her body have undergone dramatic change.

Alison's heart has grown larger, her stomach has elongated and the rest of the digestive system has grown in proportion. Her sweat glands have become very active leading to constantly damp hands and feet together with recurrent worries over 'B.O.' and personal hygiene. The increase in the length of her arms, and in the size of her feet, embarrass her and presents a problem with jackets and shoes which she has outgrown at an alarming (and expensive) rate.

It is Alison's nose which causes her most worry. She thinks it is too big, and she spends many hours in front of the mirror despairing over this obtrusive organ. Her mother has told her that, in a few years time, the same nose will be quite at home on a face which is of fully-adult proportions.

In addition to her nose, Alison is fretful about her skin. As her sebaceous glands become more active, producing an oily secretion, so the skin has undergone changes: the pores have enlarged, and the texture of the skin has become coarser. The result, in Alison's case (as with many teenagers) is acne (blackheads) and other facial blemishes, about which Alison is very self-conscious. She has searched for the right skin tonic soap or ointment to cure them with little success. Her mother pointed out, quite rightly, that such blemishes are temporary and the best cure for them is to splash the face with cold water after each and every wash.

Between the ages of twelve and thirteen Alison grew three-and-a-half inches in height. The next year she grew another three inches. These rapid growth spurts lead, as far as her mother was concerned, to a problem with food. 'My daughter,' her mother told me at the time, 'seems to spend most of the day looking for something to eat.'

Changes in the digestive system and in the metabolic rate (i.e. the speed at which chemical processes to maintain the function of the body take place) mean, inevitably, that Alison would be likely to eat more. She was growing — and growing fast!

To further reassure her mother, I told her the story of Klaus, a fourteen-year-old German boy who came to stay with us one summer. I was playing tennis with Klaus and, throughout the game, he was nibbling chocolate, apples, sweets and crisps. In the interval he bought himself a large ice-cream.

As soon as we arrived home after the game, Klaus headed straight for the kitchen, famished. 'What about fish fingers, Klaus?' I asked him. 'Fisch haff no fingers,' he replied despairingly. Klaus was always hungry. He did not have hollow legs. He was a six-foot boy with an enormous appetite, and very normal for his age group. Adolescents, as every parent of an adolescent knows, eat an enormous amount.

To summarize Alison's changes in her body: her pelvis has widened, her body has become more rounded and her breasts have enlarged. The areolae (the areas surrounding the nipples) have increased in diameter, become more deeply pigmented, and become elevated and more conical in shape. Alison, five years ago a child, is physically a woman. However, as I shall show later, she still has some distance to travel both emotionally and socially before she can claim to be fully adult.

What about Mark? What has been happening to him during the last five years?

Mark has a deep voice, and facial hair (he shaves every day). His hands and feet are enormous, compared to when he was twelve years old: he now takes size eleven shoes (yet another expensive item for parents). His genital organs have increased in size.

In boys, the development of the external genitalia is more obvious than in girls. The penis, together with the testicles and scrotum (the fleshy bag in which the testicles are held), increase in size and become more pendulous. The boy becomes capable of producing sperm cells; these need a constant temperature in order to survive (which is lower than body temperature) so that, as the temperature decreases, the testicles are drawn closer to the groin as a source of body heat. When the outside temperature increases, the testicles hang further away from the body. This is nature's way of providing a heat-regulating device to the sperm-producing part of the boy's body.

The shaft of the penis grows in length and circumference and the glans (the head of the penis) grows until, in many cases, it emerges from the foreskin. Boys tend to worry a great deal about penis size, and there is great individual variation in this aspect of the body's growth. It cannot be stated too strongly that the size of the penis, flaccid, is not related to the size of the penis when erect. Also, a larger penis can be accommodated by the woman's vagina as can a small penis; there is no relationship between penis size and the ability to satisfy one's partner during sexual intercourse.

The male sex hormone — testosterone — serves to increase the sexual and aggressive drives within the male. Erection of the penis is accompanied by strong feelings of sexual desire. Adolescent boys may have spontaneous emissions of semen ('wet dreams') during sleep. Ideally, the boy will have had, either at school or at home, some preparation for this event. It can be very upsetting to more sensitive youngsters who may feel that they cannot control their nocturnal emissions or erections and that these, occurring at frequent intervals, will in some way 'weaken their mind'. There is nothing either wicked or weakening about this 'rehearsal' functioning of the boy's sexual parts.

Although Mark, at fourteen, went through a very ungainly or 'gawky' stage his period of being an ugly duckling was relatively short. He did suffer from acne, and from food fads (very common amongst adolescents). He, like many youngsters, suffered from constipation, since he did not eat (about the age of fifteen) regular or suitable meals. However, since his mother insisted that he should eat vegetables, fresh fruit and plenty of 'roughage' (as provided in bran cereal) these helped to keep his digestive system in good order and helped to absorb and eliminate waste products within his body. The first good rule of a good complexion, and regular toilet habits, is a sensible diet.

Mark, at seventeen, rather than being an ugly duckling shows distinct signs of being a swan. His complexion is less spotty; his hair is glossier and more manageable; his body is less angular and far more graceful than it was at thirteen or fourteen. Mark's motor movements are better co-ordinated and he is beginning to appear quite graceful, despite being so tall.

Interestingly, it would have been possible to predict Mark's stature from the use of skeletal analysis techniques. These can be used to determine, and to forecast, the physiological growth of young people. This is because alterations in bone tissue (or ossification) show up clearly on X-ray photographs of the wrist-bones (or other parts of the skeleton).

Ossification has a positive relationship with (i.e. it provides a good clue to) sexual maturity. The adolescent's *bone age* increases in line with sexual development and girls are normally well ahead of boys in this respect. At seventeen, a girl's skeleton is almost fully developed. It is possible that Mark will not reach full skeletal maturity until the age of nineteen or twenty.

Mark's heart has grown larger during adolescence in proportion to his arteries and his veins, and his blood pressure has increased. His thyroid gland, situated in the throat, is sometimes slightly over-active, producing feelings of excitability and tension which have no apparent cause. They can, if they underfunction, lead to feelings of tiredness and lethargy.

The adrenal glands, located near the kidneys, are involved in fear and anger 'moods' (together with being responsible for the development of secondary sex characteristics and with the production of adrenaline and the stimulation of the sympathetic nervous system). Adrenalin is required when we want to summon up extra performance from the body, as we would if we entered a race. Too much adrenalin can make us anxious and lead to underfunctioning (as any youngster who has made a mess of an exam paper will know).

The pituitary gland, in the brain, the adrenals and the thyroid should work in harmony. During adolescence temporary disharmonies (mostly very slight) inevitably occur and the youngster is seen as being moody, offhand and 'difficult to handle'. Moods, and a certain amount of quarrelsomeness or withdrawal are part and parcel of the adolescent stage and, often, a reaction to the tremendous turbulence of bodily changes.

During adolescence the mind, too, grows up (though not completely: many of us, as adults, are prone to regress when angry, hurt or disappointed to more immature levels of behaviour). There is a growth in the *intellect* of the teenager marked by a greater capacity for abstract thinking.

In the process of becoming who he or she is, the teenager develops the power to compare and to contrast; to make assessments and judgements about situations and about people.

One of the consequences of this is that the adolescent scrutinizes his parents more closely, taking a good look at them (probably for the first time) and noticing that they have faults. The erstwhile perfect parent may be seen as insincere, or confused, or dishonest; certainly far from omnicompetent. It is one of the tasks of adolescence to see parents as they are (rather than what the youngster would like them to be) and still try to retain love and respect for them.

As the teenager's intellect develops he learns to act more purposefully, think more rationally, perceive more closely and to deal more effectively with the environment. The more stimulating his environment, the better the chance of his intelligence developing to its maximum capacity.

The Intelligence Quotient (IQ) of each individual is arrived at by the formula

$$\frac{\text{Mental Age}}{\text{Chronological Age}} \times 100$$

The mental age is gauged from the person's performance on an intelligence test. Most people have IQs between 85 and 115. Educationally-subnormal youngsters have IQs of 70 and below; gifted youngsters have IQs of IQ170+ and are 1 in 10,000 of the population at large.

I am very much against judging people by their IQ. It would be much more useful to gain a profile of an individual's abilities: to find out, in other words, just what it is that he can and cannot do. This gives us the information we need to help the youngster concerned (rather than giving IQ a god-like status and using this arbitary index of ability to label people).

We are beginning to realize the limitations of IQs and the British Intelligence Scale (an intelligence test now used in this country) does emphasize the profile approach. A youngster with a lowish IQ may be, for example, a brilliant mechanic, good with his (or her) hands; a non-scholastic boy or girl may be good practically, or in dealing with people. The academically-gifted child may be totally impractical. These are things we need to know if we are to get each and every youngster to make a contribution to society.

As the youngster's general intelligence develops he will show abilities which are, to some extent, not linked to his all-round capacity. One youngster will be good at maths, another hopeless; yet another good with words but unable to understand how the electric light works. The sort of abilities we need to look for in the young person include:

1  Verbal ability
2  Numerical ability
3  Spacial perception (i.e., seeing the relationships between areas and shapes: an ability used in, for example, dressmaking)
4  Manual dexterity
5  Mechanical aptitude
6  Musical and artistic ability

The job of parents and schools is, of course, to help the youngster to develop those abilities which he has, and to remedy the gaps in the young person's learning. This can be done without robbing young people of their confidence providing that each and every youngster is regarded as an individual with skills to offer to society.

It is very tragic when the youngster of eleven or twelve, who is not academically-minded, is sent to a grammar school (often as a 'border-line case'). Such youngsters usually end up struggling, somewhere near the bottom of the class, their self-confidence diminishing as the months go by. Nobody tells them what they are good at; what is emphasized is what they are bad at. Their suffering arises from a poor assessment, by the responsible adults, of the young person's own individual mix of abilities.

Liam Hudson, a British psychologist, has suggested* that young

*Contrary Imaginations, L. Hudson. Methuen, 1966

people can be divided into *convergers* (who do well on IQ tests but with relatively poor imaginativeness) and *divergers* (who do poorly on tests but who are very artistic and original in their thought). These two groups differ in their personalities and in the type of work that they are attracted to. Convergers will move towards such things as the physical sciences, accountancy and repetitive work; divergers will be attracted by the arts and working alongside other people.

Hudson found that convergers are more likely to show respect for authority, to adopt conventional attitudes and to avoid the expression of humour or violence. They differ, it is claimed, in the way they sleep and dream. Though these differences are interesting, it seems to me that we should always avoid putting labels on youngsters. Convergers/divergers, like introvert/extravert is, of course, too simple a dichotomy. The thing we must learn to do, as I have stressed, is to treat each person as an individual.

There is evidence that there are innate differences between the sexes with regard to performance on intelligence tests. Girls do better on verbal tests, especially in tests of verbal fluency, whilst boys succeed better on tests of spatial ability. However, these differences may well spring from cultural factors (i.e. the way we treat boys and girls, and our expectations of them) rather than from inborn factors. When it becomes widely accepted that girls will become engineers, pilots and doctors (whilst boys will move into domains previously reserved for women), these differences in the patterns of ability between the sexes may become less noticeable. Also, as social change accelerates — as social opportunity for girls and women increases — we should see an increase in the number of outstandingly creative and successful women who are recognized as such.

I have mentioned the development of abstract thinking during teenage. At the age of six a child might define a bicycle as: 'You ride it'. By adolescence, the bicycle is more likely to be defined as 'a machine' with a description of how it works and what it is for. The bicycle, in other words, belongs to a class of things. The teenager is able to relate the various aspects of his or her experience and becomes interested in (and can attempt to define) such abstract concepts as 'happiness', 'success', 'truth', and 'justice'.

There is, during adolescence, an increase in the capacity to understand poetry, allegory, cartoons, satire and 'double-meanings'. The youngster is able to stand outside his or her own experience, to make objective judgements and to ask such questions as: 'What sort of person do I want to be?' 'What is it I like about my friends?' 'What is it I like, or dislike, about myself?'

*Possibility* becomes as important as immediate reality. 'What can I be?' 'What ought I to be?' These are two questions that preoccupy adolescents as they reach out to expand their experience, sharpen their minds and 'get it together'.

The difference between what *is* and what *ought to be* (their own yearnings for an ideal world) can be a great source of disillusionment to the adolescent. The gap between reality and possibility, which yawns so wide during the teenage years, may explain why young people are drawn into areas which present them with an alternative world: films, pop stars, humorous TV programmes, even political activism. Many adults, it seems to the adolescent, are too complacent, too accepting of an imperfect world. The adolescent wants to change the world and make it better.

How to do that is not too clear, and the difficulty of creating excitement, stimulus, may be very frustrating to the adolescent, causing him or her to take long solitary walks, write poetry, become interested in politics, admire 'rebel' pop-stars who denigrate society or, perhaps, just stay at home and feel rather depressed or moody.

Many youngsters suffer from this kind of cosmic unhappiness — what the Germans call *Weltschmerz* (world pain) — and it may lead the adolescent into the plight of the oppressed, into religion, or into some other area where he or she can express the idealism and sensitivity that is often associated with the teenage years.

As their interests widen and change adolescents become capable, like Sherlock Holmes, of seeing the connection between things — of *hypothetico-deductive* thinking. They can pose alternative explanations to explain what they see and can dispose of those that seem wrong or do not fit the facts. This makes their thought much richer than that of, say, a ten-year-old who is more likely to take on trust the first explanation that presents itself.

Unlike the ten-year-old the teenager can take his own thoughts and think about them. He becomes much more critical of statements made by adults, and can ponder them and reason out why they are right or wrong. He learns to monitor his own arguments and can see if he has made a mistake in his reasoning. The adolescent, therefore, becomes more critical of his own thought processes, and of the logic of others.

Some parents find this hard to cope with. Instead of an accepting, non-critical child they are often faced with an argumentative, critical young person who wants to know the whys and wherefores of decisions. The only answer to this new situation is for parents to present the truth as they see it and to be prepared to give the reasons for their points of view. The 'because I say so' attitude may well work with the ten-year-old; it is unlikely to succeed with an all-too-aware teenager.

One of the needs of teenagers is intellectual stimulation. It is a great source of annoyance to many teenagers that their parents watch television so much and show so little interest in what is going on around them. Conversation over meals is a good way for teenagers to examine their ideas and test their reality. 'Television snacks' eaten whilst doing other things, are not a good way to encourage family discussions.

To get to know what is going on in their youngsters' minds parents have to be prepared to talk to teenagers, elicit ideas from them and, above all, listen to them. There is a danger that, during teenage, the physical, intellectual and emotional life show wide discrepancies: a youngster may be intellectually very bright but emotionally immature, or good at school work but socially very gauche and awkward. The teenager, because of the disparities in physical, intellectual, emotional and social development, needs constant support from his or her parents. Few teenagers that I know are, underneath, quite as confident as they look.

Now let us turn to the *emotional* development of teenagers and to some common signs of stresses and strain that accompany the dramatic changes going on in both their bodies and their minds.

Mark, you will remember, at the age of seventeen has the broad shoulders, fully developed sexual organs and the facial and bodily hair of a man. However, his emotional development is far from complete. He is still extremely self-conscious and unsure of himself. His mother says: 'He goes as red as a beetroot if Alison brings a new friend home and introduces her to Mark. It is then that I realize just how sensitive and shy he is and that he is still very much a teenager.'

It is the same with Alison. Her physical growth has (and this is usual with teenagers) been accompanied by a certain amount of emotional upheaval, as a recent letter about her from her mother reveals:

Alison is doing well in school now and has decided to go into the Sixth form and try for her A-levels.

She has a thing about her neck, which she thinks is too long (though I can't see anything wrong with it myself) and about the spots on her face. When we go on a bus, or go shopping together, she thinks everybody is looking at her!

She is still very untidy and her room looks like a jumble sale. She gets very upset if I shout at her and accuses me of 'going on and on'. Sometimes, she claims I don't care about her at all which is an awful thing to say, but she *is* very touchy and I only have to mention her neck or her wretched spots for her to burst into tears.

Alison is very keen on the church now and goes every Sunday morning to sing in the choir. She's in the church youth club and seems to be going through a religious phase. Where she gets it from I don't know as neither her father or I go to church.

She wants, at the moment, to buy a pony but I've told her we cannot afford it. It's a shame, really, as she is genuinely fond of animals (especially horses) and very good with them. She's still having riding lessons on Saturday mornings.

She's very moody and creates a terrible scene if Mark touches any of her things. Her bedroom is 'no-go' territory and she has a five-year diary in which (she tells me) she writes poems and all her secret thoughts. She hopes to sell them to a publisher at a later date — for an enormous sum of money!

She is into disco music and the latest fashions. We discuss clothes together and, sometimes, we're more like sisters than mother and daughter. One minute she seems like a grown woman, the next she's more like the little girl you used to know.

This letter illustrates some of the emotional characteristics of adolescents: *moodiness, a heightened sensitivity, self-consciousness* and *a need for approval* which goes along with *a fierce need for independence and privacy*. Also, there is a tendency towards *dramatization*: set-backs (such as a missing hair-brush) are seen as disasters; small victories (a compliment from an attractive member of the opposite sex) send the teenager straight up to Cloud Nine. *Daydreams* are an important part of adolescence as *ideals*.

An excellent portrait of an over-sensitive, lonely, rebellious adolescent is presented in J.D. Salinger's *The Catcher In The Rye*\*. Holden Caulfield is rebelling against the selfish materialism of modern society; his pet hate is people who are 'phonies' (which, as he sees it, most people are). Holden finds it difficult to communicate with others; he frequently telephones acquaintances (gives them 'a buzz') in a desperate attempt to establish some kind of contact with people. He has a desperate need to belong *and* to be himself. He ends up as he began, an outsider, and as unsure about himself as ever.

The great majority of teenagers are insecure; as they try to establish the parameters of their own personalities and seek a consistent identity, they need a great deal of reassurance from within the family and from friends of their own age group. More and more, it may seem to parents, the teenagers of today are the 'Me' generation: only interested in themselves.

Some parents claim that their youngsters do not appreciate the

---

\*Hamish Hamilton, 1951

sacrifices that adults have to make for them. 'I've worked hard to give them *their* chance in life,' a mother told me, 'but they (her teenage children) never help *me*.'

The teenagers, on the other hand, may feel that they are constantly criticized by adults, 'put down', never listened to. There are usually clashes between parent and adolescent over such matters as tidiness, pocket money, staying out late in the evening. To the teenager, the parent may seem at best parochial and, at worst, materialistic and with little understanding of the emotional needs of younger people.

In the transition from childhood to adulthood the adolescent faces some tricky emotional problems. If he or she accepts too readily the standards and behaviour of adult society then there is a chance that over-conformity, refusing to think for oneself, will lead to a shadowy Uriah Heap sort of youngster, lacking in personal integrity and individuality.

However, the opposite strategy — to rebel, and to drop out — has its own danger: that of rejection by the adults who have control over the society in which we live. 'I am going to set up an alternative way of living,' more than one young person has told me. This, sadly, is easier said than done. I have no doubt that *some* youngsters manage to set up alternative communities — living in a tepee in North Wales, 'squatting' in a London borough or settling down in a commune in Devon — but my own experience is that of youngsters who have found it difficult to avoid altogether the adult world that surrounds them.

Nobody wants youngsters who, by over-conforming, lose their own souls ('He was born a man, and died a grocer,' said Voltaire, referring to this loss of individuality.) At the same time, each one of us in society must play a role, must conform to some extent, this is the society we have; we must live in it; we can still try to change it for the better.

Erik Erikson, in his book *Childhood and Society**, outlines 'eight ages of Man'. Adolescence he refers to as the age of IDENTITY v ROLE CONFUSION. The young person must find an answer to the recurring question: 'Who am I?' At the same time he must conform to society (do his school work find a job, meet family demands) in ways which seem to blunt sensitivity and blur that inner picture of the 'real self'.

The answer, of course, is compromise: to accept the limitations imposed by the real world (since nobody is free to do as he likes: the needs of others have to be considered) and yet strive to

---

*Pelican Books, 1965

develop the central core of one's own being. This compromise is accepted by primitive societies: they give young adolescents 'freedom' — the opportunity to play — and yet expect conformity to the adult values of society when this period of experimentation is over. Similarly, communist countries encourage young people to be themselves, to use their own initiative, to take responsibility, *but* this freedom (and the sense of adventure it encourages) is later harnessed to the goals of society rather than being allowed to work against society.

Clearly, in the Western world, there are many organizations and schools which develop a sense of responsibility and team spirit in young people. The young person is not asked to lose his own soul; he is invited to find that soul in the service of his fellow human beings. This is, though, an area where many adults in our society fall down, by failing to stress that it is in service to others, rather than selfishness, that most satisfactorily develops the inner person.

The basic emotional needs of teenagers are really quite simple. They are: to love, and be loved; to belong; to be given some responsibility; to be accepted for themselves. I have listed these more fully in Chapter 1, and what I want to say here is that these needs can only be met by the group; whether it be the family, the school, the peer group or the world outside the front door. It is essential for a teenager to feel that he or she belongs to something or somebody and it is up to adults to provide the opportunity to young people to gain these feelings of belongingness in ways which are not anti-social.

What parents of teenage children have to do is to keep the lines of communication open between the two generations. Jaw-jaw is better than war-war and, after years of advising teenagers (and their parents), it seems to me that the constant complaint of youngsters is that their parents do not understand them. Alison and Mark, from time to time, show all the signs and symptoms of disturbed teenagers: anxiety, shyness, tantrums, moodiness, anti-social behaviour, solitariness and hypersensitivity. Their parents are not dismayed. They know these things will pass, their teenage children are destined to grow up into two well-balanced adults. During teenage, it is usual to be slightly abnormal and symptoms of stress come and go like the tides.

What should parents do to ensure that the emotional life of teenagers is as unfraught as possible? My advice is — listen to them. Believe me, very few of us parents listen and *listening* is the halfway house of understanding. Parents, in dealing with the emotions of teenagers, must learn to use their ears more and their mouths less.

It is clear that all teenagers have an inner, private world and a social world, the world shared with others. In an attempt to establish his or her adulthood, the adolescent shuffles back and forth between two different worlds: that of adults and that of his own age group. He spends less and less time at home; the family, once a major part of his world, is seen more as a base (secure or insecure) from which he can launch his personal plans and social ambitions. The family becomes background; friends, acquaintances, peer-group values come to the fore.

Nowadays, the values of the teenage group are manipulated by the mass media. Youngsters used to get their standards and values from the family, the neighbourhood. Do they now get them from newspapers, magazines, television? In my view, the effect of the media on youngsters is exaggerated, the lives of teenagers is the family and the standards and values picked up in the home tend to last whilst the group (and the media) has but a transitory, superficial impact on the youngster's inner world.

In Chapter 9 (The Pop Culture) I want to explore the world of the teenage group a little further. What I want to stress here is that the physical, intellectual, emotional and social development of the teenager are all closely interwoven, but it is the *emotions* which are of crucial importance. The basic emotions — fear, joy, love, hate, optimism and anxiety — are learned in the home. The home, as I shall stress in the rest of this book, is the major influence in a teenager's life. It is the parents who determine how the youngster looks out upon the world. It is the parents who act as the launching pad from which the teenager may follow his or her own star.

## Chapter Three

# Common Mistakes Parents Make

At heart, I'm sure all children would like their parents to be terribly old-fashioned. 'Wear a suit,' my three children say to me before I go to a Parent-Teacher Association meeting. 'Put a nice dress on,' they tell my wife. They don't want us to show them up by being too 'with it'.

On the other hand, my three teenagers are proud of the fact that their parents are somewhat eccentric. ('This is dad,' my daughter introduces me to her friends. 'He's slightly odd.') Both of *their* parents are determined to be individuals, real people, as well as the joint heads of a family.

How do we retain our own identities, as well as acting the role of parents? How do we steer a course between the Scylla of being too distant, too authoritarian and the Charybdis of being too close, too friendly, so that they don't have any space in which to lead their own lives?

It isn't easy. Consider the following letter:

My daughter, aged sixteen, never tells me anything about what she is doing. I have found out recently that she has been lying to me. I know for certain that she has been drinking in a pub with her friends (one evening we waited outside in the car and saw them go in) and yet she swears to me that she is only drinking orange squash. I might add that my husband and myself are both teetotal and not in the habit of lying. Where is our daughter getting these habits from? She is rapidly becoming quite out of our control, and is defiant, moody and refuses to answer when we ask her questions. Please help.

It is interesting, in cases like this, to have a look at the problem from another angle. Let us put on the daughter's perceptual spectacles, see the situation through *her* eyes, listen to what she has to say about it.

'My parents,' the daughter, Gillian, reports, 'are too perfect. They never seem to do anything wrong. In fact, they never do anything except watch television, and discuss the price of food.

My mother, when I was eleven, left a book on the mantelpiece for me about sex. We've never discussed sex together, or anything else. How can I talk to them? I sometimes think that they want to see me as an immoral person, which I'm not, so that they can congratulate themselves on being so goody-goody. I'm an only child and bored out of my mind at home. That's why I go out so much. I cannot stand television or talking about the old days. Why can't they *do* something — my parents, I mean — get out a bit more, lead proper lives, and leave me to get on with mine?'

This is a cry from the heart and, I must admit, my sympathies are very much with the daughter. The parents are making two common errors with regard to Gillian: (a) they are too distant from her, and her needs and (b) they have settled into a sedentary, too-cloistered world which is quite inappropriate for a couple still in their early forties.

A word about lying. Young people may tell lies for a number of reasons: to avoid social embarrassment, to salve a guilty conscience, to avoid (just or unjust) retribution, or to attract sympathy and attention. Some youngsters tell lies because their parents do, some to gain revenge on their enemies, and others to protect their friends. There are young people who tell lies to make up for real, or imagined, inferiorities.

None of these reasons appear to apply to Gillian. She lied to her parents because she had little in common with them, didn't respect their reality, didn't consider that they were people who were interested enough in *her* problems to share her confidences. Where people have a real bond of affection, a real respect for each other's humanity, there should be no need to lie; where standards are set too high, too remotely, we may be forced to tell lies to protect our self-esteem.

Consider this family. Many families I know are spit-and-string, fairly rickety parcels of common humanity operating on a basis of give-and-take, a little consideration for others, and working things out together. Few families I know live in an idyllic state, with no problems, no tensions, no quarrels.

Gillian's family *is* too perfect. The house is immaculate (the mother doesn't go out to work because father thinks 'a woman's place is in the home'). In the bathroom, the toilet seat is covered by white terry towelling and the toilet paper is to be found under a little pink fez. There is not a spot of dust to be seen anywhere.

The conversation is equally astringent. The parents have few topics to discuss; they rarely go out together; they seem to spend a great deal of their time worrying about their daughter.

In the corner of the living-room is a large water tank containing tropical fish. The occupants seemed to be watching me closely as I talked to the parents; after a short time, I began to feel we were all in a fish tank together.

'Please excuse the mess,' were the mother's first words to me as I entered the room. There wasn't any: compared to our own living-room ('very like a farmyard er — farmhouse,' as one of my friends commented with a Freudian slip of the tongue) the whole place was a palace.

Father is a bespectacled man of forty-odd, wearing a fawn cardigan, grey trousers (beautifully creased) and smoking a pipe. He looks like one of those ideal fathers portrayed in children's reading books. Mother is an anxious tiny woman, dressed in a white blouse and navy-blue skirt. She is as spotless as her home.

Gillian sits at the dining table while I talk to the parents. It dawns on me that the parents are not quite as perfect as they appear; they call each other 'darling' and 'dear' but tend to be on the verge of an argument over silly things like whether to switch on the electric fire or whether to offer me tea or coffee. To my surprise I learn that Gillian is not expected to do anything in the house other than to keep her bedroom tidy — she is given no part, no responsibility, in the running of the home.

A few days later, I see Gillian in school, and she asks me what I think of her home. 'It's very tidy, isn't it?' I comment. 'It's like a morgue,' she says.

I don't want to take up too much time with this particular family. Suffice it to say that I persuaded mother (with father's permission) to take a part-time job, working at the check-out counter at the local supermarket. She absolutely adored the job, going out and meeting people.

When the father knew me a little better I was able to cajole him into taking mother out. Curiously enough, considering their sedentary habits, they both loved walking and the countryside. I encouraged them to join a Sunday rambling group *and* to join the Youth Hostel Association (as adult members). To my astonishment, that summer they took themselves off on a walking tour of the county leaving Gillian to stay at home and fend for herself. Gillian, needless to say, was delighted; both at the trust shown in her, and the opportunity she had to show that she could act responsibly and cope with her own life.

Most important of all, the parents took themselves a little less seriously, and life a little more joyously. The forties, in my view, is not the time to start to prepare for a sedentary old age. We still have, on average, thirty years to live. The best example we can offer to our teenage children is to be active, alive and make the most of it.

The next time I saw father he had on a pair of baggy corduroy trousers and an old sweater. Mother looked much more relaxed. 'Gillian's lies have stopped,' she told me. I wasn't surprised. Why should Gillian lie? She was now relating to real people who trusted her and had interests of their own. We don't lie to our friends, only to those people with whom we have no common bond.

Moral? I think there are four lessons to be learned:

1  *Don't* try to be too perfect.
2  If in doubt about something your youngster is doing discuss it openly and humanely. Please, *don't* set up as Sherlock Holmes.
3  Don't atrophy at the age of forty. Life is to be lived — by you as well as your children. Get out and live it.
4  *Never* pretend to be anything, or anybody other than you are. Nobody (and especially our own offspring) is so awful or inhumane that we need to pretend to them.

On the theme of being honest let me say something simple that has taken me years to learn. *It is what they don't know that hurts children.* Children, and young people, can face up to pain and disappointment; they have tremendous courage providing that they can locate where the pain is. If the pain and disappointment is within the parents then it is the duty of parents to talk about it, come out into the open with it. Otherwise, the pain is passed on.

One of the greatest gifts that parents can pass on to a child is a sense of joyousness, a feeling of being happy to be alive. Misery in a mother or a father is passed on to their children (and, sometimes, to their children's children). The only stop to this process, to say 'the pain stops here', is to be absolutely honest and open about one's disappointments, hopes and fears.

Excuse me, at this juncture, being autobiographical to illustrate what I mean. When I was a child I often noticed that my mother seemed worried, preoccupied and, at times, depressed. She coped quite well with her four children, but it was always there: an unhappiness which she would never discuss.

No doubt, this maternal mystery is one of the reasons why I entered the profession of psychology: to try to solve it. I never did. I studied psychology, I would tell people, because the human mind is the last, great unexplored terrain. The real reason was rather more personal.

Then, when I was thirty-five, the mystery was solved — and without the help of psychology. I had invited my mother to dinner and she told me about her life as a teenager. Her father was very strict; she had to be in the house at 9.30 pm even when she was engaged to be married. At one point in her life, her father had thrown her out of the house for disobeying him. She was his eldest daughter in a family of twelve children.

When she married, my grandfather refused to come to the wedding. He thought that my father 'wasn't good enough' for my mother. He bought them a home, furniture, a piano (he was a relatively wealthy man; my father came from a poor home) but he refused to give his blessing to the wedding. He was always distant and cool towards my mother thereafter.

That is what she told me and, in my thirties, it all became clear: the looks of despair, the flashes of misery, the brief evidence of unhappiness (for which I thought, as children do, that I was responsible). In telling me, she swept away, in one evening, years of guilt, doubt, and worry on my part.

I hope I haven't dramatized this. Years of seeing disturbed and unhappy children and young people have convinced me of one thing: *whatever the sorrows of parents, children would prefer to be told.* Many of the children I have seen have lived in situations which would frighten the US Marines, yet, they always coped, if they knew what was going on.

Do tell your children if you are, or have been, unhappy. They'll understand and forgive. Make sure the pain stops right there.

Now, to lighten the mood, let us turn to a mistake that is all too common these days and which has its humorous as well as its (sometimes) disastrous side.

There is going to be a conflict between youngsters' needs to have a static, ever-available mother and that mother's needs to be a real person. One mother I know stays at home all day, always has her children's meals ready, and is always willing to repair their clothes, run little errands for them, and look after them. She is, as you can imagine, very popular with her children.

Because she herself eats, and eats, and eats, she is now enormous. She sits in her armchair, knitting, and chats to her children, helping herself to the occasional chocolate from a large box. In her flowered dress (she is fondly referred to by her children as Rent-a-Tent) she is, like her youngster's notepaper, colourful and stationary. Teenagers, her own and others, love her.

Few of us could be like this: we want to be up and about doing something. Fair enough, but some mothers are so active that their children rarely see them. They serve on various committees, are interested in community projects, and always seem to be rushing off somewhere, usually to help people worse off than themselves.

All this is very laudable, providing that (a) the mother tells her children what is going on (otherwise it is rather like living in a whirlwind) and (b) the mother sets aside a definite time of the day, or even the week, to talk to her own children. Some parents have such fear of growing old, becoming cabbages, that they miss a great source of pleasure and satisfaction in life: talking to, being friends with, members of their own family.

There are, of course, 'super-mums' who seem to be able to be pillars of strength on the local PTA, attend clubs and committees, organize jumble sales and fetes *and* still have time to relate to their children.

Most of us, however, can only do so much and the first community in our lives is (or should be) the family. It is embarrassing to hear teenagers say: 'Everybody thinks my mother is marvellous. I wouldn't know. I rarely see her.' Sometimes, in all the rush, it is useful to sit still. Teenagers want to feel that parents do have a moment of calm, a few minutes to spare to listen to *their* events of the day.

Sadly we live in a very busy world. Again, I think that youngsters will accept a busy family routine providing that time is set aside for the family to talk together, be with each other.

One family I know has a weekly conference: decisions are made, plans are hatched, worries are discussed. This is very formal, perhaps a grand Sunday lunch (or supper) together (and making a real meal out of it as the French do — so that people can talk) is a better idea. There are families who never eat together; meals are eaten 'on the move' — prior to going out, watching television, or going upstairs to do homework. I know it is hard, these days, to be static for long; on the other hand, family life does not have to be led as though it were a scene from the *Keystone Cops*.

Still, as I have suggested, young people will put up with the most bizarre households and regimes *providing that they know what is going on*. A delightful family of my acquaintance have a large peg-board in the kitchen to which they pin notices and messages to each other. They are all active, imaginative, highly likeable people determined to get the most out of their lives.

On Saturday, at tea-time, they have a meal together. It tires me out to listen to the topics they cover. From 5 pm until 7.30 pm (when they all dash off again) we have pocket money (how much?), household duties (who does what?), any complaints (there always are, even in the best-regulated households), affairs of the heart (with an astonishing, and very refreshing openness about sex), *feelings* about this and that, worries.

The father and mother sit at either end of the table; they don't abdicate their roles as parents, but they do allow their children a full say in any decisions to be taken, and they do listen. It must be reassuring to the teenagers of this family to know they can bring up *anything* that is on their minds; it is equally reassuring to know that, whatever the week brings, they will be able to talk about it (if they wish to) on Saturday.

I'm not completely unrealistic. I know that few of us are as organized as that. However, the principle of the family get-together is a worthy one: youngsters find a sense of continuity and belonging when they sit around a table and talk and listen to the other members of the family group. I'm not advocating the elaborate family 'do's' of my childhood, with aunts, uncles and cousins from miles around. I am saying that members of the same family should occasionally meet each other, and get to know each other. Often we are in such a hurry, get so anxious, that we never see anything (or anybody) clearly. In rushing about we miss so much.

The next parental error is one that includes a great many of my dearest friends: the problem (to the teenager) of the 'with it' parent. As one of my friend's teenage children put it, rather cruelly: 'If that's being with it, thank God I'm without it.' The mistake is a common and very human one: trying to be the same as, adopting the standards of, one's own teenage children.

To be honest, the problem includes my wife and myself. There is always a rush in our house for the best seats to watch *Top of the Pops*. I like, I explain (as I grab the armchair) to know what's happening in the pop music scene. To make up for it, I always sing old-fashioned tunes in the bathroom — selections from Vera Lynn and Paul Robeson which place me well and truly in the ice-age.

Teenagers have fun and, from time to time, we want to share that fun with them. There is no harm in that. It is when we compete with them (for fashionable clothes, for up-to-the-minute musical taste, even for friendships) that the trouble occurs.

Let me give an example. Jean is sixteen and on the Pill. She has a boyfriend who is ten years older than herself. Jean is still at school and seems to have very little in common with the man; Jean's parents find him difficult to talk to but try hard to like him.

'We want to be loving, understanding parents,' her mother tells me. She is a young-looking woman of about forty who wears denim trousers and T-shirts, and looks more like her daughter's older sister than her mother. So far, so good, except that it was mother who insisted that Arthur, the boyfriend, had hidden depths. 'His maturity is good for you,' she tells her daughter, moving towards prescription and over-control rather than seeing what develops from the situation.

Then Arthur is invited to come and live with the family and share a room with Jean. It is noticeable, on visits, that mother spends more time talking to Arthur than her daughter. Before long, mother is planning holidays for them, telling them where to go at weekends, and generally running their life.

The inevitable happens. Jean becomes fed up with the massive family involvement in what should be a personal relationship; she tells Arthur to clear off; she reverts to a 'little girl' role within the family, concentrates on her school work, gives up the Pill and boyfriends. She felt, I suspect, that she was being forced to grow up too soon, and being asked to take part in a human drama of which her mother, rather than herself, was the author.

I re-iterate: *teenagers don't like parents to interfere with their lives tob much.* They need space in which to make their own decisions. Teenagers will forgive the parent who imitates, who copies their speech, their clothes, their dances (though it irritates them). They will not forgive the parent who runs every little aspect of their lives for them or who, worse still, gets emotional satisfaction from moving into their space, and into their relationships. I think the message is clear: they don't want us to ignore them, leave them to their own devices; they do want to feel that they are responsible human beings who can form relationships, make mistakes, live their lives, without the parents constantly looking over their shoulder.

Now, I want to talk about a crucial matter: the *feelings* of parents. Firstly, anger.

One dreary, wet morning, a friend of mine (a doctor and, incidentally, a marvellous mother) threw a large pan of porridge at her teenage children. 'They were making a terrible racket at breakfast and I was feeling frustrated,' she explained. This untypical incident had a marked effect: for months afterwards, if one of the youngsters played up at breakfast the others would whisper: 'Shush. Remember the porridge.'

My friend, despite the immediate results, does not recommend the porridge approach to teenagers. 'However,' she did admit to me, 'the incident made me feel a great deal better. It got rid of a whole lot of pent-up frustration and anger.' I won't condone my friend's actions, nor praise her accuracy with the pan; I will sympathize with her need to give vent to her feelings.

Many of us adults consider that it is wrong for parents to express their feelings. This is silly: we are human beings and we have a right to have, and express our emotions (though not, admittedly, in the form of identified flying objects). Children, and young people, are baffled by adults who feel one thing and say another. They don't want to spend their early lives decoding the obscure messages that we are giving out, trying to decipher our moods and our real feelings on some issue.

There is such a thing as righteous anger and, if we are angry, then we should be angry. By showing sadness when we feel sad, joy when we feel joyful, anger when we feel annoyed, we give youngsters a chance to learn about the emotions, and their importance of life. The emotions are the driving force, the motor, in the human engine: if we hid them, live as though they never existed, we give a curious view of existence to our offspring.

One father I know is what I call a berserker. He will, if his son damages his drill or leaves a garden tool outside in the rain to rust, say: 'Don't worry about it.' If his daughter borrows his razorblades to shave her legs or leaves the bathroom untidy, he says nothing. In the face of loud transistors late at night, clothes on the landing, untidy bedrooms and bad manners, he maintains a stoic calm.

Until he goes berserk. This happens, on average, every three months when, suddenly, and for no obvious reason, he rants and raves at everybody in sight, rushes round the house accusing members of the family of being sluts, vandals and no-goods, and insists that everybody should stop what they are doing and tidy up. Then, just as mysteriously, he will resume his equanimity and become uncritical and accepting of his lot.

This is very curious behaviour for his children to interpret, but they have managed. 'Dad's going off his trolley again,' says the son. 'Oh, dear, dad's just entered his maladjusted phase,' says his daughter. They do nothing to alter their ways. Why shouldn't parents show annoyance when they are annoyed? Why let it bubble away inside of you until the lid blows off the human kettle? I don't think teenagers need to be indulged, or be required to act as psychoanalysts; I do think that what parents say should be as near to what they feel as is possible. Then everybody knows where they are.

Life is puzzle enough for teenagers — they don't benefit from being presented with emotional enigmas. Some parents, however sad or grief-stricken, will never argue. Why? Human beings do cry, do argue. We should not give youngsters a too-sheltered, false picture of the world, or of adults. Sadness, and sometimes tragedy, is a fact of life; so are arguments. The stoic, too-perfect parent who never shows his or her feelings, is a very bad preparation for leading one's adult life to the full.

Even more vital is the ability to show happiness. If you're happy, why not show it? This seems, on the face of it, a foolish question but there are parents who rarely smile, rarely laugh; everything is serious or fraught with difficulty. I cannot believe life is that bad. I cannot believe that we cannot show pleasure at simple things. Happiness, like mumps, is contagious: we catch the potential for happiness from our parents, just as we catch the tendency to be miserable. Whilst adults are worrying and wasting away their days, their children are watching and waiting for them to show some signs of enjoyment, waiting for them to be happy so that everybody in the group may learn this vital skill.

Next, a widespread affliction — depression. Every mother (and father), believe me, sometimes gets depressed. The depression may be serious: the adult may feel that he or she is walking through a long dark tunnel with no light at the end. Or the depression may take the form of being 'fed up', 'out of sorts', 'permanently tired'.

Again, I do not think it helps to deny that these feelings exist. I do not know of anybody who has not had a period in his or her life when everything seems to go wrong and 'the world is out of joint'. My view is that it is better to talk about such feelings without too much self-pity, and to discuss them with the family. It is, at the very least, reassuring to learn that such emotions are commonplace and that others, who look so competent and managing, are quite vulnerable to exactly the same depressions. Life is an up-and-down business: we don't need to pretend to young people that it is all plain sailing.

A word about family dynamics. In some families there is what is usually referred to as a scapegoat child: the one who gets the blame for everything (a scapegoat was a goat which, in the days of the Old Testament, had the sins of the people laid upon it by the chief priest and was then sent out into the wilderness).

Some years ago, before battered babies made the headlines, I saw a little girl who had been brutally treated by her parents. She had been injured so badly that there was no alternative but to involve the hospital, and the police.

The father was most indignant at this. 'You don't understand,' he said. 'That girl is a twin. The other twin is a boy. In my culture the boy is a lion — he gets all our love. It is unlucky to love the girl.' Father, an immigrant to this country and an educated man, was adamant that he had committed no injustice, no crime, despite the fact that his daughter had suffered grievously at his hands. This was my first, and startling, introduction to the scapegoat child.

Every group, large or small, is drawn together if they have a common enemy: it may be the weather, a person, or another group of people.

There are scapegoat families where the enemy is the outside world; within the family there may be tender and loving relationships and the family's collective aggression is directed on to the world outside. As long as the members of the family stick together, they can cope; yet, as soon as one member of the family goes out into the world alone, his fear and oddness show up immediately.

When a family has no obvious outside enemy it can solve the problem by designating one of its own members as the scapegoat for all the woes of life — the one who's fault it all is.

Tracey, aged thirteen, was a scapegoat child. She cooked, sewed, did the laundrette and the shopping and looked after her four younger brothers and sisters. Her father had run off three years previously with a woman in the next street.

Mother disliked Tracey intensely. 'She's dirty, idle and you can't trust her,' she told me. Looking at Tracey, and her role in the family, I placed her in the same bracket as Florence Nightingale and Mother Theresa — a heroine. Then, I began to understand mother when she told me: 'She's got the same character as him' (her husband). Tracey was getting the blame for what her father had done.

It was possible to counsel mother and to show her that she was using Tracey as the family scapegoat, a coat-hanger upon which mother could hang all her resentments. In fact, Tracey, it was suggested, was immensely supportive and helpful to her mother. The situation was resolved; mother was given a home help and Tracey was allowed to live her own life, and be herself, rather than a 'baddy' in her mother's imagination.

Scapegoat children are usually fairly innocuous, there is nothing particularly harmful about them. Often, like Tracey, they are extremely likeable. The scapegoat teenager, blamed for the family's troubles, is no exception. It is a convenient, and very unfair way of escaping making fair judgements and taking any responsibility for failure.

Just as children in school may create a scapegoat child who is picked upon, excluded, bullied, teased, or made to feel rejected, so parents may pick upon one member of the family to be the recipient of all their less worthy feelings. Scapegoating, to some extent, is part and parcel of human adaption to the stresses and strains of life. It becomes pathological, grossly unfair, when it is used against completely innocent (and even positively good) youngsters like Tracey.

A related error to scapegoating is that of favouritism. In my opinion, parents are bound to show some favouritism from *time to time*. It is when they have permanent favourites within the family, when roles are fixed and fixed unfairly, that trouble ensues.

'John is very clever.' 'Susan is always neat and tidy.' 'Jane is no scholar.' 'William is the wild one of the family.' If we label children in this way we can be sure that they will live up to their labels.

'Benjamin (or Angela) is a delinquent.' The snag in saying this kind of thing is that the youngsters involved *will* get into trouble in order not to disappoint us. We create a self-fulfilling prophecy which does not allow Benjamin or Angela to show their better natures. They are trapped in the roles we have allocated to them.

Staying with Jewish friends some years ago I can remember being very impressed at how they never stopped praising *both* of their teenage children. 'She's very intelligent.' 'Isn't he handsome?' 'Aren't they both marvellous youngsters?' They were too. They grew up, as they were bound to do, into confident kind adults. When people tell us we're clever, or good, or lovely, we usually are in order not to disappoint, and to live up to our label.

It's difficult to avoid favouritism, and labelling. In one family I know very well there are two teenage girls, one of them is very talkative and very pretty. I find myself preoccupied with her when I visit, chatting away to her, asking her about what she has been doing. I have to remind myself to talk to the sister as well; she is equally likeable, but quieter, and not as good-looking. It is so easy to be inadvertently hurtful in this sort of situation.

We may find, as parents, that we can love one child more easily than another; find one child easier to talk to than his or her sibling. We may find, as fathers, that we feel more emotional warmth towards our daughters; or, as mothers, that we love our sons more dearly than our daughters. As fathers, we may treat our sons differently, 'more sensibly', to make up for the more emotional and over-protective relationship with the mother.

All this does not matter, providing we realize that (a) each child is different (how different!) and each has his or her own good qualities and gifts to offer to the world and (b) children need our looks, the tone of voice, touching, overt displays of affection and other indications that you are fond of them. It is as well to give these signs to each member of the family, rather than share them out unevenly. Affection costs nothing but is worth a great deal to the recipient. Lastly, if you cannot give equal affection to each child, don't feel guilty about it: merely remember that your non-favourite youngsters are human beings as well (and that simple reminder should help you to act appropriately).

Teenagers do not have to experience constant traumas whilst going through adolescence — when they do it is often parents who are making things too difficult for them. 'Pushy' parents (who force a child to follow academic pursuits, even a career that *they* have chosen), over-involved parents, too-distant parents, parents who don't give straight answers to straight questions all make life more difficult for them than it needs to be.

I remember a child who was forced to follow an academic career from the age of four (he learned to read and write at nursery school)! His father, a farmer, badly wanted his son to be a doctor. Not once did he consult the boy over the question of his career. At secondary school the lad, under intense pressure to succeed, simply 'opted out'. His school work deteriorated and he failed his exams. He never did become a doctor; the last time I heard of him he was working as a market gardener (and was very happy). It is quite wrong to pressurize children in this way. They can be motivated through interest, through enthusiasm but not by force; nor should they be expected to carry the banner of parental fantasy on their shoulders through life.

Lastly, those awkward questions that teenagers sometimes ask and which embarrass some parents dreadfully. My advice is to answer them straight from the shoulder as truthfully as you can.

'Is there a God?' my thirteen-year-old daughter asked me. This is a question you can answer honestly, giving some different viewpoints perhaps, but stating firmly what your own experience of life has led you to believe. Why dodge the question? I might add that my eldest daughter is a committed Christian: a decision she came to herself, neither rejecting or following the family's particular views. My thirteen-year-old, whatever she decides, will make up her own mind.

'What do you think about abortion?' is a query once raised by my sixteen-year-old son. I explained that it was a difficult question: on the one hand life is regarded as inviolate but, under certain circumstances, it appears permissible to end it. I tried to describe the predicament a woman, expecting an unwanted baby, might find herself in. I gave the viewpoint of the Roman Catholic Church. I mentioned a man's responsibility to a woman when he has sexual intercourse with her. The pros and cons were debated. I said what I genuinely thought. Then, it was for my son to come to his own decisions.

Sometimes, questions are more factual. 'How,' my youngest daughter asked, 'does a man get a big penis into a woman's vagina? Is there enough room?' (At the back of this query may lie an adolescent doubt as to whether she — my daughter — is 'normal'.) I told her that the female vagina is capable of stretching sufficiently to receive any size of penis; it is so marvellously elastic that it can stretch to allow a baby to pass through. I added that there is no pain involved for the woman in sexual intercourse if she is fond of the partner she is with. In other words, I answered as factually as I could, and in the spirit in which the question was asked.

She followed up with: 'What is homosexuality?' I told her, a person who loves, or is attracted to, another person, or people of the same sex. I explained about lesbians, and told her about men who were 'gay'. I made no moral judgements since I hadn't been asked my opinion. I had been asked for the facts and I gave them, as best I could. This openness is far better than a secretive embarrassed approach to what are, after all, very important topics.

With teenagers, honesty (and I mean intellectual and emotional honesty) is by far the best policy.

Let me end by saying something which is a truism but is

38

nevertheless true: *there are no perfect parents.* It solves many of our problems when we realize that most other parents are just as bad as we are: erratic, prone to fatigue, annoyance, despair. The fact that we are not perfect makes us human.

In every Persian carpet there is a deliberate mistake because, Muslims believe, only God or Allah is perfect. When my children criticize me I look at them and say: 'I'm like a Persian carpet.' I never tell them why. I expect them to work it out for themselves.

## Chapter Four

# Parents Have Needs As Well

Do any of us ever fully grow up? This is a question we must answer honestly if we are to understand the problems of parents. I think some of us do grow up eventually. I also think it takes a long, long time. Many adults never reach full maturity, and for good reasons. In fact, I doubt whether most of us ever reach our full potential in life because of our inner conflicts and the pessimism that sets in as we see life slipping by.

To be aware of the conflicts that beset us it is as well to know something about the mind, and the way in which it develops. Although I don't subscribe to everything that was written by Sigmund Freud, I do think his early model of the human mind helps us to comprehend some of our own irrationality. Used as a rough map it can help us to traverse some of the more difficult territory deep down within each of us.

Freud thinks of the mind as divided into three parts: the id, the ego and the super-ego. At birth, the id comprises the total personality. It is really a vast reservoir of instinctive urges or impulses: the totally irrational, 'gimme, gimme', 'I want it now', part of the personality. The id is greedy, impatient and selfish. The feelings, and needs of others are irrelevant. When a baby wants to cry, it cries, regardless of the time, or place, or convenience to parents or siblings. When a baby wants to be fed, it wants to be fed *there* and *then*. The id seeks immediate gratification, instant tension reduction. It operates by THE PLEASURE PRINCIPLE. It wants pleasure, and it doesn't care if that involves animal urges, evil desires, chaos, catastrophe, aggression towards others, or other people being hurt.

Since we all live in society, and since nobody can have what he wants when he wants it, the id has to be controlled in the interests of others. The dark side of the personality, the id, has to be brought to adapt to the conditions of the environment. A different part of the psyche, or personality, develops: the ego. This layer of our inner life has to take cognisance of the real world. Its purpose is to perceive conditions accurately and to *plan* life in such a way as to achieve as much satisfaction as is realistically possible.

The ego operates on THE REALITY PRINCIPLE. It takes into account the needs of others. It grows by achievements in the real world, and by the praise and encouragement of others. Gratification of emotional urges is postponed until proper approved conditions in the environment make such gratification possible. The ego has to try to control the egotistical, impulsive, unrealistic urges. It has to plan ahead; it has to take into account the wishes of others; it has to compromise between what it (the id) wants and what the world wants.

The task of the super-ego is to help the ego in its struggle to control the id. The baby perceives that the parents have a code of behaviour, a system of 'do's' and 'don'ts'. At first, the baby or infant obeys the parents in order to gain their approval and avoid their anger. But, later, because he identifies with the parents (or one of them) the child internalizes these rules of behaviour and they become his conscience. That conscience gives the child a system of prohibitions, things to do, and things not to do. The other part of the super-ego, the ego ideal, is what the individual comes to believe is morally good: the code of behaviour, and the expectations of the parents are carried about within the child and the reward for being good is self-respect and the approval of the parents, even when they are in absentia (which they never are — some image, some of the expectation of parents resides within us permanently).

The battle between the id and the ego (helped by the super-ego) is just as epic, and bloody, as the Battle of Waterloo. It goes on ceaselessly, and on an epic scale, within each and every one of us. It may diminish slightly as we get older and as reality impinges upon us more and our emotional urges become less strong. But our irrational, deep, emotional needs are always there — when the battle is over we are dead.

I may have given the impression that the id, the ego and the super-ego are equivalent, take up the same space, with the mind. This is incorrect. The human mind is like an iceberg and the largest part of the mind is unconscious: it lies below the water-line of awareness. Often, we behave irrationally and the id breaks through the constraints of the id, and super-ego. Sometimes, we behave out of character: the id holds sway and its mighty waters flood over the forces of rationality and decency in an attempt to gain what we want, despite the feelings of others. The battle is always there, in our minds: it would not be a battle worth mentioning unless the id, as it undoubtedly is, were such a formidable opponent.

This is how the iceberg of the mind looks in simple, diagrammatic form:

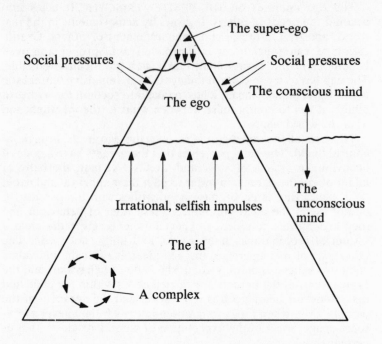

When, within the id, there are powerful forces of sex, aggression, hate or fear which are repressed (refused admittance to awareness) but which still have a strong influence on our behaviour, we are said to have *a complex* about something. Freud claimed that all boys loved their mothers and had feelings of aggression towards their fathers (because they wanted their mothers to themselves). The incestuous, irrational demands of the child's id towards the mother, Freud called the *Oedipus Complex*. Girls, too, love incestuously the parent of the opposite sex. Freud named their wish to have father to themselves, and their (repressed) feelings of aggression against the mother the *Electra Complex*. The important thing to understand about complexes is that we are unaware of them. We behave in particular ways which may be non-productive, silly or damaging. We don't know why we behave like that. Freud believed that many of the reasons we behave as we do, much of the true motivation in life, is totally hidden from awareness. The real reason for behaviour swim, like inaccessible fish, within the dark, deep, murky waters of the unconscious mind.

We can picture life as beset with troubles (or joys) as a result of contact with other people. It is true that we have inter-personal strife — we don't get our own way all the time. Other people are trouble enough. Yet, besides problems concerning others, we also have problems within ourselves — intrapersonal conflict. We have to face the battle of life and we have to face the equally fraught battle that rages within us. Life isn't easy; sometimes, it's rather as though we are walking over land bestrewn with pot-holes, traps, land-mines and trip wires. Without some balance between the id, the ego, and the super-ego, without some harmony within us, it is as though we were to undertake the journey in the dark.

Let us continue the analogy. We set out, in life, to make the best of ourselves, to make some impact on others. On one side, we have the super-ego urging us to be good — to play it safe. On the other, we have the id urging us to live dangerously, take risks, live for the moment. In the middle, the poor ego is fighting for harmony, self-respect, and the approval of others. If we stray off the straight and narrow, we may get lost in the wild terrain of our own unconscious urges; if we play life too safely we may forget to utilize the powerful forces of creativity, spontaneity and individualism that lie deep within the id.

The journey looks something like this:

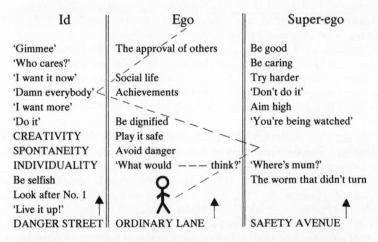

| Id | Ego | Super-ego |
|---|---|---|
| 'Gimmee' | The approval of others | Be good |
| 'Who cares?' | | Be caring |
| 'I want it now' | Social life | Try harder |
| 'Damn everybody' | Achievements | 'Don't do it' |
| 'I want more' | | Aim high |
| 'Do it' | Be dignified | 'You're being watched' |
| CREATIVITY | Play it safe | |
| SPONTANEITY | Avoid danger | |
| INDIVIDUALITY | 'What would — — — think?' | 'Where's mum?' |
| Be selfish | | The worm that didn't turn |
| Look after No. 1 | | |
| 'Live it up!' | | |
| DANGER STREET | ORDINARY LANE | SAFETY AVENUE |

Most of us follow an erratic path, veering from one road to another, sometimes in the course of the same day. By and large, though, our journey through life takes us along the Ordinary Lane, especially as we grow older and realize that there are many of our ambitions which will never be fulfilled.

There are many great artists, like Van Gogh, who have trodden Danger Street at the cost of their personal happiness. Others, like

Picasso, appear to have coped fairly well with the traps of Danger Street, and yet to have led productive, satisfying lives. *They* have moved back and forth between the lanes without endangering their own egos.

How do we know this scheme of the mind is true? Freud may have stressed the importance of the unconscious mind but what proof have we of its existence? It is only when we consider hypnotism, dreams, 'forgetting' to keep a dental appointment, sleep-walking, and our own irrational behaviour, that we realize that there *are* parts of the mind (including those minds which we know best; our own) which remain totally hidden from us.

In order to illustrate the workings of the human mind I want to turn now to another psychologist: Alfred Adler. His theories help us, I consider, to gain insight into the conflicts that go on inside of us which we adults carry around with us like excess baggage all our lives.

First, a word about Adler himself as a child. As an infant, Adler suffered from rickets and from an involuntary spasm of the glottis: his Adam's Apple would, out of his control, move up and down. At the age of four he caught pneumonia and was rather alarmed to hear the doctor tell his mother that he, Alfred, wasn't long for this world. As well as all this, Adler was an odd-looking child with a curious, moon-shaped face, small, piggy eyes and hardly any chin. He was also very small in stature.

Alfred Adler's childhood was unhappy because of self-consciousness over his appearance and because his elder brother was his mother's favourite child. The young Alfred tried hard to emulate his more successful sibling but, in his own mind, never succeeded. As an old man Adler complained that the brother was 'still ahead' of him.

Central to Adlerian theory is his notion of 'the inferiority complex'. The neurotic person tries too hard — over compensates — for real or imagined inferiorities. His (or her) goal in life is to be superior at all costs. Instead of forming real friendships, having a sense of community, the neurotic is possessed with his own individual advancement. He wants to out-do others, to be the best, the most-loved. He wants to be first.

It is easy to spot that Adler himself suffered from an inferiority complex during his own childhood. He suffered too from sibling rivalry — jealousy of other children within the family. Adler thought that the child's ordinal position in the family gave a clue as to how he would behave in later life. The second child tries to out-do the first; the third child will try to out-do both the first and second. It is middle children, sandwiched between the first- and last-born, who feel rivalrous impulses most strongly.

Adler wrote: 'To be human means the possession of a feeling of inferiority that is constantly pressing towards its own conquest.' The antidote to this feeling of inferiority is the group, the community; social involvement rather than selfishness. Adler understood only too well, from his own experience as a child, the pain and frustration springing from sibling rivalry, and intense feelings of inferiority. Power, he concluded in later life, is no substitute for love.

What has all this got to do with the needs of parents in relation to their teenage children? A great deal, especially if we concede that few parents are perfect, fully mature adults. There are very few parents whose lives run absolutely smoothly, like a Swiss watch. Most parents have conflicts, stress, jealousies, frustrations and emotional set backs. Teenage is a crisis time in human development; often, as teenagers struggle with their problems, the parents are approaching a crisis within their own lives.

The couple who marry very young, say at nineteen or twenty, will be in their mid-thirties when their children are teenagers. This is still relatively young, but is getting on towards forty: the mid-life crisis, the time when we have to face up to the fact that we are no longer young, and we will never do all the things that we wanted to do with our lives. In my view, forty is a critical age; it is when we reach forty that we realize that we are mortal, that most of us have already lived more than half of our allotted span. Parents of teenage children are approaching forty, past forty, or getting on for their half century. *They* are growing old, rapidly; their children are full of the exuberance of youth. At a time when parents could do with therapy or counselling to help them through their middle-age crisis, they are called upon to play the role of therapists, counsellors, and wise, contented human beings to their own roisterous children. It is not easy.

This interaction of middle-aged parents and teenage children is asking for trouble, especially in these days when most 'nuclear families' live far away from relatives of all ages who give moral support as they did in the days of the 'extended family'. We live locked inside of our own houses with these young people who want action, excitement and fun, when over-worked and over-tired parents need, more than anything else, a bit of peace. It's asking for trouble, and trouble there often is.

When parents look at teenagers they can see that they (a) mature earlier than their parents or grandparents did — they are taller, and many of them look older than their age; (b) teenagers have more money that their parents had; (c) teenagers look more sophisticated than their parents looked at the same age. Though some of this sophistication is spurious — many teenagers are still

45

*emotionally* insecure — it is true to say that, because of television, cheaper travel, more emphasis on educational opportunity, many teenagers know more about life than their parents knew at the same stage.

Parents are often envious of teenagers. Why on earth shouldn't they be? Teenagers, now, seem to 'have it made'. They have far more sexual freedom than we ever had; they seem to be able to go out and buy expensive clothes and hit records; they seem to have more opportunity than previous generations. 'I want my son to have the things that I never had,' one father said to me. The he added, ruefully: 'He's had those things, believe me, and a few other things besides.' I asked that father if he was slightly jealous of his son. 'You bet,' he answered, honestly, but with a laugh. Here is a father who is well aware how fortunate some of today's youngsters are and, yet, is able to have a sense of humour about, as he put it, 'missing the boat and being born thirty years too early'.

Not all parents can take the same objective view. Some parents, disappointed in their own teenage, try to re-live their own youth through the lives of their teenage children. They take too close an interest in the 'teen-scene', identify too closely with the interests, fashions, and ambitions of teenagers. This, of course, is unfair — it is their teenage, their time of being young, not ours. For good or ill we have had our turn, and it would be wrong to try to have a 'second helping' of youth by living vicariously through the lives of those teenagers who depend upon us and want us to provide some values, some standards of behaviour, against which they can rebel. If what *we* believe, do and feel is a pale copy of what *they* believe, do and feel, then what do we leave them to rebel against?

Back to Adler and his notion of sibling rivalry. These feelings of jealousy with a brother or sister may be transferred, at middle-age, to feelings of rivalry, or jealousy, over a son or daughter. It is common for men at middle-age to have some doubts over their sexual attractiveness. By then, the first grey hairs, an incipient pot belly (if not a full-scale pot belly) will have begun to appear. The father may find young, teenage girls sexually attractive; he may start to dress in younger fashions to give the impression (if he can) that he is not as old as he is. If he does not enjoy sex as much as he once did, his feelings of inadequacy are exacerbated by his son moving, in front of his eyes, towards sexual attractiveness and potency.

No wonder that middle-aged fathers sometimes rant and rave about the sexual morals of the young; no wonder a father may deprecate the way in which his son (or daughter) dresses. If the father is disappointed, depressed, about his achievements in life (including his love life) he may frequently 'blow his top' and provoke arguments with his teenage son about some trivial matter. The son will be hurt, and annoyed, and will not suspect the real reason for father's outburst. The real reason is no more than frustration at the dissatisfactions within his own life and old-fashioned, green-eyed jealousy of his son's youth, and all the opportunities for love, life and learning that go with being young. Irrational, you might say? How many of us (as Freud was keen to enquire) are rational?

In much the same way, a mother may see her teenage daughter as a rival. For sure, the girl's teenage is freer, less restricted, more exciting and less irksome than mother's was (or at least, that's how it seems to mum). The teenage girl has probably matured sexually at an earlier age than mother, and will discuss sex in a much less inhibited and self-conscious way than her parents' generation. The teenage girl of, say, fifteen may be pretty, elegant, self-assured. Mother may, at this time, be worried about the effect of grey hairs/lines around the eyes/false teeth/spectacles/burgeoning waistline upon her appearance. As the mother sees the first signs that she is growing old, her teenage daughter is blossoming into a terribly pretty, sexually attractive, young woman. Why shouldn't the mother feel more than a twinge of jealousy? Some of us age gracefully, but, however we do it, we age; nobody should pretend that it's a pleasant experience.

Often a mother will joke about her teenage daughter: 'When we're out together, people take us for sisters.' This is fine — there is some humour behind the remark; the rivalry of mother and daughter is playful, not bitter. Other mothers will try to outdo their daughters in dress, poise and looks; they will feel jealous, or angry, if the girl's boyfriend does not pay a lot of attention to *them*. This is wrong. Most teenagers are proud of their mums; most teenagers know that their mothers (however young-looking and pretty they are) are thirty years older than they are. They don't mind the mother looking young. They *do* mind the mother who pretends to be a teenager, or twenty-one. 'You'd never think my mother was forty-two, would you?' they may sometimes say, in company. As you shrink under the table, they smile. They have put you in your place, reminded you, once again, it's their youth, their springtime, not ours. I'm not saying that adults, by the age of forty, are decrepit, half-dead; I'm saying that we should live our lives and the young people should live theirs.

We don't *have* to be over-serious when it comes to considering the errors parents make in relation to their teenage children. All parents make mistakes; our children do not expect us to be perfect. They do, however, expect us to have a bit of commonsense. They want parents who are viable, interesting parents in their own right. They want parents who set *some* standards. They want parents who are out there, battling with the world, and not using their own children as emotional props and crutches. They want parents who are in there, fighting their own pain, disappointment and frustrations and not projecting their fantasies and frustrations on to their children.

The Ten Commandments for parents are:

1 *Learn something of your own psychology.* Learn what it is that makes you tick, what it is that makes you angry, or sad, or ineffective. Only then will you avoid the danger of passing on your own hang-ups to your teenage children.

2 *Believe in something.* If you don't you can hardly expect your children to respect you. They will gauge whether you believe that life has some sort of meaning, whether you are religiously-inclined or not. If you don't believe that we are here on earth for some purpose, it is hardly surprising that children look elsewhere for a code of behaviour, and a philosophy of life.

3 *Be aware of the crisis of middle-age* and try to avoid passing on the emotional conflicts which you will inevitably encounter at this stage of life to your teenage children.

4 *Accept your own limitations,* and life's little ironies and disappointments. Few people, including famous psychologists, get as much as they had hoped for. Make sure that your children get a better deal from you than you had from your own parents. Avoid passing your frustrations on to them.

5 If you had an unhappy childhood, *don't live in the past.* Say to yourself: 'The pain stops here.' Live in the present, where you are, and try to understand why you were unhappy, rather than project your unhappiness on to others.

6 *Be honest and humble* (after all, we cannot know all the answers). Don't 'waffle' if teenagers ask you your views — they're your views and you have a right to hold them.

7 *Don't envy teenagers* their greater freedom and affluence. We paid the instalments on their behalf, and there is no sure way of knowing whether greater freedom leads to greater happiness. Freedom can be very frightening.

8 *Don't ape teenagers.* Learn to know yourself and your own hang-ups. If you are 'a square' accept it gracefully. Your children may rebel against you but they will respect and love you because you are yourself.

9 *Talk out your problems* with your teenage children. In view of the vicissitudes and pain of life, and the difficulties we all face in growing up, there is a lot we can share.

10 *Don't expect to be perfect* but try to be human, the more

problems are shared, without dragging up the past, the closer you will feel to your teenage children.

To deal effectively and openly with teenage children we have to understand something of our own unconscious impulses, our own irrationality. We all have a chronic tendency to project on to others our own irrational desires, fears, anger and spite even though we know, at heart, that those others are not the main cause of our frustration. The only way we can guard against this kind of projection and irrational behaviour is to know how our own minds work, to know ourselves better, and to accept ourselves more, warts and all. Others will love us if we are real; they will accept us if we can learn to accept ourselves, and our unconscious minds, and our constant struggle towards love, status and integrity.

What is your real self? Which is your real personality? Parents cannot dodge these two questions and the way in which they set about providing an answer to these two crucial queries will affect the way in which they relate to their children. In order to have real children, one must be real oneself. In order to have happy children one must first be happy. That is why it is important that parents should know something about the theories which I have sketched in above. Without knowing who *we* are, what *we* are, what makes *us* tick, how can we know what *they* are and how can we expect them to cope with *their* emotions.

In *The Prophet* by Kahlil Gibran there is a passage on children which is one of my favourite pieces of writing. Your children are not your children, says the prophet, they are the sons and daughters of Life's longing for itself. With my own children I have always had a deep awareness that they were on loan, on trust; they are very much people in their own right and we, as the Prophet says, are the bows from which they as living arrows are sent forth. We can house their bodies, but not their souls; we can offer them what we have to give, but we cannot make them take it.

Our need, as parents, is to count for something, to be respected (and, if possible, loved) and to have a feeling that we still have a valid contribution to make in the world. We will never, many of us parents, grow up completely. Who wants to? It is in the battle to become mature, really wise, that the interest and excitement of life resides. Let our children enjoy their teenage. We, as adults, have our own enjoyments; and they're no less curious or pleasure-giving as those odd things that young people seem to get up to.

*Chapter Five*

# Reward and Punishment

I have a friend who is called Ambrose Mark Jones. He had a problem. 'People call me Mark,' he told me, 'but I want to be called Ambrose. What shall I do?' I gave him the best advice I could.

'Let it be known,' I said, 'that you want to be called by your first name. Then, and this is the vital bit, ignore anybody who calls you Mark and smile at everybody who calls you Ambrose.' Sure enough, after a few weeks, nobody called him Mark again.

This advice, though I say it myself, would have received the approval of B.F. Skinner, America's most eminent psychologist. Skinner tells us that *behaviour which is rewarded tends to recur; behaviour which is not rewarded tends to extinguish, or go away.* In practical terms, the rule is to reward the behaviour we want, and to ignore the behaviour we don't want. It sounds simple enough but it is a rule which is broken by parents every day.

In my local supermarket, day in and day out, mothers can be seen unwittingly teaching their young children to behave badly. This is what they do. When the child is good, the mother ignores it. When the child offers, say, to carry the wire shopping basket, or to wheel the trolley, the mother takes no notice. The occasions when the mother *does* pay attention to the child is when it shouts, knocks something over, or generally begins to behave abysmally.

The same system of reward (and paying attention *is* a reward) is operated in thousands of homes. The child is taken notice of, or punished, when he or she behaves badly but completely ignored when behaving well. Is it any wonder, then, that children behave badly? We all make this mistake: when my three teenagers play their transistor radios too loudly, forget to tidy their bedrooms or otherwise behave in ways of which I disapprove, I shout at them, take notice of them; when they behave well, I tend to take their behaviour for granted and forget to praise them.

Skinner maintains that we must always reward the *specific* behaviour we wish to establish, and that it is very important to make sure you know what sort of behaviour you want. If you do reward certain types of behaviour they will recur.

As a psychology student, I can remember the day when we put Skinner's theory of reward to the test. We were listening to a lecture and all the students sitting on the left-hand side of the hall avoided the lecturer's gaze, or scowled at him, when he looked in their direction. Those of us sitting on the right side of the hall smiled at him throughout. Before very long, the lecturer was addressing his remarks only to those sitting on the right-hand side of the aisle. We told the lecturer what we had done afterwards, and he agreed with us that Skinner's idea certainly seemed to work!

How can we apply Skinner's theory to teenagers? Can it help us to explain why, on occasions, they behave so badly? To answer these questions let us have a look at a modern phenomenon — football hooliganism.

Recently, I had tea with a headmaster and his wife. The couple had two teenage children — a boy aged sixteen, and a girl aged fourteen. Both teenagers were keen supporters of their local football team. 'What about the violence at football matches?' I asked them. 'Doesn't it put you off? Doesn't it make you feel that you would rather do something else with your Saturday afternoons?' To be honest, I couldn't imagine a worse way of spending an afternoon than amongst thousands of people shouting their heads off at two football sides.

The boy answered first. He told me that going to football matches was the real excitement in his life; he liked dressing up in his scarf and woollen hat and joining the team's supporters to urge his side on. 'It's great,' he said, and he meant it. The girl said that the members of the football team were her heroes. 'What point is there in having heroes if you don't support them?' she asked me. She, too, found Saturday afternoons exciting; she found the atmosphere in the football ground, the tension during the game, 'a real turn on'. Both teenagers, in their own terms, were being rewarded for their determination to support their local team.

I found the conversation interesting. Many adults consider that most young football supporters are hooligans, that they consist mostly of 'nutters' and rowdies. I wonder. There is a distinct possibility, to my mind, that thousands of young football supporters of both sexes are ordinary, normal youngsters. Why, if this is so, do they behave so badly on the day of the match? Why do rival gangs of supporters sometimes fight each other? Why are law-abiding citizens, who live near football grounds, often forced to stay at home (and sometimes board up their front windows) on the day of a football match?

You will agree, I think, that most young people need excitement and heroes. No measures to combat football hooliganism will succeed when the one opportunity young people have for adventure is at football matches; when the Saturday match gives those concerned a lot of attention, and therefore reward, from the rest of us. This is particularly true if the young people concerned are failures at school or, having left school, are unemployed. For youngsters like this, football is a main interest in their lives; Saturday afternoons is a time when they (in their own minds) become important, step into the limelight.

Imagine a large housing estate, or an inner-city area, containing hundreds of bored teenagers. On Saturday, these young people dress up to pay their respects (using the accepted chants and rituals of the day) to their own heroes, or gods, the football team. If there is some violence at the game, it is then that the media take notice of them. The youngsters may see themselves on the television, or there may be news of them in the local or national newspapers — *Fans Run Riot,* scream the headlines. The young people have succeeded in getting what they want, attention. We have rewarded them for *bad* behaviour.

What we do, every Saturday, is to reward young people when they behave like hooligans (by paying them attention) and ignore them when they behave well. Nothing is more calculated to make teenagers behave in a mindless, rowdy and irresponsible way.

Sometimes, to teenagers, a violent encounter with a rival group of supporters is seen as an opportunity for personal 'heroism'. At a football match (where I was, to be frank, watching the fans, not the game) I saw a teenage fan become so enraged by the fact that his side was losing that he climbed a ten foot-high wire fence and jumped into the enclosure where the opposition was gathered. There he was, alone, surrounded by hundreds of rival fans. After a moment's hesitation (he was a big chap) the opposition set upon him and beat him up very badly. In a war, that young man would have been awarded a VC for heroism. I'm sure that, in his own mind, he *was* in a war; he *was* a hero. Even his cuts and bruises could not take away the reward of the adulation and praise of his fellow supporters, freely expressed when he managed, eventually, to climb back over the wire.

My advice to parents concerning their teenagers going to football matches is (a) go with them (the more adults there are about, the better) (b) forbid your youngster to go unless he, or she, does go with a responsible adult. Having said that, the vital point is that we *must* find better ways to give these youngsters the adventure and excitement that they need. Boredom is an ever-present danger during teenage. Why cannot we divert these youngsters' need for excitement into more positive channels? They could *play* football or rugby (rather than be spectators); they could join the YHA or some other organization catering for youth; they could, with our encouragement, take up a new interest rather than searching for 'kicks' in such non-productive ways.

If the only time we adults take notice of teenagers is when they get up to mischief, or behave violently on football terraces, then they *will* get up to mischief, they will learn to behave violently. 'It's fun on Saturday,' the headmaster's son told me. 'It's a good day out,' said his daughter. They were two normal, otherwise law-abiding and sensible, teenagers. It is a pity that adults cannot provide alternatives for them to find adventure, even danger.

Back now to B.F. Skinner, and to further consideration of his theory. One important aspect, says Skinner, is to *reward frequently at first*; the rewards can become more variable once the behaviour has been established. This sounds complicated, but isn't. Take an example from your courting days. The suitor usually has the sense to lavish on his loved one plenty of boxes of chocolates, or flowers, during the initial stages of courtship. When the relationship has been established (or the couple get married?) these tokens of affection may tail off, or disappear. Usually, despite this, the relationship continues, though (sadly) on a less rewarding, or romantic note.

To avoid accusations of bias, let me say that the same variation in reward patterns can be observed amongst women. In the first stages of marriage, a wife may put her husband's slippers out to warm, and make sure he is woken with a piping-hot cup of tea. Over the years, such rewards may (again, sadly) become less frequent without diminishing in any way the affectionate behaviour of the husband. Indeed, if the rewards are intermittent (only given occasionally) they may be appreciated more and, hence, be more effective.

A fixed interval reward tends to work less well than a fixed ratio. Somebody who works for a weekly wage, or a monthly salary, may have less inducement to work hard than somebody who is paid by results (piece work). To give a simpler example, it is not advisable to smile at someone all the time with whom we may be conversing; it is better to smile at them now and again, perhaps when they have paid us a compliment or made a witty remark. Rewards, like everything else, can be over-done. To succeed best, they should be related to the behaviour which preceeds them, and they should whenever possible be given *immediately after* that behaviour. There is little point in praising a child for behaviour which occurred three weeks before; the trainer of animals rewards the animal immediately after the appropriate behaviour has been enacted; the successful horse, for example, doesn't receive a sugar lump days after jumping a high fence.

That there should be a relationship between behaviour and rewards seems only commonsense yet, here again, parents can go wrong. Sylvia, a thirteen-year-old, is a teenager whose parents own a shop and work long hours. They rarely see their daughter. To compensate her, and to alleviate their own guilt, the parents buy Sylvia expensive presents: she has a new bike, a camera, a new record-player, and a gold wrist-watch. Sylvia's mother feels sorry that her daughter (an only child) has to spend so much time in her own company. To everything that Sylvia does, whether in school, or at home, her mother comments: 'That's very good, darling.' The girl is unhappy and it's easy to see why: she is being rewarded without any demands being made on her. She is rewarded without regard to her behaviour, or true identity. *Whatever* Sylvia does is approved, and she feels more and more wretched about it. Too much reward, without regard to what has gone before, doesn't work.

Rewards should not be erratic; the same behaviour should not be rewarded handsomely on one occasion but evoke little response the next. If parents act like 'one-armed bandit' machines, doling out rewards at odd intervals and of varying amounts, it is difficult for the teenager to see the connection between his or her behaviour and the amount of praise, or some other form of reward, that is doled out. The truth, often, is that there is no connection; the rewards within the family are doled out randomly; the mother is like the 'one-armed bandit' machine in that her offspring are never sure, if they behave in a certain way, 'feed her' with certain behaviour, whether she will come up with three bunches of cherries or nothing at all.

A teenage son rushes into the house; he shouts at his mother that he wants his tea straight away. She is in a good mood, and rewards him by giving him his tea. The next day, the same thing happens but, this time, the mother is in a different mood; she upbraids her son for being so impolite; she does not give him his tea but, instead, tells him to go upstairs and wash himself! The same behaviour is, one day, rewarded; the next day it is punished. *That's* something that happens in many homes and it is the sort of erratic reward pattern that can have a very bad effect on young people — treated in this way they simply do not know where they are, or what is expected of them.

In a laboratory experiment with rats, the animals are trained to jump to a card with a black circle on it. If they do so, they are given food as a reward. If the rat jumped to a card with a white circle on it he bumped his nose against the, immovable, card and fell to a net below. The rats soon learned which card to jump to. After some time, the learning situation was made insoluble: if the rat jumped to the black circle he sometimes bumped his nose and, at the same time, the food was sometimes given with the white circle. The result was that the rat did not know what to do; he didn't know what sort of behaviour was expected of him. He was neurotic — faced with a problem he could not solve.

Rats are not human beings, I know, but human beings become similarly confused if faced with insoluble reward and punishment patterns. If a mother is kind and loving one day, rejecting the next, without regard to the child's behaviour then we cannot be surprised if the child is totally bewildered. Or, if in response to a particular piece of behaviour, the mother becomes angry one day, but accepts it the next, the child will see no consistent pattern of reward. The lesson is that rewards, to be effective, must be consistent.

A teenage daughter enters the house, ignores everybody, sits in an armchair, turns on the television and watches while mother is preparing tea. The mother says nothing. The next day, the teenager behaves exactly the same way; this time her mother 'flies off the handle' and shouts at her. 'Why do you never offer to help me?' mother asks. 'Why do you treat this place like a café?' The daughter is, justifiably, confused. She is looking for some consistency from the mother but receiving very little. All parents make this mistake, I feel. It is one which, whenever possible, we should do our best to avoid. Otherwise, the teenager feels, rightly, that he or she lives in an irrational, inconsistent and utterly confusing world.

I have said a lot about reward but, so far, very little about the other side of the coin, punishment. Let me say, straight away, that too much punishment is as bad as none at all. Punishment, in the words of the Gilbert and Sullivan song, has to fit the crime and, to be effective, it must be administered as soon as possible after the crime.

A great deal of nonsense is spoken, or written, about punishment. I am quite clear in my own mind that a short sharp rebuke never did a child any harm whatsoever. At the very least, the expression of righteous anger certainly does *the parent* good — better to chastise and forget, than to bear a grudge. Children should learn that adults have a right to be angry if annoyed or let down but being angry does *not* mean that the parent doesn't care, or is being rejecting. Most children, and young people, do understand this quite clearly. *They* accept punishment and anger, providing it is fair and justifiable.

Two years ago, my teenage daughter was 'larking about' at home and (unintentionally) broke my ruler. I was furious, and shouted at her, telling her in no uncertain terms that she ought to be more careful with other people's property. She went upstairs to her room to sulk, but emerged five minutes later. 'Sorry, dad,' she said. The incident was forgotten and there were no bad feelings. Shouting at her had done *me* good; she accepted the fact that I was, temporarily, very angry but such anger did not mean that I had ceased to love her.

I remember telling a group of health visitors, a long time ago, that I once had occasion to smack my five-year-old son. They were very shocked; I thought it was less important than they did that I should smack him. He had, like my daughter, broken something and he was given a sharp rap on the hand for doing so. Like my daughter, he went away to sulk and like her he came back to apologize. The whole incident, as far as any recriminations were concerned, was forgotten. He had been naughty; rightly or wrongly, he had been punished, swiftly and in righteous anger. I cannot believe that the smacking has left him with a permanent psychological scar.

You may agree with me that parents have the right to smack their own children but what about corporal punishment in schools? Do teachers have the right to act *in loco parentis* — i.e. in place of the parents — and cane children for misdemeanours in the classroom?

I would be most annoyed if any of my children were caned in school without my prior approval. In fact, I would prefer that some *other* form of punishment were used (lines, detention, foregoing of privileges) rather than the cane or smacking or any other form of physical violence.

In the Western world most schools seem to manage without the use of the cane. Only in Great Britain, the Republic of Ireland and America (where corporal punishment is banned in just two States) is the use of physical sanctions against children condoned. Ought we, in Britain, to fall in line with the rest of Europe on this issue?

Most British teachers favour the cane. In 1977, a National Opinion Poll survey found that only twenty-two per cent of primary school teachers, and thirty-nine per cent of secondary school teachers, were in favour of the abolition of the cane. To be fair, most teachers see the cane as 'the ultimate deterrent': to be used sparingly, and mostly when all other measures have failed.

Most pro-caners hold that corporal punishment is the answer to the bully, the school tyrant, the violent child (and some children *do* attack teachers) and the vandal. By using the cane, it is argued, we make the punishment fit the crime and we administer justice rapidly and with the least fuss. Teachers, a survey in the mid-seventies showed, were convinced that the cane was more effective than detention, extra work, loss of privileges and, especially, calling in social workers or educational psychologists to deal with the child.

56

There is evidence that heavy use of the cane is counter-productive, making the pupils' behaviour worse rather than better*. Anti-caners would argue that violence breeds violence and that, in our society, physical violence against other adults isn't allowed. Why should physical violence against children be condoned?

Most of our children are in schools that use corporal punishment. What do the children concerned think of it? Of the ones I have questioned on the matter about half think it is necessary and should be left to the teacher to decide. The teachers themselves see the use of the cane as an option left open to their professional discretion; to take that option away from them would seriously weaken their authority within the classroom.

One real difficulty, it is argued, is to think of something to take the place of corporal punishment. Excluding a child from school seems a very radical measure indeed. In my experience, those youngsters 'suspended' from school may be left without any form of schooling for weeks, or even months. Tuition at home is both expensive and lacking in any attempt at re-socialization.

Fairly recent surveys have shown that between one half and one third of youngsters questioned considered that corporal punishment should be retained in schools. This seems to support the pro-cane lobby and to suggest that children prefer the cane to other forms of punishment.

Despite this finding, I find it hard to agree that corporal punishment is necessary in a good school. Nor do I consider that schoolteachers have the moral right to use physical punishment against their pupils. 'Punish, get it over quickly, forget it and make friends,' is sound advice to parents but I cannot acknowledge that the same dictum applies to teachers. However knowledgeable they are, teachers cannot teach without discipline, but discipline must come from the example set within the school, its atmosphere, and its concern for the pupils. I believe that every time a youngster is caned there has been a breakdown in discipline for which the adult, rather than the child, must be held responsible.

I have no doubt that our schools will come into line with European schools on this matter. Before we do, we must all ask ourselves if we, as parents or teachers, are giving enough to children to have to resort to caning when they reject what it is we offer.

If schools must cane pupils they should do so for specific offences about which the pupils have been told, and warned against. The punishment should be administered quickly, and with

*See *Corporal Punishment*: a discussion paper written by Peter Wilby for the International Year of the Child (published 1979 by the UK Association for the International Year of the Child, 85 Whitehall, London, SW1).

the minimum of fuss; pupils would seem to prefer this to lasting resentment and antagonism.

It is when the punishment, in the form of recriminations or resentment, goes on for weeks, months or even years that it is objected to so strongly. In our method of dealing with delinquents, for example, it may take many weeks for the young offender to come before the magistrates to be dealt with. By that time, the offender may well have forgotten (or would like to) what it was that he, or she, did in the first place. Long, drawn-out systems of punishment are much less effective than short, sharp reminders that follow the crime, and are fitted to it, as nearly as possible.

With young offenders it would seem commonsense to suggest that they should make some sort of retribution to the person that they have hurt in some way; they should also make retribution to society. Few of them expect to be 'let off' for what they have done; at the same time, they do want to see that there is a link between the punishment that they receive and the crime that they have committed. From this point of view, Community Service Orders (or any method of making the offender pay his or her debt to society in a useful and practical way) are far better than recommending that the youngster be placed on probation (without any punishment) or be given 'therapy' for his or her misdeeds. Young people know when they do wrong; they do not resent being punished; they do ask, and rightly, that the punishment be both fair and appropriate.

Punishment has its limitations — it is, by and large, far less effective than reward. In the nineteenth century, it was the law that sheep-stealers, and petty thieves, should be hanged for their crimes. The hangings were often public events at which large crowds gathered to see the criminal on the gallows. The atmosphere was rather like that of a fun-fair, with nobility, farmers and peasants alike gathered to watch the ghoulish spectacle of the hanging of a man, or a woman, to deter others with the same inclinations.

Curiously, at these hangings, pick-pockets would ply their trade, moving in and out of the crowds, stealing money and jewellery, even though the person swinging from the gibbet, in front of their eyes, had been punished for exactly the same offence. Stranger still, since farmers liked to attend on these macabre occasions, many sheep-stealers took the opportunity to get on with their job whilst the farmers were elsewhere. It is *not* true to say that punishment is always a deterrent!

One of the difficulties with administering punishment is that, even where it stops undesired behaviour, it may also stop behaviour which *is* wanted. For instance, a maths teacher at a secondary school criticizes a girl for being poor at maths (this, in itself, is

58

dubious: we could argue that if the teacher was really good at his job, he would be able to encourage the girl to higher attainments). Because of her fear of, and resentment about, the maths teacher the girl stays away from school completely, and says she dislikes PE, English Literature, and every other subject in the curriculum. Her loathing of maths has spread to become a loathing of school; her resentment of the maths teacher has fanned out to become a resentment of all teachers. Punishment, when it is unjust, can give rise to lasting resentment.

We can punish through words, as well as through actions, and, as with actions, inhibit the other person from acting positively. A friend of mine played a Russian Grand Master at chess, and drew with him. The Russian, to be honest, was playing thirty-nine other games at the same time; all his other opponents lost. My friend thanked the Grand Master for the game. 'I olvays draw wiff somebody,' said the Russian. 'Good for publicity.' My friend was dismayed. 'Why mé?' he asked. 'You vere the smallest,' said the Russian. My friend, treated in this frank and insensitive way, never played tournament chess again. A word of praise, a smile, would have been sufficient to encourage him to greater heights; instead he was verbally punished, patronized.

People are quicker to punish than to reward. A smile is a powerful reward, as is the phrase 'Well done'. If we must punish, we should do so quickly; we should also remember to praise where praise is due. Children, and young people, like firm (even stern) kindness; they want to know where they stand; they want some information about the standard of behaviour that is expected from them. Where a child is rewarded consistently for his or her efforts there will be little resentment over punishment, particularly where young people have been told what the rules are, see the sense of them, but are remiss and break them. It is adults who make too much fuss over punishment, and refuse to punish, or who don't understand its limitations and punish too much. Both approaches are equally disastrous in evoking cooperative behaviour from youngsters.

My conclusion after many years spent dealing with young people, is very much the same as that of B. F. Skinner: *reward works better than punishment.* Very well, but we still have a problem. It is to decide how best to give young people the rewards that *they* want? How do we provide them with adventure, excitement and danger (if they want it)? How can we stop them from becoming bored and apathetic?

During my own adolescence all eighteen-year-olds had to serve for two years in the armed forces; if a young man went to university at eighteen he still had to complete his National Service when he had finished his degree course. I remember, when I was eighteen, looking for the Mau Mau in Kenya. I'm glad to say I didn't see many Mau Mau; I did enjoy the opportunity to travel abroad and I did mix with a great variety of young men of the same age, but from very different backgrounds.

This is an old chestnut but I'd like to bring it up again — do we need, in the eighties, some kind of National (or Community) Service, perhaps of one year's duration, which would be compulsory for young people *of both sexes*? Can we organize a scheme which would provide the youngsters of today with the new experiences that they need? There is a lot within the community, to be done; if youngsters were asked to do it, and given adult support, there is no doubt in my mind that they would get on with the job. If the scheme involved community living, perhaps in camps or disused army barracks, it would help teenagers to stand on their own feet, and to think of others.

Aren't there, though (you might point out) already teenagers who go out of their way to help others? There are those youngsters who participate in the Duke of Edinburgh Award scheme; there are those who, from school, go out to help at the local playgroup or adventure playground. There are those who visit old people and chat to, and do practical tasks in the home for, our senior citizens. That's true. My point is that the enthusiasm and idealism of youth should be better organized, more skilfully harnessed, by the adults living in their neighbourhood.

There are still a large number of youngsters who seek their 'kicks' in anti-social ways. I spoke to one of them, a young man of eighteen, who lived on a large estate of some 20,000 souls; outside a large town. Ben (not his real name) had been in trouble with the police since the age of sixteen. He had been convicted of burglary and had just served a sentence in borstal for the crime. I asked Ben about the burglaries and why he did them. This is what he said:

> Well, me and a gang of mates just wandered about the streets 'cos we were unemployed and we stole a car because we were so bored standing around doing nothing. We decided to go and get some money by doing a burglary so we got in the car and went to see if there were any empty houses. We knocked on doors, pretending to be looking for a friend at a fictitious address. If nobody answered we broke in. We were a bit frightened, but we were excited as well. It was very exciting.

At the same time as I spoke to Ben, I met Terry. He was a young man of nineteen who lived on the same estate as Ben. Terry had been unemployed for a year: the firm for which he had worked since he left school had become bankrupt and Terry had been left without a job. I asked him about his situation:

MYSELF: Terry, can you tell me what it's like to be unemployed. What do you feel about being without a job?

TERRY: I sometimes feel depressed. Well, yes, I get very depressed. I've learned to accept it, though. It's just one of them things.

MYSELF: How does your mother react to your being unemployed? (Terry's father was separated from his mother.)

TERRY: Well, she goes on about it. It's not so good being at home all day.

MYSELF: Have you made any efforts to find a job?

TERRY: I've tried everywhere. It's hopeless.

MYSELF: How does it affect you when your mother gets on to you?

TERRY: It gets on my nerves. It's not my fault I'm unemployed. I blame it on society really.

MYSELF: When you were at school did you ever suspect you might reach twenty and find yourself out of a job?

TERRY: No, and I'm fed up about it.

Two young men. One had sought rewards, turning to delinquency to do so. The other had very few rewards in his personal life. How can we help youngsters like Ben and Terry to find some rewards, in legitimate ways, within the society in which they live? To answer that, it would be useful to look at what is happening on another estate, again at about twenty thousand people, in another part of the country. *Here,* efforts have been made to give youngsters something to do in an attempt to stop them drifting into crime or anti-social behaviour.

As we walk about the estate we notice that there are things going on. There is a large adventure playground used by the young children of the estate and supervised by the (voluntary) efforts of the mothers. It looks rather a dangerous place to me, with climbing frames, ropes to climb and a pulley and rope to slide down. Then, perhaps even young children need an element of danger in their lives? There is a very successful football team (for teenagers) and a girls' netball team. The young people are supported by their friends: on Saturday afternoons, participation is the watchword, since people take part in something they have built up rather than just spectate. Both teams have helped in building the adventure playground because they wanted to do something for the children living on the estate.

There is a community centre with a 'tea and a bun' club for

senior citizens; the young mothers meet there, too, and bring their babies along with them. There are social functions, bingo for the parents, discos for the young people and a room where people can drift in from the streets to enjoy a cup of coffee and a chat. There is a well-supported youth club, and a *detached social worker*. He meets, talks to, advises, young people wherever they may be found — at lunchtime outside school, in the day on the estate, in the evening at the youth club or disco. He is a facilitator, an enabler. His job is to help the youngsters to achieve what they want to do, to give them advice, to listen to their worries. This is not an estate with plenty of houses but nothing for people to do. People help each other; old people support the football and netball teams; the young people help, and arrange social events for, the senior citizens.

It's lunchtime at the local secondary school. The detached youth worker is on his rounds. He stops at the school field to chat to a group of girls about a play the school has put on. The subject was Women In Society. The girls want to share their experience with a sympathetic adult and Ted Taylor, the detached youth worker, is there to *listen* to them and to give them practical advice if they need it. To the girls, Ted is a friend, somebody who cares about them, their problems, their ideas and their ambitions. In the evening, Ted will see some of them again at the youth club, or at the disco. He always has a word of praise and encouragement for them. He makes them feel that they count for something; he rewards them, by taking them seriously and treating them as responsible human beings, for their efforts to reach maturity. He also instils in them a sense of community and caring for others.

Then, there's Johnny. He has started the disco. On a Saturday night it is attended by hundreds of young people who live in this, and surrounding areas. He's not a professional but he cares about young people, and wants to provide some activity which they will enjoy. Johnny is a valuable person in the young people's lives. As he walks about the disco he, too, is rewarding the youngsters by taking notice of them and making them feel that they are important and worth looking after.

The incidence of delinquency on this estate has dropped since the young people have started to take an interest in their own neighbourhood and been encouraged to develop a feeling of community. It is we adults who are responsible for instilling into youngsters this community spirit, both by encouragement and example.

Many young people are *not* helped by any kind of youth service; many youngsters have nobody to whom they can go for advice. The kind of help that youngsters need, the advice they seek, should be provided by the community in which they live, by you and me, and not by experts. It was Alfred Adler, who said that the antidote to neurosis and depression was *Gemeinschaftgefuhl* — community feeling. There will be far fewer aimless youngsters when the adults who live near them take a keen interest in the welfare of the young and help them to contribute to the lives of others.

Talking to a motor-bike group one of the youngsters explained to me why they kept themselves to themselves, provided their own rewards, and rejected the rewards that society was prepared to offer them:

It's not that we won't mix in society. Society doesn't want to mix with us, because we wear leather jackets and ride motor-bikes. They're not prepared to give us a chance. You get somewhere, say a pub or a youth club, and you want to go in and they say: 'Sorry, no bike boys, no leathers. You can't come in.' Why? *We're no different from anybody else.* If you've got a special type of car, say a Jag, you don't break away from the rest of society.

How do we include young people like these? How do we make them feel that they belong in society? It's easy enough to reject them but harder, and yet more beneficial to all of us, to think of ways in which *they* can be persuaded to give a hand to those less fortunate than themselves and to take an active, positive role in the community of which they (as the next adult generation) are an important part.

We have got to think of more, and better, ways of rewarding young people by involving them in community projects. Skinner claims (and I think rightly) that reward works better than punishment. By all means punish where appropriate, or necessary. Yet, isn't our job, as adults, to think in terms of rewarding youngsters? The best way of rewarding anybody is to give him, or her, something worthwhile to do; and to give praise where praise is due. I don't think youngsters will let us down if we think up personally rewarding projects for them within their own community. I hope we don't, as adults, let ourselves down by not caring enough. That, to my way of thinking, would be unrewarding to us, and disastrous to them.

*Chapter Six*

# Maladjusted Teenagers

Some time ago, in the United States, a group of High School teachers were asked who, in their opinion, was the most normal member of the school staff. The majority vote went to an intelligent, attractive blonde teacher popular with both students and colleagues alike. Here was a person who was good at her job, who had lots of friends; she fulfilled Sigmund Freud's two criteria of adjustment: *arbeiten und lieben* — to be able to work and to love. The teacher, in school, had a friendly word for everybody and invariably looked cheerful.

After the vote, the same teacher was subjected to a battery of personality tests by a group of psychologists. The results indicated her to be under a severe degree of emotional stress. The psychologists next questioned the teacher about her personal life. The 'most normal' member of the school staff confessed that she had often felt near to complete nervous breakdown, that her marriage was extremely vulnerable, and that she was worried about the effects of the marital discord on her six-year-old son. Of all this the staff knew nothing; her home life was a closed book as far as her colleagues were concerned; the general impression the teacher gave in school was one of cheerful competence.

This story leads me to ask two important questions. Who is normal? Who amongst us could bear to have our personal life probed by a team of psychologists?

It is my contention that happiness, contentment and misery move in and out of all our lives; few of us are happy all the time. We cope with our troubles; we learn to live with our own limitations. We try to sympathize with the troubles of others; we learn to accept *their* limitations, and their eccentricities. Laurence Sterne says, in *Tristram Shandy*: 'So long as a man rides his hobbyhorse peaceably and quietly along the King's highway and neither compels you or me to get up behind him — pray, Sir, what have either you or I to do with it?' The only answer is that we try to be tolerant of the differences between people and we intervene only when it is clear that the other person is suffering and is asking for help.

Understanding, here, is better than over-concern or complacency.

To understand the concept of maladjustment it is useful to approach it from our own experience. We might picture a child who lived in the same neighbourhood as us when we were children, and who we considered to be maladjusted. What was it about the child that made you think so? Did he, or she, tell lies, or steal or show persistent anti-social behaviour? Was the child very aggressive, or very shy? Did the child wet the bed, or blush, or avoid the company of other children? Having answered, now ask how many of these characteristics applied to *you* as a child. Were *you* never shy? Were *you* never over-aggressive? Maladjustment, I contend, is part-and-parcel of human development: it comes and goes like the tides.

There are not two distinct groups of human beings: Us (the normal) and Them (the maladjusted). We cannot be placed neatly and bimodally in two piles, like the humps on a camel's back. Maladjustment lies at one end of the normal distribution curve of human behaviour and too much stress, a series of painful or disappointing experiences, can send any one of us to the wrong end of the continuum.

What counts in our maladjustment is its *duration* and *intensity*. I am somewhat maladjusted every Monday morning, especially after an enjoyable weekend, but my Monday morning blues do not drive me to despair or thoughts of suicide. Usually, I recover by lunchtime. The feeling of dislocation — maladjustment — is real enough but, happily, it doesn't last too long. As for intensity, I may, for example, become angry or withdrawn from time to time but I do not chase the person who has aroused my wrath around the room with a carving knife; I do not lock myself into my bedroom and stay there for weeks on end.

When we say that a young person is maladjusted we should bear in mind the transient nature of most of its signs and symptoms *and* we should ask: maladjusted to what? There are three main areas of a teenager's life in which maladjustment may reveal itself: at school, at home, and in the inner, personal life of the child. There are three salient types of maladjustment. These are (a) educational maladjustment (b) social maladjustment and (c) personal maladjustment. Let us look at each in turn.

EDUCATIONAL MALADJUSTMENT Elizabeth, aged thirteen, was referred to me by her headmistress. She was a capable and pretty child who had difficulties in both reading and spelling. Elizabeth was given an intelligence test and her IQ was 121 — well above average. Her reading was more than two years behind her own age group and her spelling was that of a nine-year-old.

Elizabeth was a very good musician and excellent at games. She described herself as 'hopeless' at 'batty' spelling and 'terrible' at 'horrible' reading. She was well aware of her failure in both subjects and it worried her and she knew it worried her mother. Elizabeth was found to be a crossed-lateral child (left eye dominant, right-handed and right-footed). Her scanning of the printed page was poor; she had a tendency to read from right to left instead of from left to right. A programme of individual remedial help was designed to build up Elizabeth's sight vocabulary, and to train her eyes to scan the page more effectively. She had particular difficulty in building up the component parts of words and in synthesizing them (putting them together). Materials were provided to correct this, to be used by the remedial teacher.

At the end of the programme Elizabeth was just half a year behind her own age group in spelling and had caught up with her classmates in reading. She was much more confident about the subjects, now that she was succeeding in them. Her general adjustment to school was described as 'excellent'. Mother was no longer anxious about her daughter's scholastic progress and there was a natural, friendly relationship between the two of them.

Elizabeth, with appropriate remedial teaching, was helped through her temporary educational crisis. It was the suitability of the help which was crucial, and the timing: if Elizabeth had not been in the right place at the right time it is possible, even likely, that her educational maladjustment would have spilled over into her social and personal life. From a happy, adjusted child she may have turned into a frustrated and depressed youngster with a poor self-image, because of her low school achievements.

What is clear about Elizabeth is (a) her problem was firmly located in the school setting and (b) she did not need to see a child psychiatrist in order to be officially deemed 'maladjusted'. In fact, she was a lively, outgoing teenager with a great many friends. Her problem was educational and there would have been no point at all in conducting a psychological, or psychiatric, investigation of her family or personal life. She did *not* require to be sent to a special school; the remedial help could be, and was given, within the setting of her own school.

SOCIAL MALADJUSTMENT David, aged fourteen, lived with his mother and his grandfather. His father had died when he was an infant. In the same year, when he was thirteen, his mother was killed in a car accident and his grandfather died six months later. David was placed in a children's home and was referred to me by the headmaster of his secondary school. 'David,' wrote the headmaster, 'is very sad and depressed, which is understandable enough, but he refuses to talk to anybody and I am very worried about him. Can you help?'

I saw David in the child guidance clinic. He wore a black

mackintosh, his face was pale and he looked the picture of sadness. The first session, and the second, he refused to say anything and just sat in the chair opposite me, looking at the wall. During the third visit to the clinic I suggested that we play chess, and he nodded his head in agreement. The chess games, each Wednesday afternoon, lasted for four months. They were played in complete silence. One afternoon, David looked at me and said: 'Your move.' Those were the first words I had ever heard him speak. From that moment, he was able to talk to others; he joined a cycling club at school; he spoke to the headmaster and to the staff at the children's home about his mother and about his grandfather. The last time I heard of David he was working well in school, had made some friends and was on his way to getting over the tragic happenings in his life.

The home is very important to teenagers; it is the base from which they go out to explore the world. David was a boy from whom, in a very short space of time, the home was taken away, plus the major emotional props in his life — his mother and his grandfather. His reactive depression was severe. Yet time heals most wounds and with professional help David was able to overcome the disaster and sorrow in his life and return to a reasonable level of social and educational adjustment. It was in his social life that the symptoms — withdrawal and depression — appeared; his school work remained acceptable.

SOCIAL MALADJUSTMENT, *Case 2* Jane, aged twelve, wrote some essays in school which shocked her teacher. In one essay, the matron of a nursing home killed off the babies in her charge, one by one. In another, a toddler was pushed into a pond by a drunken tramp and left to drown. Jane was referred to me by the headteacher because she was worried about the stories. It transpired that Jane, an only child, had been presented with a baby brother; she was very unhappy about the arrival of her sibling because 'he cries all the time and keeps me awake at night'. The mother, and Jane, were counselled about the arrival of the new baby; Jane was encouraged to become involved in looking after him, and the importance of her role in helping mother was emphasized. The essays about death stopped; Jane returned to being her friendly, cheerful self.

PERSONAL MALADJUSTMENT Jean, a dark-haired, tall fifteen-year-old was referred to the child guidance clinic by the family doctor. She had nightmares, walked in her sleep and suffered from frequent headaches. Physical investigation, including assessment of Jean's vision, had produced no cause for any of the symptoms. The GP asked: 'Are Jean's problems psychological?'

Jean was assessed by myself in the clinic. On a test of intelligence she scored an IQ of 95. Her reading age was average for her age group. She appeared timid and shy during interview; her remarks were guarded and she did not converse freely. Jean did voice some resentment of a younger brother, however. A school report sent by Jean's headmistress described her behaviour and work at school as 'very satisfactory'.

The consultant children's psychiatrist saw her and Jean, more relaxed on her second visit to the clinic, chatted about her bad dreams and her anxieties. Mother was seen; she, like Jean, was highly strung and 'a worrier'. Mother and daughter identified with each other strongly. The mother was counselled by the psychiatrist, and Jean by myself. After a few weeks, each was able to voice her own fears and anxieties. Both were reassured and promised further help and counselling should they need it. Jean's symptoms abated, and both she and her mother seemed much more confident and outgoing on a 'follow-up' visit to the clinic six months later.

What is interesting about Jean is that the headmistress had written to say that: 'There is absolutely nothing wrong with this girl.' Yet, there was no doubt about Jean's pain, even though she showed no symptoms in school or, indeed, in her social life. Her problem was real, and it was personal though caused, to a large extent, by her mother's tendency towards fears and chronic worry. Jean needed help, despite the fact that she had no difficulties in school, or in making friends.

It is essential to stress that the educational, social and personal problems of young people will more often overlap than not. Teenagers like Elizabeth, where the problem is in the school alone, are in the minority; the vast majority of youngsters have problems to do with the home, and with the parents. As a result of home discord there are *secondary* effects in the school life of the young person, or in his or her personal life. In my experience, about ten per cent of problem youngsters are maladjusted, like Jean, in a clinical sense, and have neurotic and personal problems which need clinical diagnosis and treatment. Another ten per cent of youngsters have educational problems and need to see a good remedial teacher or, perhaps, an educational psychologist, like Elizabeth. Eighty per cent of youngsters have social problems, reacting to conflicts within the home.

Take the case of Raymond, aged eleven. He was a boy who drew pictures of clowns in school; they were always depicted as crying. This was slightly strange in that Raymond was a noisy, ebullient boy and the comic of the classroom. The teacher asked me: 'What is the significance of the drawings?' I called on Raymond's mother and it transpired that the lad lived in a tense and unsettled home where there were frequent rows between father and mother. By talking to the mother, and chatting to Raymond, and by giving him some encouragement over his school work the problem was eased. The rows between the parents did not stop, but they became less frequent. The problem was not cured, but Raymond was aware that the school knew something about his problem and that he did not have to face it alone. The drawings were distress signals and, in this instance, help was available. The problem was based in the home; the signs that there was a problem showed up in school.

This is often the case, and it points to how useful it is for teachers to keep in touch with parents, and to work as closely as possible with the home. Events at home can have marked effects on a young person's school attainments. Some years ago, I saw a twelve-year-old boy whose school work had deteriorated over the previous six months. He was an able, polite boy who showed no obvious symptoms of maladjustment. His IQ was 129 and he was working well below his true capacity — his school work was poor, careless, and badly presented.

I asked Geoffrey about his home. He was an only child and lived with his parents and an elderly great-aunt. The parents were very keen on their social life and left their son on most evenings of the week and most weekends, to look after the old lady, who was becoming rapidly more eccentric and senile. I visited Geoffrey's parents and suggested to them, as diplomatically as I could, that they were placing too great a responsibility on the shoulders of their son. They agreed to take a larger part in the care of the elderly relative. The change in Geoffrey, following this one visit, was dramatic: his school work quickly started to reflect his ability; he became more sociable; he looked happier.

Once again, a problem at home had reflected itself in the youngster's school life. Once again, the young person was not primarily seeking a cure to the problem — he was signalling his distress. Many youngsters are far worse off than Geoffrey was; they live in homes which, in their sheer neglect, or violent treatment, of the young people would shock and frighten many, many adults. Youngsters living in such homes do not expect a magic cure; they hope for, and deserve, a feeling that some adult, somewhere, knows about their plight and is sympathetic. We *cannot* protect young people from every injustice; we *can* try to get to know them better and to help them when help is needed.

Let us turn now to a closer consideration of the teenagers within our own family, and the ways in which they may run into emotional difficulties, and the best ways in which they may be helped. All human beings have (as has the whole of the animal kingdom) three inbuilt biological mechanisms to cope with stress: *fight, flight* and *imitation.* Faced with danger we can battle against it, we can run away, or we can camouflage ourselves and hope that we won't be noticed.

Teenagers who fight back, *act out* their difficulties, are easy enough to spot. They may intimidate others, 'show off,' behave rowdily or defiantly or, perhaps, turn to violence or vandalism to 'make their mark' on a society from which they feel rejected. Girls mostly, but some boys, will get into sexual difficulties in order to gain attention from, or reject the values of, adults. Conventional values will be rejected, too, in the form of anti-social behaviour such as stealing and lying.

Youngsters who run away suffer desperately from *anxiety*: the psychological concomitant of the pumping of adrenalin into the bloodstream and the stimulation of the sympathetic nervous system as a prelude to action. They are anxious because they cannot resolve their conflicts and neurotic in the sense that they have a problem to which there is no clear solution. Running away, either physically or by becoming withdrawn, is not a solution to human problems; it is simply avoiding them.

The teenager who resorts to imitation suffers from the same failure of courage as the youngster who runs away. Of the two survival mechanisms, imitation is the more self-destructive. Imitation is a poor form of defence: our ability to believe that we can be liked or loved for ourselves, to believe in our own unique worth, is part of our insurance policy against the slings and arrows of life. If we pretend, if we do not trust ourselves sufficiently to be as real as we can be, we exacerbate rather than solve the problem of relating to others.

Having said this, it is my contention that maladjusted teenagers do not become maladjusted out of thin air. They fight, or run away, or pretend, because they cannot relate to those who are closest to them; the parents. It is a truism to say that there are no maladjusted teenagers, only maladjusted parents. Like many truisms, there is more than a grain of truth in the saying. I have rarely seen a socially or personally maladjusted teenager who came from a home in which the parents were contented and in which there were good lines of communication running between the parents and their offspring. It is because *parents* go wrong, somewhere, that teenagers go wrong. This is an unpalatable truth, but is *is* the truth.

*Chapter Seven*

# Violence and Vandalism

Violence hurts. Of that I am totally sure. What always strikes me about violence as portrayed, for instance, on television is that it doesn't seem to do much damage. The thug, or policeman, or spy, is beaten up but usually manages to stagger back on to his feet, shake his head, and walk off.

In real life, we read in our local papers such headlines as: 'Air Pistol fired at Bus'; 'Teenager thrown through Shop Window'; 'Shopping Trolley hurled from Car Park Roof'; 'Gang fight — Innocent Passers-By Injured'. What is never dealt with fully, under each headline, is the pain of the victim.

Let's take an example. A teenage boy (well known to me) was unlucky enough to say 'boring' when another teenager was performing his *pièce de résistance* on a skateboard. For this remark (admittedly, a silly thing to say) he was unceremoniously kicked in the mouth — but he didn't get up, shake his head and walk off. What happened to this victim was that he lost two front teeth, his face was a mass of bruises, and he spent a night in hospital under close observation having had his mouth sewn up.

I have to admit it. I *am* disgusted when I hear young people blithely talk about 'putting the boot in'. I am equally sickened by the frequent portrayal of violence on television. If the heroes are depicted as living violent lives can we be surprised that young people follow their example?

I don't want to get too involved at this stage in arguments as to whether television violence makes youngsters more violent or not. Some studies* say that boys who have watched a lot of violence on television are more likely to commit acts of serious violence. Other studies claim that television programmes have no effect on behaviour.

What I would say is this. Only a fool would spend thousands of pounds advertising his product on television if it had no influence on the mind of the viewer; and whatever else it does, television

*See, e.g. *Violence and the Adolescent Boy*, William Belson, Saxon House, 1978.

71

violence cannot have beneficial effects on young people and it may well confirm the view of life held by tough, urban youngsters who will ('for a laugh') commit violent acts for sheer excitement. Theft, violence, vandalism becomes a pattern for such youngsters and violent television programmes do nothing to deter these young people from a philosophy of 'might is right'.

There is a great deal of violence and non-caring in our society. A statistic which fascinates me (though I am less than enamoured of statistics) is that, in the United Kingdom, over £7,000m is staked, each year, on various forms of gambling. When I hear that a youth club is having financial difficulties, or that a housing estate is struggling to set up an adventure playground, I wonder just how much we *really* care about the youngsters in our midst? If we spent on young people just one-hundreth of the money we (as adults) spend on gambling we could set up facilities which would go a long way to curing the delinquency of which we complain so loudly. Adults, I'm sad to say, are part of that delinquency.

Just one more statistic. There are (as I discuss further in Chapter 13 Where's Father?) three-quarters of a million children in this country whose fathers are not living with them. Fathers are not an optional extra in family life. They are, or should be, a vital part of the youngster's upbringing and they can be a great source of emotional support for wife and children in the family context. There are thousands and thousands of mothers bringing up children without a husband; there are well over a million children who (if we count intermittent fathers, 'ghost fathers' — call them what you will — men who see very little of the family) are living without an effective father.

Is this not a massive deprivation in a youngster's emotional life? Is this not part of that adult non-caring attitude which, through its own selfishness and lack of thought to others, adds to the unhappiness and the violence in our midst? The family is the basic unit of society and yet the family life of many of the youngsters whom we label as delinquent is violent, fragmented or non-existent. Can we be surprised that young people, seeing the behaviour of the adults in their life, resort to aggression and destruction? After all, it is we adults who are supposed to set an example of how to live.

Let's get down to brass tacks. Where does aggression come from? Basically, there are two theories — the *learning* theory and the *frustration* theory. Both theories are easy to understand and both, to my mind, contain an element of truth.

The learning theory states that if we live with aggression we learn to be aggressive. We learn that aggression 'pays off'. It may be the only way that we can gain attention or impose our will on others. We learn what we live — if we live in peace, we learn to be peaceful;

if we live with love, we learn how to love; if we live with violence and aggression we learn to be violent and aggressive. Aggression, like mumps, is caught from (and taught by) others with whom we come in contact.

This seems to accord with common sense. I saw a boy in a playgroup. Aged four, John spent most of his time running about shouting 'bang, bang, you're dead'. He liked to knock other children over or, where he couldn't succeed in that, hit them.

I went to see his father, a smallholder and a man who owned a shot-gun and liked to shoot rabbits, birds, grey squirrels and, it seemed to me, anything that moved. The father had a very loud voice and a brusque manner. It was suggested to him, as diplomatically as possible, that he might show a little more tenderness, and a little less roughness, towards his son. Dad got the message and, within a short time, John's behaviour in the playgroup altered for the better.

These 'like father like son' cases are not always so easy to solve. I had a case referred to me of a persistent school refuser — a fourteen-year-old boy who would not go to school. Father was a burglar and a tough man. He told me, with some pride, that he only 'did' country houses; the homes of the rich. He boasted that his son, Wayne, could find his way home from miles away, over fields, without a torch.

I managed to cajole the boy back to school but I could not do much about his aggressive (and criminal) outlook on life. He got his standards and values from his father who was a tough, criminal character. Whether Wayne will follow in his father's footsteps, I don't know; I *do* know that his chances of leading a law-abiding life are far slimmer than boys brought up in non-criminal, honest families. Like us all, Wayne learned, and learns, from parental example.

In this easy-going society of ours there are homes which are regular thieves' kitchens where latter-day Fagins produce modern artful dodgers reared in the art of theft. There are homes where certain goods 'fall off backs of lorries', where dad regularly steals from his place of work, or where mother steals from the local supermarket and enlists the help of her children as she goes about it. Youngsters who come from homes where stealing is not regarded as wrong will learn the obvious lesson.

Curiously enough, and this is a most important point, there are youngsters who come from dishonest, and even violent, homes who are neither dishonest or violent. We all know adults brought up in the most appallingly deprived circumstances who have grown into honest, law-abiding individuals. There are children, brought up in terribly unhappy, warring families, who have later married very happily and produced a successful family unit. It is not true to say that, if our parents (or other adults in our lives) are thieves, or violent, or vandals, that we are inevitably destined to be the same. All human beings have choice. It is merely more difficult to choose to be honest, and loving, if those who are near and dear to us are dishonest and aggressive. By and large, we live what we learn and we learn a great deal from our parents.

Let us turn, before discussing the influence of the home more fully, to the *frustration* theory of aggression. This states that severe, or recurrent, frustration leads to anger and, sometimes, violence.

An example. One wet, dreary morning I rushed outside to get to work for an urgent appointment. I sat in the car, switched on the ignition and nothing happened. In pouring rain, I opened up the bonnet.

I checked the plugs, and the points. I looked at the electrical contacts and fiddled about with them. I checked the battery — that seemed to be all right. By now, standing in the rain, I was soaking wet. I sat in the car, switched on. Again — nothing. I was so angry I kicked the car — totally irrational behaviour.

Another, more common, example. I, like you, have to cope with my share of the household chores and with looking after the garden. If I'm doing a repair job in the house and nothing goes right (shelves fall down; thumbs, rather than nails, hit with hammer — DIY was never my strong point) I can feel the frustration rising within me, and I become angrier and angrier. It is at times like this that my wife and children avoid me; they have learned to read the signs of mounting annoyance, bad temper, even violence.

Granted that *some* people seem to manage to 'keep their cool' under the most frustrating circumstances. Granted that some people lose their temper much more easily than others. There *are* individual differences as to how much frustration we can all tolerate. Yet, I would argue, we all have our breaking point. When frustration becomes overwhelming even the calmest person will become angry and aggressive.

This frustration theory has enormous implications. If frustration *does* lead to aggression we have a ready-made formula to explain the anger and the violence we see all around us. We could argue (and I do) that there are millions of people, both adult and children, in our society whose basic psychological needs are not being met. Consider these four needs: *spiritual needs, the need for love, the need to belong within a community* and *the need for status.*

SPIRITUAL NEEDS It was Carl Jung who said that he was besieged by middle-aged men, in their late forties and fifties, who had made money, raised a family and yet were still unhappy. They all asked Jung the same question: 'What is the meaning of life?' (These men

74

were all financially successful but their success hadn't brought them the contentment they'd hoped for.) They knew there was something missing in their lives. But what?

I personally believe that men and women do have a spiritual element in their make-up. They need, in my opinion, to believe in something greater than themselves; they are entitled to wonder what life is all about, and to reject the theory that it is a will-o-the-wisp, a passing show, totally meaningless. I do not think that political credos, or the pursuit of material goods will satisfy the yearnings of the human spirit.

In 1979, Pope John Paul visited his native land, Poland. He was accorded a spontaneous and massive welcome by the people. It was, in my view, an occasion to remind us that motor cars, transistor radios and other earthly goods are simply not enough. They do not offer sufficient motivation to human beings — sufficient explanation of what life is about. Most people, both young and old, need something which will feed their souls otherwise, they will suffer (as did Carl Jung's patients) from a feeling of meaninglessness and frustration.

It is interesting that, in the USSR, a non-religious society, there are some fifty million devout Muslims, thousands upon thousands of practising Roman Catholics, many who observe the Jewish faith. These people are, to my mind, a living witness to the importance of the spiritual dimension within human beings. Man cannot live by bread, or pleasure, or Communism, alone.

When men and women are given explanations of life which are inadequate, faulty or facile, they feel cheated. We know that the acquisition of wealth does not necessarily lead to happiness but all around us we are exhorted to work harder, earn more, spend more, as though *that* were a satisfactory answer to living. It isn't. People need a higher purpose than that. The churches are empty; they do not seem to be able to express or to provide that purpose. So the frustration remains within many of us, and the anger. We know, somewhere along the line, that we are being cheated; we can't say where or how, but a large gap remains in our lives, a hunger for meaning, and that gap is, in my view, a rich source of desperation, aggression and potential violence.

One more point about religions. Not only do they cater for the spiritual elements within Man's nature but they, all of them, provide a code by which to live, a scale of values, a system of right and wrongs. If we give up, say, the Ten Commandments we, in effect, abandon a set of rules by which to live our lives. If we put nothing in their place, we become existentialists, living for the moment and for ourselves. I do not think that people can live in a society without rules; I do not think that people can be happy when they make up the rules as they go along. Without over-stating the point, a society without religious beliefs, and a society without rules to which everybody keeps, is bound to produce conflict, selfishness and violence. If we abandon God, choose to live without Him, we must be prepared to take the consequences. If we vandalize the human heart and spirit, we must not be surprised when that violence and vandalism, perpetrated on our souls, is reflected in our surroundings.

THE NEED FOR LOVE How many young people (not to mention adults) feel that they are not loved sufficiently? Wouldn't it be true to say, with some justification, that a huge number of children feel that nobody loves or cares about them? A great many youngsters in our society, inhabit an emotional wilderness, a psychological slum.

I would agree with Dr Winnicott who, in *The Child, the Family and the Outside World,** states: 'The thief is not looking for the object he takes. He is looking for a person. He is looking for his own mother, only he does not know this.' However, I would be less specific than Winnicott and merely re-assert the old psychological adage: He (or she) who steals, steals love. Many youngsters steal (and commit acts of violence and vandalism) out of an acute sense of despair and abandonment.

These feelings of 'loss of love' are not confined to children or young people. Much of the anti-social behaviour shown by members of our society (whether adults or youngsters) is, in my view, an attempt to combat helplessness and loss of identity in the face of what appears to them to be an uncaring and unjust society. This deviant behaviour often results from a sense of powerlessness and 'lovelessness'; both feelings being exacerbated by the day to day demands of modern living.

If anybody were to ask me, as an experienced educational psychologist, what children and young people need most in our society I would answer: more love. Where they are to get such love from (since many parents seem incapable of giving it) I cannot say. There just doesn't seem to be enough love, genuine concern, and caring, to go round. For those children who don't get their share of this precious commodity the outlook is bleak. Love is as essential to human beings as air, water and food. People who are not loved are capable of the most immoral, uncaring, dastardly deeds. Let's face it, what have they got to lose?

THE NEED TO BELONG WITHIN A COMMUNITY The loss of a sense of community is a vital factor in many people's feelings of unhappiness and frustration. When most of us lived in small villages we could give everybody a role, a part to play, an identity. How do

*Pelican Books, 1975.

76

we do so in the large, impersonal towns and cities in which most of us live?

Gordon Rattray Taylor, in his book *Rethink,** comments upon this loss of community, the lack of a feeling of belonging. 'The village shop assistant,' says Taylor, 'remains an individual, known to most of his customers and knowing them. More insidiously, the state treats men as ciphers, and with the growth of computor methods will do so even more. Letters from people who object to being 'simply a number' are constantly printed in the papers and reflect this feeling.'

Not far from my home is a large housing estate with row upon row, street upon street, of identical houses. Here, young mothers (living, in many cases, away from the children's grandparents and other relatives) try to rear young children. There are no facilities for community life: no community centre, no shops, no playgroups, no nursery schools, no adventure playground, no places where mothers can meet, compare their experiences and talk together.

Those families who live in large blocks of flats are even more at risk — to depression in the mothers, to violence and vandalism amongst the young people who lack social facilities and who get up to mischief, for the most part, for want of something better to do. To herd people together in such large, impersonal estates or 'high-rise' dwellings is asking for trouble.

Admittedly, walking about such estates one will see houses that are beautifully cared for; spick and span dwellings, with trees blossoming in the front gardens. Yet, in the same roads, one will see the other side of the coin: houses which are delapidated, run down, lived in but almost derelict. In 'high-rise' dwellings there are people who are courageous, responsible citizens. There are also hordes of vandals, totally alienated from their environment, bent on destruction. In some instances they have achieved complete success, where the amount of vandalism has been so great that the tower blocks have had to be blown up, razed to the ground, and the tenants rehoused. Who can say that, living in such community-less, soul-less circumstances, the fault lies entirely with those youngsters who created such havoc and destruction?

There are solutions. You will find estates on which there are community schemes which involve the mothers: 'cuppa clubs', community projects, thriving playgroups, school holiday organized activities for the children. The mothers on such estates do not need to take drugs to calm their nerves; they have organized themselves, sometimes with 'enabling' help from professional organizations, and they are doing something about their environment. For every

*Secker & Warburg Ltd, 1972

community scheme, for every unattached social worker giving his time to those who live in such places, there is a saving to the rest of us. We foot the bill when young people end up in detention centres, borstals or prison. Prevention is always cheaper than cure.

Where the human sense of belonging sinks, the taxes that we pay rise. It is you and I who must pay for the cost of boredom and of alienation. We pay for the violence and vandalism that arises from the feeling of not belonging in a community. Wouldn't it be better to explore ways in which we can develop the *Gemeinschaftgefuhl* — that community spirit — which seems to be so essential to the mental health of both young and old?

THE NEED FOR STATUS Let us return to the example of the village and consider the village blacksmith, a fast-disappearing trade. He is a man who is known within the community and is respected because of his skills. He can do a job which others can't and he takes great pride in that job. He is valued within the community for the work that he does.

Compare the blacksmith, with a man (or woman) working in a large factory, or as part of the clerical staff of a large business concern. He, or she, is not indispensable: if he or she falls ill there will always be somebody available to fill the job. Indeed, on a production line it is essential that individual needs do not get in the way of the job. The line must be kept moving.

If people cannot get status from the job that they do, from their skills, where do they get it from? The answer is that they buy status symbols: motor cars, freezers, dish-washers, mink coats and fox furs, expensive clothes and various other goods which distinguish them from the less well-off. To prove his unique worth, to establish his identity, a man may be forced to buy goods that he does not really need. They are essential items in his own eyes since they establish his status: they are quick-and-easy guides to social standing, within the community.

This, as we might imagine, is a dangerous business — satisfying for those who have the money to buy the goods they see advertised in the colour supplements and on television but frustrating for the 'have-nots'. These days, we have a tendency to compare our status with that of others. There is more relative deprivation. Few of us are starving, but most of us know (and mix with) people who are better off than ourselves. This gives rise to envy and greed. We all expect more. We are, most of us, disappointed in our expectations and our disappointment and frustration at not being amongst 'the in-crowd' turns to anger.

The need to 'be somebody', 'to make one's mark', is a fundamental human need. In our complex society the opportunities to make one's mark are limited. Those who do not have any status — few possessions — may be driven to anti-social acts, even criminal acts and acts of terrorism and murder, to impress upon society that they, the perpetrators of barbarous deeds, are indeed 'somebody'. The punishments that we mete out to them are less of a deterrent than their deep fear of loss of identity and status of being nobody.

The village blacksmith knew who he was and he was respected by others. How many youngsters are respected for the skills that they have? Indeed, what have many of them to offer society? Only themselves. It is up to society, to adults, to ensure that the identity that they have is not set at nought, and their potential contribution to others discounted.

Trade unions go on strike to give them more money to buy the goods which will give them higher status within the community. They also go on strike, I suspect, because they fear that they are not respected sufficiently for their skills, for fear of becoming 'factory fodder' — a source of industrial wealth rather than real people. How do we, in large and complex societies, give each member of society sufficient status to maintain his self-respect? That is a problem to which I shall return later. It is not an easy one to solve.

Let us summarize the argument so far. Where do violence and vandalism come from? They are *learned*; they spring *from frustration*; they come *from a sense of injustice,* a grudge, a feeling that society has dealt the individual concerned a very bad hand of cards in the game of life chances. (Life is unfair; it is the fact that it is so blatantly and shamelessly unfair that makes a great many people in society react with anger.)

Not only this. Chronic frustration, the denial of the opportunity to find legitimate outlets for the expression of our own identity leads to irrational behaviour. We may, like a three-year-old child stamping his foot in anger, *regress* to childish forms of behaviour. We may lash out at those we imagine have hurt us, or project our anger on to completely innocent bystanders. We may daydream of winning the pools, or withdraw into ourselves. On the other hand, we may spray walls with aerosol paint to express our grievances, or break the aerials off cars, or burgle houses, or highjack planes, or kill. Better, the philosophy is, to be somebody and anti-social, than nobody.

In explaining why I think some sections of the community resort to violent or criminal behaviour, or to 'mindless' vandalism (not a good description: there is usually a reason for behaviour, however 'mindless') it may appear that I am trying to excuse it. That is not my intention. We have to try to understand the violent youngster and the vandal. That is not to say we excuse their misdemeanours. Society has to punish wrongdoers; if people do wrong they must make retribution to society. Nobody would argue about that. What we can argue about is the crux of the matter which is contained in three questions. What sort of punishment? How effective is it likely to be? What are the alternatives?

Before we discuss this we should bear in mind that there is a masochistic streak in human beings. Some people like being hurt: they are never happier than when the weather is bad, or they are uncomfortable, miserable or in some sort of emotional turmoil. It is a curious thing to say but, with certain people, as soon as they establish some happiness in their lives, they start to feel guilty.

These people behave like the rats (referred to on p. 54)* who jumped at the black and white cards. Like the rats, the human beings continue to launch themselves at a particular target; even though they know that they have a very high chance of being punished, a very low chance of being rewarded. It is as though they were (a) getting used to pain and (b) positively seeking it out.

I believe that there *is* an urge to punishment; that some of us, whether neurotic or not, are never happier than when we are being punished. Indeed, some people seem to arrange their lives so that they will receive maximum punishment. If things are going well, they will land themselves in matrimonial, financial or legal difficulties so that their own pessimism about life can be justified. They seek out punishment and, usually, they find it.

This urge to punishment has been called the *Polycrates Complex,* after Polycrates, the Tyrant of Samos, who threw an emerald ring into the sea to placate the gods. The ring turned up inside a fish, served to Polycrates at a banquet. Polycrates took this as a sign that the gods had it in for him, that they were lining up something really nasty to happen to him. As in all good Greek tragedy he came to a very sad end, just as he expected (and, some would say, engineered). The need for punishment is, with some human beings, a recurrent theme in their lives. Like the rats they see where the rewards are, despite this, they opt for disaster and punishment.

Let us leave Polycrates, a gangster of 380 BC and consider how best to punish the vandals of modern society. That's easy, you might say. Put them in prison, and for as long as possible, and make them work whilst they're inside. That will teach them the error of their ways.

It's a readily understandable viewpoint, especially if one has been the victim of crime. I have in front of me a newspaper. In it is a letter from a reader who returned from holiday with her husband to find

*Studies of abnormal behaviour in the rat,* R. N. F. Maier *et al.* Journal of Experimental Psychology III, 1940.

her house burgled and her valuables (which had taken fifty years to acquire) stolen.

Obscenities had been scribbled on her walls. The thieves had vomited on her carpets. 'Are we,' the writer asks, 'to let do-gooders and fuddy duddies in high office continue to allow this increasing tide of violence, crime and senseless vandalism?' One can appreciate this housewife's feelings, and her anger. At the end of her letter she advocates longer sentences for criminals who are caught.

Prison sentences certainly keep the criminal away from the rest of us. They remove him from society, but do they deter him from subsequent crime? I think, in a few cases, they do; in many cases, they don't. The burglar I have mentioned before, the one with the son who had been a school truant, had been to prison several times, and the last occasion was a deterrent sentence. It had inconvenienced him. It had punished him. It had *not* deterred him: as soon as he came out of prison he continued his criminal activities. Prisons cost a great deal of money. They cannot (by their isolated nature) rehabilitate the criminal. Only an optimist would claim that they were a kind of therapy. They do punish, but does that punishment deter sufficiently to prevent crime? The answer must be no. Our prisons are filled to overflowing.

Let's take another example. A friend of mine, a social worker, was woken at two o'clock in the morning by sounds in his kitchen. He went downstairs to investigate. He saw a burglar making a hurried exit through the kitchen window.

A chase ensued. My friend caught up with the man, took hold of him and said: 'You're going to come with me.' The man replied, in an educated accent: 'I don't think so.' He broke free, ran off through a maze of side roads and made good his escape. 'He was no more than sixteen or seventeen' said my friend, 'but I could have killed him. I hope they find him and put him away for a very long time.' His wish was granted. The youth was, subsequently, apprehended by the police, tried, and sent to borstal for several years.

Good, you say. But is it? Borstals, like prisons, are very expensive institutions and it is we, the taxpayers, who pay for them. Do they work? Do they deter criminals from committing further crimes? The answer, again, is no — many youngsters who go to borstal return to borstal within a very short time.

Is it, when we think about it, surprising? Another friend of mine, a teacher, worked in a borstal for many years. During her time there she befriended one inmate who was due to be released. His day of freedom came and, two days later, he 'phoned her. 'Can I come and stay with you?' he asked her. He had no friends, nowhere to go. My friend, because of her family commitments, couldn't help. Within a week, the lad was in trouble again. The causes which led him into crime in the first place had not been removed and those same causes led him back to his well-worn path.

How silly to spend enormous sums on preventive institutions like borstals and yet to provide inadequate help to prisoners once they are released! If the prisoner goes back to the home circumstances which made him turn to crime in the first place, we must not be hypocritical enough to express surprise when he continues his life of crime and 'fails to see the error of his ways'.

Leo Tolstoy, in *Anna Karenina,* tells us that all happy families resemble each other but each unhappy family is unhappy in its own way. I'd like to alter that and say, all happy families resemble each other, and unhappy, delinquent-producing families are remarkably similar when we come to look at them closely. Loving, caring families do not produce violent youngsters, or criminals, or vandals. Those families which do produce such youngsters have certain things in common. The more we examine the cloth of delinquency the more we realize that there are certain recurrent patterns running through the weave.

Based on my own experience as an educational psychologist I should like to list the ten most common factors present within those families which produce criminal, delinquent or anti-social youngsters. They are:

1   Defective discipline within the home (usually it is too lax; less frequently, far too strict).
2   Inadequate (or missing) fathers.
3   Lack of overt affection shown to children within the family.
4   Quarrelling (or violent) parents.
5   A depressed, inadequate mother.
6   Sheer lack of interest in the lives of the children.
7   An emotionally disturbed mother, who is too obsessed with her own problems to look after the children.
8   A drunken, or criminal, father.
9   Low IQ on the part of father or mother and a chaotic, haphazard pattern of family life.
10   Rejection, either overt or concealed, by the mother of a child, or children.

Parents should set a good example to their own children. Those parents that fight, quarrel and constantly argue with each other can hardly be surprised if they produce aggressive, anti-social children. Many adults, if they found something valuable in the street, would pocket it. Children notice such things, just as they notice the father who boasts about cheating the tax inspector or the mother who, when given too much change in the shop, walks off with it. The way father treats mother, and vice versa, may set a pattern for the children; and that pattern may be one of non-caring, neglectful or even violent relationships.

What can we do to help families which produce anti-social, delinquent children? It has been suggested that we tackle the problem at governmental level by introducing a new ministerial post, a Minister for Families. Certainly, I would have no objection to this; we have a Minister for Sport; sport is important, but hardly more important than the family which is the bedrock upon which societies are built.

I think, too, that Child Guidance Clinics, the local Social Services Departments and charitable organizations such as the NSPCC all have a part to play but I do not think we will solve the problem of violence and vandalism until parents realize that it is their duty to build up, within the child, self-discipline and a stable system of moral values. Mothers who go out to work, fathers who are frequently absent from the home, the absence of moral values within the parents; all these factors add up to neglect of the child (and neglected children do strike back at a society which has hurt them).

Not all mothers who work do harm to their children: many mothers manage to do a job and to be a good mother as well. It isn't easy. There are women who benefit from going out to work: they are more cheerful when they come in, have more to give to the children when they are with them. There are mothers who prefer work to the family, who (having had children) place a low priority on family life and would rather be in the factory, the office (or the bingo hall) than in their own living-rooms. This is asking for trouble (since it is a rejection of the children that they brought into the world) and trouble there often is. That trouble usually takes the form of aggressive behaviour; not directed at the parents but at society at large — you and me.

We all know the sort of families I am talking about. What can we do to help them? First, for mothers (and fathers, many of whom may be unemployed) 'cuppa clubs', local playgroups, youth clubs and neighbourhood organizations all have a part to play. They should try to involve parents. We must develop a better sense of community, of mutual help, *within the neighbourhood, by the neighbourhood*. The street, the estate, the high-rise flats ('slums in the sky') must be given a sense of self-respect. The only way that they can gain self-respect is by self-help. The professional can set up various clubs and organizations. Then, the professional must move out, and the people must run such self-help institutions themselves.

Schools can help. They can be community-based, family (rather than factory) institutions, which remain open in the evening and support a wide range of community activities embracing all age-groups within the neighbourhood. Teachers and parents should work together for the good of the child. Teachers may be able to offer a boy or girl a wide range of activities (swimming, football, netball, camping, cycling, judo and other worthwhile pursuits) which give him or her something to do during leisure hours and provide an opportunity for aggression to be worked off in a non anti-social way.

The police can also help: by having more men on the beat, by visiting schools regularly and by talking to the youngsters about the work of the police. *By being seen to be an essential part of the local community* the police can take a preventative role with regard to juvenile crime. When we see young police constables (men and women) in track suits at the local recreation ground, in 'civvies' at the local youth club, mixing with and making friends with local youngsters, then we can point to a positive approach to policing and young people. All too often, the police become involved only when the damage is done and the youngster has already broken the law.

The *Zeitgeist,* the spirit of the times, is too lax, too casual, particularly with regard to young people. Youngsters do not respect adults who say, in effect: 'Anything goes'. If we treat young people with a negligent casualness can we be all that surprised when they reject our attitude and values and lash out at a society which so undervalues them as people?

What do we need to do to stop violence and vandalism? I am sure you have some ideas of your own. Here, I list just a few measures I think we could take to prove that we adults really are seriously involved in the business of rearing the next generation of parents. We should:

1 *Have a Minister for Families* He or she would be charged with ensuring that society was doing its very best to help families, and the youngsters in our midst.

2 *Pay mothers with young children to stay at home* The loving care of a mother is vital to young children and the mother's place (when children are not yet of school age) is in the home.

3 *Encourage more community schemes* to give youngsters something to do. On the stage of violence and vandalism, the chief villain is boredom.

4 *Encourage more collaboration* between primary care-givers within the community (i.e., social workers, youth leaders, teachers) and the police and all other agencies involved with young people. Put in every office of all these agencies, in a

prominent place, the slogan: THERE IS ONLY PREVENTION. THERE IS NO CURE.

5 *Have citizenship classes within schools* (helped by the local police and other statutory and voluntary agencies) to encourage young people to live law-abiding lives and to help people who are handicapped or worse off than themselves.

6 *Have a massive drive to tidy up the country* (especially cities) to restore some of our self-respect. This would involve the unemployed as well as secondary school children. Our cities look shabby, vandalized. This encourages further vandalism. Isn't it time we cleaned up the environment in which we live?

7 *Provide a wider variety of (and more pertinent) punishment* for young offenders, including work camps, 'short, sharp shock' punishment (e.g., weekend detention centres) and a greater variety of community service orders. It is of dubious value, and very costly, to send youngsters to borstals and other long-term institutions which are often 'universities of crime' as well as ineffective deterrents.

8 *Have an emphasis on television on socially-minded behaviour* instead of implying that the solution to problems is violence and physical aggression. Violence on television may effect the behaviour of only a small number of youngsters. It, on the other hand, does nothing to give young people of all ages an example of how to behave decently.

9 *Tighten the law to put more pressure on parents to be responsible for their children.* When youngsters commit a crime, put the parents on probation and ask *them* to make some restitution to society.

10 *Set a good example* All of us, but especially the leaders within society, should show youngsters adequate patterns of responsible behaviour. We, adults, must learn to act honestly and decently and with consideration towards each other.

The violence and the vandalism that we see about us is a symptom of the neglect of young people by their parents, by their neighbours and by the leaders of society. We are all implicated. If we, the adults, don't care you can be sure that youngsters will not care either. In that case, we lose, they lose and their children lose.

## Chapter Eight

# Sex, Love and Relationships

The letter from the headmistress read as follows:

> Denise is sexually precocious. She flirts outrageously with the boys in the school and even with men on the school staff. She is known to my women teachers as Denise the Menace. In my twenty-two years of teaching, I've never met anybody like her. Can you advise?

When Denise and her mother turned up at the child guidance clinic it happened to be a beautiful sunny day. Looking through the window of my room I saw a sports car turn into the car park at the front of the clinic and glide to a halt.

Two very attractive women got out of it, one dressed in yellow, with shoes and handbag to match, and the other in white. A few moments later the clinic secretary told me: 'Your next appointment has arrived.' I went into the waiting-room to learn that the woman in yellow was Denise, aged fifteen.

In my office I asked them both to sit down.

'Cigarette?' asked mother. I declined. She lit hers and puffed away as we talked. 'Denise is very fond of older men,' said mother. 'I think she's going to like you.' Denise smiled at me. Then, she winked.

'Men of your age are more interesting,' she said.

Clearly, giving Denise advice about anything, never mind sex, did not promise to be easy.

Let me interrupt the story to confess, straight away, that my own sex education can only be described as appalling. Teachers, in all my years at school, never mentioned sex. My mother discussed it with none of her children. My father referred to it obliquely, when I was in my late 'teens, by telling dirty jokes in the pub.

As a teenager, the little information that I had on the topic had been gleaned from other boys of my own age, and from embarrassing encounters with girls in the local park or in draughty bus-shelters. At the age of nineteen, whilst on active service in Kenya fighting the Mau Mau, I could reflect to myself that I was old enough to die for my country but not old enough for any adult to have had an open discussion with me about sex, love, and relationships with females — the other half of the human race.

My wife's sex education had been no better. It consisted of her mother whispering to her nervously: 'There's something for you to read on the mantelpiece.' This 'something' was a brief pamphlet about menstruation. The fact that my wife and I produced a family, and cured our mutual ignorance of sex, is a tribute to human forbearance and curiosity.

Reacting against our own upbringing, both my wife and I insist on a major rule of sex education: *it should begin as soon as children start asking questions.* Having been fobbed off with evasive looks, avoidance of the topic, we were both keen to answer our children's questions honestly, factually and without 'flannel'.

The second lesson we learned was that it doesn't matter that one's own sex education was so awful but *it does matter that we are open about our own doubts, confusions and uncertainties.* We, as parents, may find ourselves giving advice to the first generation of teenagers who have received formal sex education in school. It would be silly if we were to pretend to be wiser in this area of life than we really are. Teenagers expect, and deserve, complete frankness.

Sex education, it seems to me, is a basic human right. It is not a privilege, or an optional extra. It is not covered in half-hour lessons at the age of fifteen, on pregnancy, venereal disease and contraception. This is too crude, too little and too late. Sex education has to be set in the context of human relationships and it has to start early.

Teachers, and heads of schools, vary enormously in their attitude towards sex education for the youngsters in their charge. Some of them are aware, concerned, forward-looking. Others are appalling. I remember one headmaster of a boys' secondary school turning down a series of lectures by an outside speaker on sex and relationships. His reason? 'My lads don't get pregnant.' That shows a fundamental misunderstanding of the true context of sex and its part in a meaningful relationship.

A woman friend, an experienced and first-rate teacher of teenage girls, asked me recently: 'At what age should we teach them about contraception?' The subject, she opined, should be taught at the second-year level (ages twelve to thirteen years) rather than in the fourth and fifth years. The second-year girls, she added, had been taught about menstruation.

In my book this was a non-question. Sex education cannot be compartmentalized; contraception and menstruation are not isolated topics. They are part and parcel of our duty to behave responsibly towards ourselves and towards others (including the unborn); they are part of our need to understand vital human physiological and emotional processes.

Teachers *are* confused about sex education. It is silly to say that many of them are not secure in their own sexuality. After all, who is? It isn't silly to say that there is no point in hiding their own fears and ignorance by too frequent use of the word 'Don't!' Youngsters want to know the whys and the wherefores; they want to know what is positive and helpful, rather than forbidden.

Nobody has ever died, to my knowledge, from knowing too much about sex. Many thousands of people, children and adults, have been made miserable by knowing too little. It is amazing how ignorant parents are in this crucial area. Young teachers in training, at institutes of higher education, are taught very little about sex education. Parents, teachers, even members of the medical profession, still have a curious reticence on the subject. Many hundreds (thousands) of youngsters pick up their sex education where I myself picked it up — from friends. That is too casual a way of acquiring what is, let's face it, vital information.

Sex education, given by sensitive parents or by trained teachers, can play a major role in combatting illegitimacy, pornography, obscenity and the embarrassed, hole-in-the-corner attitudes of large sections of the adult population. There is nothing obscene about sex, in its proper context of caring human relationships. Now, back to Denise and her mother.

'The headmistress tells me that Denise is . . .' I could hardly say 'sexually precocious'. I took an easy way out. 'Not doing terribly well at school,' I continued, 'and having trouble with some of the members of staff.' I really wanted mother and daughter to do the talking.

'Have you met the teachers at Denise's school?' asked mother. 'They're really old-fashioned. Anyway, what does Denise want with all that English and Maths? She's going to be a hair-stylist, like myself.'

Come to think of it, both mother and daughter had very elaborate (and very fashionable) hair-dos.

It transpired that Denise had a boyfriend called Ted, aged twenty. Denise and Ted were due to be engaged on Denise's sixteenth birthday.

Mother and Denise's father had separated when Denise was ten. An only child, Denise was very attached to her father, and extremely upset when he abandoned both her and mother to 'run off with another woman'.

By the end of the interview I had come to certain conclusions. It was fairly obvious that Denise had a tendency to flirt. I did not think that her flirtatious attitude was solely, or even mainly, sexual.

Denise *was* attention-seeking with men but was this the result of the loss of her own father?

Perhaps it was because Denise was gaining very little either intellectually or emotionally in school that she was using sex as a weapon, to ensure that she did make some kind of impact on the staff. My problems were (a) how could I advise the school without making the staff (and the headmistress) feel that they had failed with Denise? (b) how could I help Denise to make good use of the ten months that remained to her of her school life?

I discovered, during the interview, that Denise was interested in art and in young children. I therefore asked the school to arrange for her to spend more time doing art, and practical subjects such as dressmaking and child care.

It was possible for Denise, with the co-operation of the headmistress, to help out at a local playgroup for two mornings a week. This Denise greatly enjoyed and, according to the playgroup leader, she was 'marvellous with the children'.

I told the headmistress that, in my view, Denise was *not* promiscuous. Promiscuity is having indiscriminate sexual relationships with people you don't care about but Denise had one boyfriend, Ted, and the couple were devoted to each other. That is not being promiscuous, whatever our opinion may be as to the wisdom of becoming attached to one person so early in life.

Denise, after a couple of months, was a 'changed girl', (the headmistress's phrase). She had been made an art monitor, which gave her some prestige. Her maternal feelings could be expressed, and put to practical use, within the playgroup. The staff had been told about Denise's father (most of them knew little or nothing about the home situation) and were more understanding of the girl's behaviour. Denise stopped, quite spontaneously, flirting so outrageously with the male members of staff. She also gave up her habit of embracing Ted at lunchtime outside the school gates; a sacrifice on her part which greatly pleased the headmistress.

The case of Denise sticks in my mind for two reasons: (a) *the school* were wrong to brand her as 'sexually precocious' and fail to give her the praise, prestige and responsibility that she was seeking. Denise was a mature, sensible fifteen-year-old who was bored in school. She was not 'immoral'. In fact, she was a very caring person; (b) *mother* had never discussed sex openly and factually with Denise. What Denise knew about sex she had picked up from her friends, including her boyfriend.

This leads me to ask are we, as parents, any more honest about sex education than were our own parents? Many of the parents I know (most of them able, coping parents) have *never* discussed sex with their children. 'I would be too embarrassed,' a mother told me.

'They learn all about it in school,' said a father. Parental sex education is, I suspect (at best), extremely patchy and (at its worst) non-existent.

What do pre-teenage (and certainly teenage) girls need to know? They need to know about menstruation. The age at which girls start their first periods varies enormously: some girls start at fourteen or fifteen but others start at the age of eleven or twelve.

If menstruation starts suddenly, without warning, it can be a very alarming experience for the girl concerned. Often, for example, the first period is not a bright red colour, as many girls expect. It may be of a reddish-brown hue and the unsuspecting girl may think that she is ill, or has damaged part of her inside. She *must* be told about menstruation well in advance.

Mothers should tell their daughters the facts of life, bluntly and without prevarication. This is better than picking up fairy stories in the school playground. It is also better than all of the responsibility being placed on the shoulders of the school.

Sex is not to do with gooseberry bushes or storks; it has little to do with the birds and the bees, or the physiology of the frog. Sex is to do with human relationships. Sexual maturity is part of personal maturity, and what we only half know can hinder our development.

A parent *should* have a closer relationship with a child than a biology teacher. I do not think that parents can stand back in this important aspect of life and hope for the best, or leave the problem to somebody else.

The words parents should use to talk to youngsters about sex should include words such as 'vagina', 'penis', 'erection', 'sperm' and 'ejaculation'. Many children are a little embarrassed when they hear these words for the first time. The shock soon wears off, especially if parents avoid euphemisms and try to avoid making the child embarrassed by not being embarrassed themselves. Honesty and openness, in these matters, breeds honesty and openness.

A female friend told me recently that she first heard the word 'penis' when she was eighteen. She had no idea what it meant. Her parents had never, in the whole of her life, mentioned sex to her.

Sex, of course, is not only to do with having babies. It is an expression of love and an important aspect of communication between two people. We should tell youngsters that sexual desire is best gratified, and most tenderly expressed, within the context of a loving caring relationship. To be promiscuous — i.e. have casual sex — demeans both sex and the promiscuous person.

Young people want to know what seem to us obvious facts. A woman does not conceive every time she has sex with a man. It is possible to conceive standing up and/or during the first sexual experience (as many girls have, sadly, discovered for themselves).

Young people need to have a factual description of childbirth. They need to know about Caesarian births, and the reasons for them. They need to know what an umbilical cord is, what it does and what happens to that and to the placenta after the baby is born.

*Masturbation* is a much-avoided topic amongst parents. Many boys and girls do worry about masturbation; it *can* lead to intense moral conflict and to feelings of unworthiness amongst more sensitive teenagers.

At home, we have an old medical book, a volume of some 1,010 pages. On page 865 there is a photo of a happy, healthy-looking man taken 'before the habits of secret vice had begun to tell on him'. On the next page there is a 'photo of the same man, dark-eyed and miserable, taken three years later 'when he had become an inveterate victim of the vice'. The doctor's opinion? 'If this young man escapes the asylum he and his parents will be fortunate.' Thousands of young people, in the past, have been made to feel guilty and wretched because of this kind of nonsense. It's plainly silly, yet it did a great deal of harm.

What are the facts? Masturbation has *no* adverse physical side effects. It does *not* make us go blind, or mad, or make us weak, or give us a spotty complexion. It is only when youngsters feel guilt or ashamed of this quite natural exploration and manipulation of their own bodies that harm is done.

Masturbation is a source of sexual pleasure; it also serves to release sexual tension. It can provide an outlet for the young person's sexual imagination and daydreaming, his or her sexual fantasies. Most people have these fantasies and the vast majority of young men (and a large proportion of young women) masturbate. Neither the fantasies, nor the masturbation, are harmful.

An American survey showed that ninety-three per cent of men, and sixty-two per cent of women, had masturbated. Since most of us have done it it can hardly be called an unusual practice; since most of us have come through our masturbatory experiences unscathed, it cannot be injurious.

What does the damage, where damage is done, are feelings of shame, guilt and unworthiness, which most youngsters seem to feel about this commonplace expression of their own sexuality. The truth is that the shame felt about masturbation by many youngsters is a symptom of the parents' (and other adults') confused, secretive and embarrassed attitude towards their own sexuality and the sexual lives of young people. It cannot be said too strongly: *masturbation is nothing to be ashamed of.* It has helped thousands of young girls to experience and learn about orgasm; it has helped thousands of boys to understand their own bodies, to give expression to their sexual feelings. It is, most importantly, pleasurable. It is because they do not trust adults, do not feel close to them, that youngsters are so afraid to admit that they masturbate, and suffer the pain of guilt. This is the price that *they* pay for our failure to give them the facts, and to present those facts in a proper, humane context.

Young people need to learn about contraception. It is the moral responsibility of us all to make sure that our actions don't affect others in a harmful way. One of the ways we can harm other people is by bringing an unwanted child into the world. No child should ever be born as a result of a casual, passing relationship. Every baby should be a wanted baby.

Youngsters, therefore, should know about the various methods of contraception. They should be aware of the sheath (condom, French letter); the diaphragm (Dutch cap); the Pill; foaming tablets, aerosol foams and spermicidal jellies; the IUD (intra-uterine device, coil or loop). I advocate that teenagers know about contraceptives, *whether or not they have need to use them.* Nobody was ever hurt by knowing too much about contraception; thousands of youngsters have been hurt as a result of knowing too little.

It is essential to describe the drawbacks of various forms of contraception: that the 'withdrawal method' (i.e. withdrawing the penis from the vagina) is far from safe; that condoms can slip off the penis on withdrawal and sperms enter the vagina and uterus, and pregnancy results.

Even 'going on the Pill' has snags. It is essential to use it only when prescribed by a doctor. It can have serious side-effects, especially where a woman (or young girl) is overweight or has high blood pressure. A girl may not understand that she cannot just pop the Pill into her mouth and have sex — she will need to learn how soon after taking the Pill it is safe to start having sexual intercourse.

The best contraceptive of all is a sense of responsibility towards other human beings. Sexual intercourse should never take place casually, without forethought, or as a result solely of sexual excitement. Sex, to be really satisfying, should be an extension of caring.

Young people are surrounded, everywhere they look, by references to sex, on television, in the popular daily newspapers, and in magazines. This more open display of sexual material does not mean that there isn't, still, a great deal of ignorance and misunderstanding about sexual matters.

Every year, more than 13,000 schoolgirls between the ages of thirteen and seventeen become pregnant. Every year, there is a rise in the incidence of venereal infections, including schoolchildren who have caught gonorrhoea, or other sexually transmitted diseases. These are the casualties in the war against sexual ignorance, and our failure to stress the importance of the *emotional,* rather than the *physical* aspects, of sex.

Whilst youngsters need to know the facts about VD they also need to understand about the importance of *feelings* in sexual relationships; they need to realize that sexual attraction is only a part of the wide spectrum of attraction that draws members of the opposite sex towards each other. We can be friends, as well as (or instead of) lovers, and with equal satisfaction and happiness.

The danger in the teaching of sex education is that schools may leave it to the parents, whilst the parents leave it to the schools; in the middle of the two is the teenager, confused about this adult reticence to discuss openly one of the most important aspects of life. Sex is important and, like birth and death, it is part of life and cannot be side-stepped.

Parents and teachers *are* confused about sex education. Many of them think that to talk about sex you have to be 'good at it', or have had a great deal of sexual experience. This isn't so. Providing that you are honest about your own doubts, fears and ignorance, young people will listen to you and respect you for your openness; furthermore, the fact that you don't pretend to be omnicompetent and faultless is more, rather than less, reassuring to them.

There is nothing obscene about sex. There is plenty of obscenity (i.e. activities which 'tend to corrupt') about us both on television and in the streets. Violence and vandalism is obscene; so is the neglect or pollution of the environment in which we all must live. Cruelty is obscene; so is sadistic treatment of another human being. In the context of a caring relationship, sex (I repeat) is not obscene. It is certainly not 'dirty'.

How should a parent go about teaching the teenager about sex? The answer is as naturally, and as casually, as possible. If we make too much of a 'performance' of it the whole thing is driven into its secret, guilt-ridden, underground terrain. When sex is brought out into the light of day the result is far less personal unhappiness for the youngster. We must avoid passing on *our* own anxieties about sex to the next generation of parents.

Schools should eschew a biological, physiological approach to sex. Sex should be allied to child development, to the emotions and to our relationships with others. Young people must be given an opportunity to talk, not about rabbits or frogs, but about their responsibilities towards each other. They should ask questions, and have some answers, concerning friendship, love and happiness, as well as sex.

Teenage girls, but not boys, are taught child care. This is part of curious tendency to make girls morally responsible for sexual (and family) matters. Boys should be prepared for fatherhood (the husbands of the future will find it harder to avoid doing household tasks or taking their share of looking after the baby). Both boys and girls should be prepared for *parenthood.*

Fathers will, more and more, be expected by their wives to take an active interest in the physical, intellectual and emotional wellbeing of the children. Fathering, in my view, is just as important as mothering. Teenage boys will, therefore, need to be taught something of *father's* role within the family. At present, our attitude towards sex education for boys is totally archaic, and many boys leave school without having had any child care lessons, sex education or discussion of parental roles whatsoever.

At this stage, let us look at the views of the teenagers themselves on sex, love and relationships and make some comments as we go along.

'I'm not interested in boys,' one fourteen-year-old girl told me. She had been referred to me by her mother who explained that she was worried about her, since her daughter's best friend had a steady boyfriend. 'What's wrong with my daughter?' she asked. The answer is, of course, nothing. The girl will judge when she is ready to go out with boys. Some girls go out with their first 'steady date' at the age of eleven; others do not have a regular boy friend until they are eighteen, nineteen or even older. It is up to the teenager concerned to decide she (or he) is ready to date the opposite sex.

'I'd rather go out with other girls. We have more fun,' this youngster told me. Why shouldn't she? There is tremendous variation in the development of sexual awareness in teenagers, and in sexual activity. It would be quite wrong to expect teenagers of the same age to act in the same way.

The curious thing about this girl was that she dressed in a provocative, 'sexy' way, with a tight skirt, split up the side, and a sweater that emphasized her ample bosom. Rather like Denise, and many other girls, she had no idea of the misleading impression this gave. What she was after was admiration, not sex. Many girls, even with a boy who they know well, may wish the boy to hold their hand, or kiss them, 'neck with them', but go no further. Boys, whose sexuality is much nearer the surface, find this difficult to understand.

The truth is that physical sex is usually less important to a girl than being loved, cared for, or admired ('rated'). A girl is concerned with her friendships as a whole, with her 'image' and reputation. The last thing she wants to be thought of is a 'slag' or the local 'bicycle' whom everybody who chooses can have a ride on.

Teenage boys, on the other hand, may take great pride in (and boast about) being 'a stud' or 'one for the girls'. Sexual conquests may enhance their reputation amongst friends, rather than diminish it. Boys talk about sex far more than girls. They swap stories, tell each other 'how far a girl will go', and generally split off this area of life from their other (sometimes more caring) relationships.

Few girls read 'soft-porn' magazines. The fact that such magazines are read by a large number of teenage boys is an indication of how separate and apart sex must seem to them. It is linked with eroticism, and 'sexy', unavailable women rather than with real people — youngsters of the opposite sex who are usually quite keen to talk to them and get to know them.

Girls do not chat to each other about sex as sex. What they like to talk about is the periphery of the sexual, or friendly, encounter: the clothes that they wore, the make-up, what the boy looked like, his face, his dress sense, his personality. A girl usually likes her friends to meet her boyfriend; if she is going steady with him, and likes him a lot, she may want her parents to meet him too. In this aspect of sex (the social aspect) girls are often more mature than boys in that they wish to integrate sexual or loving relationships with the rest of their lives. They are quite right to want to do so — sex is not something apart, and it should never become a 'dirty secret'.

Teenagers reach puberty, and discover their own sexuality, at different times but before they are old enough to marry or to enter upon (in most cases) a full sexual relationship. As they grow towards sexual maturity the sex urge is strong: yet they must sublimate that urge, direct it towards non-sexual activities, if the concept of marriage and responsible child-rearing is to survive. When a teenager says that she is not yet interested in boys the sensible thing, it seems to me, is to believe her — she has found her own way of satisfactorily sublimating one of the strongest of human urges. Why should we push teenagers into sexual relationships when they are not ready for them or do not want them?

It is useful nevertheless to gain some experience of the opposite sex before marriage and this can range from casual friendship to an intense, passionate love affair. In any large group of seventeen-year-olds there will be a few girls who have never been out with a boy, a great many who have friendships of one sort or another and a few girls who are 'sleeping around'. It is not for me to take a moral stance here but rather to point out that a variety of non-sexual friendships during teenage can teach us a lot about other people, especially about members of the opposite sex.

Attitudes to sex before marriage amongst teenagers, as we might expect, vary enormously. One sixteen-year-old girl told me: 'Nobody is going to practise on me. I intend to get married in white. White signifies that you are a virgin and that is exactly what I intend to be. I'm told sex is marvellous but I can wait until I'm married to find out. My husband and myself can learn all there is to know from each other.'

95

Despite what one might gather from newspapers and television (and magazines for teenagers) this is *not* an unusual point of view. Many youngsters feel that they are being pressurized to be sexually experienced, both by friends and by the media. Contrary to what we might guess many girls (and boys) resist this pressure and take what is essentially the view of most churches (including most Christian churches) on this issue: that sexual intercourse should take place within the context of marriage.

Another teenage girl (also sixteen) had very different views. 'What's wrong with sex?' she asked me. 'It's just like eating an ice-cream. It's enjoyable, and it does you no harm. Also (she laughs) it's the only thing left that costs nothing. I think that adults say that teenagers shouldn't have sex before marriage because they (i.e. the adults) are so hungup about sex themselves. If you sleep around you find out what it's all about, don't you? And, besides, it's greatly over-rated, sex, I mean (pauses, then laughs loudly), I should know.'

My reaction to this view would be to make sure that the girl knew something about contraception. I would also have a diplomatic chat to her about the incidence of venereal disease amongst youngsters who partake of casual sex. Then I would attempt to discuss with the girl the meaning of a mature emotional relationship. Even a sixteen-year-old may find that sexual relationships place emotional pressures on her and prevent her from having a wide spectrum of relationships with young people of both sexes and differing ages. Finally, I would put the girl in touch with one or two useful agencies, just in case she needed further advice or practical help.*

One girl of my acquaintance, who is fourteen, has a boyfriend of twenty-two. They sleep together, with the full knowledge of all four parents. Sex with a girl under the age of sixteen is, in this country, illegal. An adult found guilty of such an offence could go to prison. The girl herself could be taken into the care of the local authority and deemed 'in need of care and protection'. A male minor can be prosecuted for having sexual intercourse with a girl below consenting age.

Having made clear the illegality of the situation let me say that

---

*Advice on birth control may be obtained from:
1  The family doctor.
2  *Brook Advisory Centres.* Registered Office: 233, Tottenham Court Road, London W1P 9AE. Tel: 01-323-1522.
3  *The Family Planning Association,* 27/35 Mortimer Street, London, W1A 4QW. Tel: 01-583-3077.
4  *The Marie Stopes Memorial Clinic,* 108 Whitfield Street, London W1P 6BE. Tel: 01-388-0662.

there are fourteen and fifteen-year-old girls who are having sexual relationships. The morality, and illegality of the situation is a matter for the youngsters (and the parents) concerned. What our major concern must be is that none of these girls bring into the world an unplanned for, unwanted baby. The agencies below do not take a moral stance: it is one of their concerns to stop undesired pregnancies. I would strongly urge mothers who suspect that their young teenage daughter may be having sexual intercourse to make sure that they contact one or other of these agencies before they take up a moral stance on the issue. If a young girl *is* sleeping with a boyfriend it is essential to reverse the normal procedure. Deal, in other words, with contraception first and human relationships and morality second.

Those who are indignant at this advice may not fully appreciate the tragedy that an unwanted baby can bring into a girl's life nor the damaging psychological effects of abortion (or termination of pregnancy, i.e. the deliberate killing of the human foetus *in utero*) on an, as yet, not fully mature teenager. Practical help is worth more to the youngster concerned than too much moralizing. *That* (ethical and legal) angle can be discussed (and it *must* be discussed) after the question of contraception has been dealt with. Nobody wants fourteen-year-olds to sleep around; by the same token nobody wants a young teenager to have a baby that she cannot love, cherish, protect and care for.

Teenagers, I have stressed, face two dangers in their sex education: (a) that schools are too biologically orientated in their teaching (where that teaching exists) and (b) that parents, despite our so-called 'enlightened' times, still do not discuss sex openly with their children. With some parents, furthermore, sex is a nasty word — a taboo subject never to be mentioned.

Parents have a tremendous responsibility in sex education. They are the major signal box to prevent their children from going off the rails and given that the relationships within the home are open and honest, it is to them that the sexually active teenager should turn for advice.

I'd now like to discuss a more appealing (though, sometimes, no less fraught) topic — love. Let us start off with something that a seventeen-year-old girl told me. 'I'm in love,' she said. 'It's really marvellous. My boyfriend is an apprentice car mechanic, and we met at the college where he goes once a week (on a day-release scheme). He's very good-looking. I think about him all the time — from the minute I get up to the time I go to bed. I dream about him, too. I'm really happy and I know I'll never love anybody else as much as I love him.'

From her description, it sounds as though this particular teenager

97

has been well and truly pierced by Cupid's arrow! Young love, particularly first love, is a very special feeling.

To be in love is exciting at any age. My wife's grandmother was courted, at the age of ninety-three, by a curly-haired stripling of eighty-four who was head-over-heels in love with her. He had been an ostler as a teenager looking after the horses used to pull coaches, before the days of the motor car. The two senior citizens would hold hands and gaze into each others eyes, even in public. They were very much in love, and very happy about it.

First love, though, is even more thrilling. Many people remember their first love all their lives. I can recall, clearly, the very first girl with whom I fell in love. I can picture her face, the colour of her eyes, her hair, the dresses she wore, even the pattern of freckles on her nose. I was eleven-years-old at the time.

With quite a few teenagers their first experience of love is a 'crush' or 'pash' on an older person of the same sex. With a boy, it may be a games master, the captain of the school football team, or some other heroic-seeming figure who evokes his undying admiration. With girls it may be a mistress at school, a guide leader, or an attractive and prestigious older girl who is the object of adoration. A smile from the loved one, a glance, will make the smitten teenager blush, and make the rest of the day bliss; a frown, an angry word, and the teenager will be plunged into paroxysms of despair. Most of the objects of teenage 'crushes', it should be added, are worshipped from afar; this makes it safer to love since the fantasy, and the distance involved means that the teenager stands less chance of being rejected.

What is love? There are many different kinds. We may love our family, our cat or our best friend; there is no romantic element (or sex) present. It might be better to say that we have warm lasting affection for them, we like them a lot, we are extremely fond of them. Used in this affectionate sense it is clear that *we can love more than one person*; indeed, we can (and, I hope, do) love a large number of people.

Romantic love, or being *in love,* is quite different. This is what poets write about and singers sing about: it is an ecstatic feeling, almost a loss of our own separate identity, where we feel a part of the person whom we love and at one with the world about us. Such a feeling must exist since so many people have tried to put it into words. 'Like walking on air,' says one. 'Being on cloud nine,' says another. Another, rather more cynical, view is Jerome K. Jerome's: 'Love is like the measles,' he tells us. 'We all have to go through it.'

I would not denigrate the power of love in human life. Perhaps the major theme of life is good versus bad (and we have to work out what is good and bad for ourselves, and for those with whom we come in contact). I would prefer to say that the major thread running through all our lives is love versus destruction, and we all have to decide whether we build, create and love or hate, dislike and destroy.

Love is a powerful waveband into which we must all tune if we are to stop manipulating, abusing and debasing each other. We can tune into love through art, through religion, through philosophy, through play, through dance and through music. We can also tune into love by means of another person. Great love stories, whether of fulfilled or thwarted love, reach out to our unconscious as well as our conscious minds. Romantic love, in our own lives, in the same way, can transform us (as the seventeen-year-old in love with her apprentice mechanic knew only too well).

There is no knowing who people will fall in love with. The loved one is often not what we expect. Plain people may love each other, as may beautiful couples; but the ugly may love the beautiful and the beautiful may love the plain. Somebody who is talkative and sociable may fall in love with a person who is shy. Tall people fall in love with short people, fat people with thin people, clever people with dull people. It is the tremendous variation within the spectrum of loved objects that makes the whole business of falling in love so mysterious.

Sometimes, a young person may fall in love with a person of the same sex. Where this is not a schoolgirl (or schoolboy) crush but an adult relationship that person is called homosexual, i.e. 'same sex'. Usually male homosexuals are called 'gays' and women homosexuals 'lesbians' (from the Greek Lesbos — the island where women ruled, and loved each other). Nowadays, there is no shame attached to being a homosexual; most universities have 'gay societies'; most cities have clubs where homosexuals can meet. There is still, we must add, a great deal of prejudice against (and ignorance about) homosexuality within our society.

If a young person feels no attraction towards the opposite sex it does not mean that he or she is necessarily homosexual. If the youngster is worried about it, help is available from the family doctor, or from local counsellors who can be contacted through the Citizen's Advice Bureau. It is important, for young people not to worry about their feelings towards those friends of the same sex and only in the light of advice, varied friendships and increasing maturity should they attempt to decide whether or not they are homosexual.

Sex and love, it should be clear, are two different things. There are many people around us whom we may love; there are those with whom there is a possibility of a sexual, loving relationship; there may be that one, very special, person with whom we are in love. Puppy love may come and go quickly, but it is no less intense for all

99

that: it draws to itself the human need to love, and the human delight at being in love. As we grow older we see that mutual respect, trust and courtesy are vital elements in any love which is to last.

What is very sad in our society is the taboo we have imposed on too-overt expression of affection. We don't touch each other enough, in my opinion, nor hug each other (as in the USSR) or even shake hands with each other when we meet (as they do in France, for example). It is frowned upon to show too much tenderness to those for whom we have affection and liking. This, in my view, is a grave error: human beings have a deep need to show affection and to love, as well as being shown affection and love. Why should we be averse to showing love (in its general sense) by kind words and loving physical contact?

The vital concept in the whole panorama of teenage sex, love and relationships is that of *friendship*. It is in the context of friendship that we learn most about ourselves and about our obligations to others. A friend is not somebody we wish to take advantage of, or use for our own satisfaction; it is not somebody whom we treat as a sexual object; it is not somebody we use to gain satisfaction regardless of the consequences. The more the teenager has relationships with a wide variety of friends the more likely he or she is likely to gain knowledge about the physical and emotional aspects of sex.

What about sex education in the future? We need:

1   To realize that many teenagers are sexually active and we have to help them to use their sexuality so that it does not harm others. This involves the 'hard facts' of contraception and venereal disease and knowledge of the misuses of sex so that they are not themselves exploited.

2   To explain to teenagers that they live in a sex-obsessed society but that they can make moral judgments for themselves; they do not have to have sex just because their friends do. The pros and cons have to be argued openly and honestly. It is foolish for teachers (and parents) to send children out into a sex-ridden world totally unprepared for it.

3   To provide sex education, set squarely in the context of caring human relationships, by which young people have a better chance to rid themselves of their fears and anxieties about sex.

4   To ensure that parents and teachers make better use of the sex advisory bodies that are available to the community.

5   To teach student teachers how to approach the task of sex education and to move firmly away from birds and bees in the direction of human beings.

6  To realize that sex education is a right and young people deserve full and objective information on such a central aspect of their lives.

7  To provide youngsters with an opportunity to consider some of the moral values which are part and parcel of every human relationship.

8  To be more open and honest about our own doubts, fears and anxieties.

9  To consider the needs of special groups within the adolescent community, e.g. the mentally handicapped, the physically handicapped, ethnic minorities and children in care. (Some people, including myself, would argue that teenage *boys* are a special group; all too often their sex education is appalling or non-existent.)

10  To stress that parents have a major role to play in sex education and that they cannot abrogate that responsibility or imagine that (as one parent expressed it to me) 'the school teaches them all they want to know.'

11  To train sex counsellors who can, in both voluntary and professional capacities, pass on their expertise to those who need it (e.g. parents, teachers, doctors and the teenagers themselves).

12  To teach young people something of the beauty of sex, its symbolic nature, and its role in communication with another loving, caring person.

Actually, I remember, my father did address a few words to me on the subject of sex. He said: 'Keep away from girls.' I hope we have, in the eighties, moved on from this sparse and fairly uninformative advice. I fervently hope that we will do our best to give the young people in our midst the facts and the understanding that they so badly need.

*Chapter Nine*

# The Pop Culture:
# Fashion, Music and Rebellion

'All the world's a stage,' says Jaques, in Shakespeare's *As You Like It*. Perhaps so. Certainly, it's very tempting to think of the youth culture as one vast theatrical production.

Call the show *The Teenage Years*. It contains lots of dancing, plenty of beautiful costumes and uniforms, plus dramatics that would do credit to the National Theatre. The plot is a little more difficult to follow.

What I want to do here is to pry into the teenager's world, take a peep behind the curtains, and try to understand what's happening: in the world of fashion, pop music* and the media. Some aspects of what we'll see will be tawdry; other bits quite exciting. None of it is without interest to those adults who want to understand teenagers.

CLOTHES Many's the parent who, on seeing a son or daughter dressed up for the evening's social event, has commented: 'Surely, you're not going out looking like that?'

At the time of writing this (and, remember, trying to track down fashions is rather like a drunken man looking down a kaleidoscope) my son is wearing his zutes to go to a disco. For those that don't know, zutes are bright, baggy pantaloons rather like those trousers worn in paintings of little Dutch boys.

Each of his friends wears different coloured zutes with a contrasting shirt. They present a riot of gold, greens, reds and yellows. Curiously, every youth has a carefully-cultivated drooping moustache (very much the fashion). Standing together they look like an outing of Chinese mandarins.

What about my daughters? At the moment, high fashion decrees a pencil-slim skirt with a slit up the side or front to give a provocative glimpse of thigh. Alternative (and acceptable) dress is suits with

---

*My thanks are due to Henry Shires, aged eighteen, and to Peter Turner, Senior Lecturer in Sociology at the Dorset Institute of Higher Education, both of whom discussed pop music with me and made many helpful comments.

tight skirts or baggy (then tapered) silk trousers worn with 'footless tights'.

Bright colours are 'in'. You should, I'm told, be wearing strawberry, magenta, rust, aubergine, wine or purple. By the time you read this these fashions will be 'out' and something new, in different colours, will have taken their place.

Fashions, like visiting fairgrounds, come and go. Those of us who were children in the forties can remember tight skirts (and the wide-shouldered jackets that go with them). My mother and aunts (now senior citizens) all wore them when *they* were young.

There is nothing new under the sun, said the preacher. With regard to clothes I have a suspicion that he may well have been right.

How important is it to teenagers to wear the latest fashion? What advantages are there to wearing stylish, distinctive and, sometimes, outlandish clothes? What do teenagers get out of it? I think there are six main rewards:

1 ATTENTION Clothes that are different make the teenager stand out from the crowd (and from adults). 'When you walked down the streets lots of people looked at you,' said an ex-punk to me, nostalgically. 'It was great.' If the adult world reacts with shock and horror so much the better.

2 INSTANT IDENTITY I know a boy, from a respectable family, who (almost overnight) became a biker, with leather jacket, badges and boots, but no motor-bike. 'Who are you supposed to be?' asked his father. 'A greaser,' said the boy proudly.

3 GROUP APPROVAL 'With it gear' (close following of the fashion) within a particular group gives the youngster status and the feeling of being part of a group. It sometimes wins the wearer's approval of members of the opposite sex ('Straight girls, especially convent girls, really went for my gear,' said the same ex-punk).

4 DISAPPROVAL OF ADULTS Clothes can be a visible sign that the youngster is 'doing his thing' and rebelling against authoritarian, formal (adult) standards. 'Teenagers want to look different from their parents,' a fourteen-year-old told me. Many of them succeed.

5 INSTANT IMPACT Clothes that are colourful, original or noticeable make some kind of statement about the wearer. More than one mother has complained that her daughter's clothes are too garish. Some clothes positively shriek at you: 'Notice me. I'm a teenager, and into (teenage) group solidarity.'

6 SELF-RESPECT It is sad, but true, that sixteen per cent of all school-leavers in England or Wales have no O or A level qualifications. Only nine per cent of teenagers leave school with

five or more O levels.* A small minority of youngsters are academic; most will seek prestige and status out of the classroom. Some will find some kind of identity through the clothes they wear.

Aren't you being a little too serious? This is a question you might well ask at this stage. Surely (you might add) *some* teenagers wear certain styles of clothes simply for fun? What's more, there are many teenagers who do not follow fashion at all because (a) their parents forbid it or (b) they're not interested or (c) they simply haven't the money.

I won't quarrel with any of this. Certainly, in discussing fashion with young people it is refreshing to find plenty of youngsters who say: 'I buy clothes that look good on me. I can't be bothered with all these new styles. It's a waste of money.' How many youngsters there are like this I don't know; I suspect that there are quite a few. There are also quite a few to whom clothes are a central part of their young lives.

For many youngsters clothes form an integral part of their search for identity and authenticity. They are a witness to the fact that the wearer is questioning established authority, traditional standards and the values of the adult world.

In the early fifties, in such working-class areas of London as Lambeth and the Elephant and Castle, certain youngsters had noticed that, over the river in Mayfair and Soho, upper-class young blades were wearing Edwardian clothes — flowered waistcoats, tight trousers, and jackets with velvet collars.

The working-class youths of East London copied the style and the teddy boys ('teds'), looking like music-hall caricatures, emerged. There they were, on street corners, in long draped jackets with velvet collars, drain-pipe trousers, day-glo (phlorescent) socks in bright colours, 'brothel-creeper' shoes and DA ('duck's arse') hair-cuts.

Many teds wore bright colours; some wore a sinister black. Either way, they were instantly recognizable and the adult world (still recovering from World War II, and rationing) had seen nothing like it — at least, not amongst working-class youth. To go with the clothes was a self-image, and a philosophy, which was aggressive, brash and disrespectful of adult opinion.

With the clothes went a new kind of music — rock 'n' roll — which was the start of a massive pop music counter-culture of the young. 'Roll over, Beethoven,' sang Chuck Berry, 'Tell Tchaikovsky the news'. The news was that pop music was here to stay and would

*Department of Education & Science. School Leavers Statistics.

play a tremendous part in the lives of young people (and many, many adults) from the fifties onwards.

The teds came and went, having spread to the provinces and having started a revolution in teenage attitudes towards dress. Before the teddy boys the vast majority of adolescent youth wore the same sort of clothes as their parents. Young boys pined to wear long trousers; older boys hoped to wear a suit like dad, older girls hoped to wear the sort of clothes that mother wore.

After the fifties, everything, clothes-wise, changed. The 'rag-trade' flourished and the newly-minted teenager, with money in his or her pocket, wanted clothes that were distinctive, and which were exclusive to this recently-created sub-culture. Teenagers had been the followers of (adult) fashion; from now on, they were to lead, not follow.

In the sixties the pattern of teenage dress became a little more complicated. Various cults and sub-groups appeared, and disappeared; one fashion borrowed from another, or from one that had preceded it. With the fashion, often, went a particular philosophy, an outlook on life, a style.

Take the mods — a teenage group which first appeared in the mid-sixties and who, at the beginning of the eighties, have (following the film *Quadraphenia*) made something of a come-back.* The mods were well-dressed, narcissistic teenagers, the first working-class teenagers to carry mirrors (and combs) and to have their hair 'styled'.

The mods' suits were expensive, smart, and treasured. I'm told that one mod (male) refused to kiss his girlfriend at a party unless she supplied (a) a coat-hanger for his suit and (b) shoehorns for his shoes. Parkas (long, khaki coats) were worn to protect the suits and to fend off the cold when riding on the scooter. There was little in the way of a philosophy; drugs ('purple hearts' and other stimulants) were popular; the attitude was anti-authoritarian, and pleasure-based: 'have a good time'.

The scooters were impressive. They often carried as many wing-mirrors as the bike would hold, two headlamps and an over-long aerial at the back of the bike, topped by a small flag. Scooters were in many ways, the alter-egos of the young people. The bikes were powerful, glossy and impressive; they gave the mods mobility and a taste of freedom. On your scooter you were no longer a wage slave, tied to a boring place, a boring job. You could get to Brighton, to Hastings, fight the rockers and gain a place, if not in

---

*Though it's important to note that some mods never went out, especially in the north. Scooter clubs, in Yorkshire and elsewhere, kept the mods alive though far less influential as far as fashions were concerned.

the Halls of Glory, at least on the front page of the popular press.

Opposed to the mods were the rockers. This group of youngsters wore drain-pipe trousers, greasy hair and leather jackets. The mods (following the teds and the fairly respectable-looking Beatles) had a certain raffishness; many of them were extremely smart. The rockers were, in their leathers, far from elegant; their clothes were functional; they went with the powerful motor-bikes to which most of them aspired.

The rockers' music was, of course, rock 'n' roll (Chuck Berry, Bill Hailey, Little Richard). They drank alcohol to get their 'kicks'. They despised ska (a type of reggae and the music of the mods), they despised mods, they were anti-authoritarian and aggressive. The worst thing that could happen to a parent of a teenage daughter was (as far as my friends were concerned) to find out that their youngster was going out with a rocker. In manner, in life-style and in dress they were instantly recognizable as being anti-adult and anti-establishment.

Clothes, for the young, became not only to be used for sexual display (and to attract members of the opposite sex) but a means of protest against the adult world. At the beginning of the sixties the beatniks shocked society by their rejection of adult values and standards, and by their dress. By the middle of the sixties the hippies had emerged. They were out to create an alternative society. They started by wearing alternative (often very grubby) clothing.

The hippies were 'into' smoking marijuana ('pot'); many swallowed LSD, a powerful drug which alters human consciousness and can induce hallucinations. The 'cool' or 'laid-back' life-style of the hippies was reflected in their dress. Their philosophy was Peace and Love. They wore old jeans and denim jackets, old plimsolls (or no shoes), sweat bands around their foreheads and old hats. The girls wore long, flowered dresses, no shoes (and no bras); they tattooed their faces with hearts and flowers; at pop festivals they wore flowers in their hair.

In the swinging sixties it became fashionable, in what had become a distinct Youth Movement, to *protest* — against war, against established authority and against the materialistic philosophy of parents. With a burst of youthful exuberance and romanticism, the young burst free from the chains of adult standards and values.

To walk down Carnaby Street in London, was an outing in itself. The clothes were often outrageous but never dull. It became fashionable to wear old army uniforms, or American Army jackets. Denim (from a cloth made originally in Nimes, France — and worn by French working men) became the uniform of the young, and a symbol of the alternative society. Protest, whatever it was directed

106

against, had become very closely linked to styles of dress.

Along with this sartorial rebellion went, at least as far as the hippies were concerned, some very serious consideration of the values of society. Some hippies moved into communes, to establish an alternative life-style and to set an example to their elders as to the right way to live. These communes, some of them, are still in existence and the latter-day hippies have remained consistent in their anti-materialistic views.

The hippies had come into being against a background of affluence; they lived, many of them, off the effluence of the affluence. By the 1970s, economic realities had begun to alter the outlook of both adults and young people. It became clear that the world did not have limitless resources which we could plunder at will. Oil rose sharply in price and the economy of Great Britain did not seem to be capable of producing the wealth that would pay for the social services that many of its citizens had come to expect as a right.

The harsher realities of life were reflected, in the early part of the seventies, in the dress of youngsters. The mods, for example, disappeared and were replaced by the skinheads, so called because of their shaven heads which were shaved for effect, and in order to 'butt' their enemies in the face more effectively.

The skinheads were racist and into violence. They enjoyed fighting at Saturday afternoon football matches. Some of them indulged in 'paki-bashing' (beating up members of the Pakistani community). The skinheads wore trousers (or dungarees) that were too short, with braces over their shirts, plus Dr Marten boots. They were frightening in appearance (at least to many older adults) and their 'mindless violence' image did nothing to enhance them in the eyes of adults: especially the police and teachers in secondary schools.

The 'Peace and Love' hippies were seen less and less as the seventies progressed. The aggressive skinheads were replaced by the suede heads, the Hairies and the Crombie boys; all less into 'aggro' but all (even the Crombie boys in their short, Abercrombie overcoats) far less elegant than the teds or the mods.

Then colour returned in the form of the punks. A surfeit of colour. The punks looked bizarre. They dyed their hair vivid pinks, reds and yellow; some youngsters shaved it down the middle, like Apache braves. Razor blades, and safety-pins were attached to raggedy clothing, or even worn through one nostril. The punks wore tiny circles, triangles and cheap jewellery (borrowed from Glitter Rock) and used glitter make-up (e.g. little coloured stars on their faces) and skull-and-crossbones (or razor-blade) earrings. 'Society is punk so we dress punk,' was a comment made to me by a latter-day follower of the trend. He certainly succeeded in looking different, wearing a long-tailed dinner jacket (decorated with safety-pins, a German iron cross and a Brownies' badge) with HM PRISON, PENTONVILLE written on the back in large white letters.

What about the eighties, and the nineties? My own view is that teenage dress will become more and more varied, and confusing to adults. Already, in 1980, the skinheads are back. The hell's angels are to be seen in many towns and cities, their leathers covered in chains, emblems and swaztikas. The mods have made a come-back. Fashion is cyclical. The big wheel turns and a style of dress goes out and, a few years later, re-emerges.

Today, mingling with the mods, and the bikers, and the hell's angels, and the skinheads we can see youngsters (like my son), afficionados of jazz funk, dressed in colourful shirts and suits. We can spot disco fans, dressed in velvet cat suits, or narrow split skirts (girls) or pleated trousers and winkle-pickers. With some young people, there is a synthesis of styles.

In future, since there are only a limited number of fashion combinations, I expect to see the emergence of pods and munks, of rods and mockers, or hinheads and skippies and other syntheses of fashion which (perhaps, thankfully) we cannot imagine. I expect to see, too, a reaction against the commercial manipulation of young people and a growing number of youngsters who will have the courage to say: 'I buy clothes like this because they suit me, are comfortable and because I look good in them.'

Clothes, and dressing-up, can be fun, and rewarding. However, dressing up to gain attention cannot, in my view, act as a substitute for the satisfaction that comes with the feeling that one is valued and respected for oneself. Many young people seem to want something a little more substantial than the latest fashion by which to steer their way through an uncertain world. They need something more than bizarre clothes to believe in.

The more alienated the teenager (from school, from his or her employment — or lack of it, or from adult society) the greater the temptation to use clothes to gain status, identity and attention.

That so many youngsters in our midst are so very preoccupied with the trivia of dress is some kind of comment on the way they see the values, principles and behaviour of the adults who surround them. We adults, let's face it, fail to offer them more sensible ways of gaining approval. Or attention. Young people wear bizarre clothes because many, many adults have nothing better to offer.

POP MUSIC With the emergence of the teds as the first, large-scale, 'uniformed' youth group came music and that music was to reflect much of the rebelliousness and yearning for freedom that was part of the new, post-1953, Elizabethan era.

Pop music emerged as a curiously non-verbal affirmation of youth identity. Mixed in with the sheer exuberance and enjoyment was an element of identity-searching and a large element of rejection of adult values. Pop music, on the surface, was an emotional pep-up, reminiscent of the music that had boosted the spirits of the 'flappers' of the twenties and the romantic songs that had provided ready-made, hand-me-down, dreams during the depression of the thirties.

But pop music was to provide more than escapism. For many young people it provided a philosophy, a way of life. Up there on the stage, or singing on the radio, were *their* heroes, singing about young people like themselves, putting into sound their thoughts and feelings. Pop music became the focus for the perennial frustrations of the young.

Before the 1950s pop music had been received by the working classes in a spirit of acceptance of the social order. In the fifties, pop music became an integral part of the protest at the injustices of life. The exuberant, warm vulgarity of the music chimed in with the new affluence of work-class youth, its greater mobility and rising standards of education, and expectations. Many young people were in dead-end jobs. Despite this, the music seemed to be saying, you exist and you are important.

In the early fifties young people could be seen circling the floor, at dance halls, to the formal strains of the waltz, quickstep or fox-trot. In the same dance halls, or elsewhere, to jazz records, other youngsters would 'jive' or 'bop' in a display of individuality, style and rebellion. So far, the teds had displayed their yearnings towards emancipation, and inclination towards violence, but they had no music which was theirs and which expressed their philosophy. In 1954 'skiffle' (self-made music on crude instruments) had come but failed to provide the exuberance which the young wanted to express.

In the mid fifties the music that youngsters wanted arrived — rock 'n' roll. By November 1955 *Rock around the Clock,* played by Bill Haley and the Comets, was the top-selling pop record in Britain (it was first heard accompanying the film *Blackboard Jungle*). Dissident youth of all classes now had their own national anthem and their very own style of music. In the same year James Dean, an anti-adult, anti-establishment hero died; he became a cult. Rebellion was in, conformity with adults was out.

In line with rock 'n' roll the popular ballads of the day (*Finger of suspicion* by Dickie Valentine; *Softly, softly* by Ruby Murray) were still extremely popular, but another (and more boisterous) kind of music was rapidly gaining followers amongst young people.

Bill Haley opened the gates yet, by 1957, was forgotten when performers like Elvis Presley, Buddy Holly, Fats Domino, Gene Vincent, Little Richard, Jerry Lee Lewis and Chuck Berry swept the musically-emancipated teenagers along on an avalanche of rock 'n' roll.

The atmosphere of dance halls changed. Once staid and formal, they now echoed the voice of Little Richard shouting out his message to the young:

'Gonna rock it up, gonna break it up,
. . . . . . . . . . at the ball tonight.*

The words were prophetic. A lot of the old, adult values were to be broken up during the next twenty-five years and, in the process of creating an in-world of teenagers, quite a few youngsters were (despite what their parents might think, say or do) to have themselves a ball. The ramparts of the adult world had been breached; the generation gap had been achieved; over the next few years that gap was to widen.

Rock 'n' roll, by the end of the fifties, had a mass following. It held out, by its music and lyrics, the hopes of a new culture: classless, non-racist and non-authoritarian. The new culture was one, not of Beethoven or Brahms, but one to which the teenager could belong. In literature, during the later fifties, there was a similar revolt: the 'angry young men' expressed their cynicism and anger, and revolted against the established values and attitudes of the time. The rebellion of the young was well on its way and the scene had been set for the swinging sixties.

During the sixties young people were to launch on a largely unsuspecting world new music, a new language of teenagers and life-styles which were totally different from (and in some cases, totally opposed to) the habits and standards of the adult world. Music would be used to find an identity, to express a newly found teenage confidence, and as a form of political and social protest. Music was no longer non-verbal, a form of entertainment, sounds to dance to. More and more, it had a variety of messages to transmit to the young. It seemed, to the young of the day, to hold out two golden prizes — participation, and freedom.

Rock 'n' roll lived on but, in 1962, a second youthquake was to shatter the peace of mind of many parents: the Beatles sold their first successful record and made a tremendous impact on the world of the teenager. The world of youth was ready for them. The sixties was to be the Renaissance of a new, participatory pop

---

*Rip it up, sung by Little Richard. Written by Blackwell and Murascallo; recorded in 1957.

music. At the beginning of the decade there were three hundred pop groups, including the Beatles, playing in Liverpool alone.

What made the Beatles so popular? First of all, they looked smart — their image was one of wholesomeness, but rather cheeky with it. Their velvet collars, on those famous jackets, were less threatening than those worn by their teddy boy predecessors. Secondly, the Beatles could sing and were musically extremely talented. Thirdly, they were shrewdly presented to the world by their first manager, Brian Epstein.

In 1962, a 'Welcome Home' show was staged at the Cavern in Liverpool (the Beatles had just returned from playing in Hamburg). The group's return broke all previous attendance Cavern records. The 'Liverpool Sound' was here and a new drummer, Ringo Starr, joined the group. In September, 1962, the Beatles went to London and recorded their first record for EMI studios. The record — A side, *Love me do,* was released in October. It sold enough copies during its first twenty-four hours to make an entry into the hit parade.

For the remainder of the sixties the Beatles were rarely out of the charts. Their early songs (*Please, please me, From me to you* and *Do you want to know a secret?*) combined outstanding lyrics and a pleasing, musically-accomplished sound. They developed as a group to create very appealing, elegant pop music and to write intelligent, moving lyrics (*Fool on the hill, Eleanor Rigby, Penny Lane*). Their music remains, to this day, outstanding of its kind.

The Beatles, in the middle sixties moved from their 'boy-next-door image' towards a more revolutionary, dissenting stance. They became associated with the hippy movement, with meditation and various other aspects of 'alternative' life-styles. Their message became Peace and Love, anti-war, 'do your own thing'. Their image remained elegant, non-violent.

In contrast, a London group, the Rolling Stones, (with an equally large following) were loud and raucous musically and the appearance of the group was an affront to the tastes of many adults. The 'Stones' were untidy, wore their hair long and their behaviour (in private, and on stage) was unacceptable to a whole generation of shocked parents. A mother might imagine her daughter going out with one of the Beatles; to imagine her daughter associating with one of the Rolling Stones would, at that time, have been too much for most parents, however liberal.

The Rolling Stones wrote a series of songs which reflected the teenage revolt against adult values and, in particular, the revolt of male working-class (and, increasingly, middle-class) youngsters. There was no tender regard for girls; no respect for elders; the charismatic Mick Jagger took pleasure in shocking the adult world.

Many parents, though they liked the Beatles, were frightened of, and appalled by, the Stones. The overt sexuality of the group's lyrics, dress and behaviour were hard for many older people to accept. As for young people, a vast number of them loved the rebelliousness of it all.

Equally rebellious, though more gentle (and with more political overtones) were the songs of Bob Dylan. He first appeared in New York, at the age of twenty, as a pop singer. His qualifications seemed doubtful: he was far from good-looking; his voice had a curious, flat, nasal quality. His first LP, recorded in 1962 (*Talkin' New York*) was a talking blues parody on folk music, aimed to satirize the in-music of American intellectuals (and pseudo-intellectuals) who adored 'folk'.

Dylan's first single had been released in 1961. By 1964, he was established as a star, a major recording artist, with a massive following. His songs included *Blowin' in the wind, The times, they are a changin', A hard rain is gonna fall* (about the Cuban missile crisis) and *With God on our side* (an attack on religious prejudice). The songs were adopted by a whole generation — the protest generation — of youngsters. They became the battle songs of the peace movement, of revolutionaries, and of the hippies. They were also adored by less committed young people in America, Britain and elsewhere. Dylan, who looked like an outsider, sang to and for the teenage outsider throughout the western world.

Bob Dylan, with the songs *Blowin' in the wind* and *We shall overcome,* became a symbol of the anti-war, anti-racist and anti-authoritarian youth of the day. Pop music became part and parcel of a vast (mostly young) political protest movement, and a reiterated statement of discontent by young people, especially in America. Music was no longer something to dance to, dream by. It became an essential part of a variety of political, social and personal credos and philosophies.

On anti-Vietnam war marches, on university campuses, at pop festivals and other gatherings of young people in revolt the strains of *We shall overcome* rang out. Pop music had reached a stage of universal appeal to the young; it had also begun to be used as a political weapon, to bind rebellious young people together and to provide them with sentiments, and words by which to express themselves.

On a slightly more homely level, in Britain during the sixties the mods fought with the rockers at the Battles of Hastings, and Brighton. The exaggerated dress of the mods was part of a changing life-style that many British groups conveyed through their music and in their own personal behaviour. Groups such as the Kinks and the Who emphasized immediate gratification and enjoyment.

The Who, with their lead singer Pete Townsend, were adored by the mods but feared and loathed by a great many parents.

There were, of course, thousands of youngsters who remained uninfluenced by the avalanche of pop music or, at least, its excesses. Pop music had become an integral feature of the lives of many teenagers but that did not mean that all these youngsters were into protest or radical philosophies and life-styles. Pop music, through radio and television, reached the masses; it became part of teenage culture; it was almost impossible for a youngster, however staid or old-fashioned, to avoid it completely.

Pop music achieved something else besides blanket coverage of our tiny island: it became a channel of expression for those teenagers who had a quarrel, or a different viewpoint, from their parents, headmasters or employers. It became the focus for a grand parade of teenage anti-establishment attitudes and beliefs. In the on-going rebellion of the young against adult conventions, dress and value-systems, pop music was the refuge for all those youngsters who believed (rightly or wrongly) that they had been badly treated.

This affirmation of youth, and rejection of established standards, was continued into the less affluent and more cynical seventies. The skinheads liked reggae, a West Indian music; the bikers and latter-day teds remained loyal to rock; Glitter Rock, with Alice Cooper (a man), Marc Bolan, David Bowie and Gary Glitter made its appearance. In the seventies, the Vietnam war was forgotten but new social issues arose: racism, conservation of the environment, women's liberation.

Pop music had become an industry, with disc jockeys, pop festivals, the incessant playing of records on commercial radio (and their frequent appearance on BBC Radio 1, and on television, especially *Top of the Pops*). The large scale pop festival could be viewed as a ritual affirmation of the youth culture; the radio pop programmes served to remind us all that pop music was ubiquitous in its appeal. From Bermondsey to Land's End to John o'Groats the transistor radios carried by teenagers boomed out the latest hit records. Pop was for the majority.

During the seventies pop music expanded to embrace, and give a voice to, minority (and overtly deviant) groups. With Glitter Rock it was sometimes hard to tell whether the stage performer was a man or a woman; with the arrival of the punks the sex of the performer was discernible but what he, or she, was singing was obscure, at least to adults.

The punks represented a synthesis of styles: there was an element of psychedelia and surrealism (from the pre-Beatles era), there were the leather jackets and leather trousers of the bikers plus the jewellery and make-up of Glitter Rock. It is said that Johnny Rotten, a member of the Sex Pistols, was first discovered miming to a record of Gary Glitter in a London shop. The owner of the shop saw the potential in Rotten, in Sid Vicious and in Siouxsie (of Siouxsie and the Banshees) and determined to break into the pop scene with a new kind of music: punk rock.

Punk was a kind of raw-energy music, made by working-class youngsters for working-class youngsters (though it was later adopted by the middle classes). The aim, at first, was to cut out the big record companies and to bring out the records without big business intervention. It was a Do-It-Yourself kind of music, crude, brash and very, very loud. Some of the performers didn't seem to be able to sing or to play the instruments that they carried on stage.

To go with the music came a dance — the Pogo. Here, the audience bounced up and down to the music, bounced into each other or hit each other. The result was chaos and young teenagers loved it. The noise, and sense of youthful exhilaration was tremendous as a thousand young people would cram into town hall, dance hall or disco and bounce to the ear-shattering sounds of the punk rock.

The punks was a young movement — many of its followers were eleven to fourteen-year-olds. It was keen on equal rights for females and it was anti-racist. Punks wore make-up and were liberal in their attitudes towards homosexuals ('gays'). It was, unlike the skinheads, a non-aggressive cult, though some of its members did take pills ('speed') or drank alcohol. In contrast to the hippies, few punks resorted to LSD or the more powerful drugs.

The seventies saw a proliferation of groups — many with curious names like the Slits (an all-women group who started with primal punk songs such as *Vaseline* and *Let's Do the Split* and progressed to a rather more sophisticated rock), the Vibrators, UK Subs and Sham '69. It became more and more difficult for adults to follow the trends in pop music and to distinguish one type of group from another.

The Tom Robinson band openly supported gays and groups appeared with both black and white instrumentalists. A Rock Against Racism campaign was instituted and pop music, as in the sixties, embraced minority views and spoke out against ugly prejudices and manifest injustice within adult society.

By the end of the seventies, with the advent of the film *Saturday Night Fever,* disco music became the pop music of the 'silent majority' of young people. Punk had been something of a minority taste; disco music embraced the mainstream and gave less radical youngsters a chance to re-join the pop scene. In a very short time, disco dominated the charts with groups like Angels, Dollar and

Street Life. Cliff Richard, a star of the late fifties and the sixties, made yet another appearance at number one in the hit parade with *You don't talk any more*. He looked no older than when he had sung with the Shadows twenty years previously.

Punk rock became, for the most part New Wave music, with groups like the Boomtown Rats, Ian Drury and the Blockheads, the Police and Blondie. The Stranglers, an ex-punk group, moved into New Wave. The Darts played doo-wop, a kind of rock, Gary Newman played New Music, a few groups were MOR (Middle of the Road). The main influence was disco; the rest of the pop scene was becoming more and more diffuse.

Curiously, as the hit singles sold the fashionable disco pop, the LPs showed the strong current of nostalgia running through the seventies. In 1979, Bob Dylan's *Slow train coming* was a best-seller (bought by twenty- and thirty-year-olds, recapturing their youth, as well as by young people). XTC, the Electric Light Orchestra and Led Zeppelin were all high in the LP charts, perhaps illustrating the following that pop music has amongst adults as well as teenagers since these groups had been popular a decade previously.

This brings us to the present day and the eighties. It seems strange that I, in my mid-forties, have lived long enough to see pop music change from the appeal of songs such as *The nightingales sang in Berkeley Square* to *A hard day's night* and (more recently) *Strut your funky stuff* or *I said you had a beautiful body (would you hold it against me?)*

At the moment of writing the mods are back, with ska music; the teds are back, with rock 'n' roll; the skinheads (or, at least, a few of them) are back. Some of the punks never went away. If I go to an under-eighteen disco, representatives of all these movements are present, dancing on the floor, in their own way. At moments like that I wonder if I'm a thousand years old. When my son asks me what I think of his zutes I tell him: 'I was there in the fifties, when it all started.'

Before the fifties the musical tastes of adults affected the musical tastes of young people. Now, it's the other way round. Some adults stay in the pop musical culture of their own youth and carry it with them into old age. When Elvis Presley, the 'King of Rock 'n' Roll', died, his mourners included teenagers *and* a great many older people who had been teenagers in the fifties and who loved him still. Bob Dylan has his ageing fans: *May you stay for-ever young* he sings for them. Listening to his music they recall and re-live their youth. For many adults the music of the Beatles is of far more importance in their lives than the music of Sibelius, Chopin or Puccini. Pop music has infiltrated, from the lives of youngsters, into the lives of parents.

Today, in the eighties, the teenager has his or her own magazines (with names like *Oh Boy!*, *Patches, My Guy, Smash Hits, Jackie, Fab 208, Blue Jeans, Disco 45* and, for older teenagers, *19*). Teenagers have their own slang, their own T-shirts, hair styles and badges. BBC Radio 1, and the commercial radio stations pipe out an endless stream of pop music from 6 a.m. to midnight, and (with some radio stations) throughout the night.

Teenagers can eat at late night take-away cafes with food (hamburgers, chinese meals and fried chicken) cooked and sold with teenagers in mind. Their dress and their pop music transcends boundaries of sex (with unisex styles), class, geography, colour, socio-economic status and religion. They are joined together in one massive, vibrant, somewhat vulgar sub-culture — that of the modern teenager.

Teenagers have their own posters; boutiques and record shops cater for them especially. They have films, on television and in the cinema, made about them. In the early fifties it was difficult for young people to make their voices heard; now their opinions, and their transistors, are heard throughout the land. In some homes the slogan seems to be: Teenagers Rule, OK? Teenagers have not only arrived, they take up a great deal of space in society.

The values of teenagers, and their opinions on sex, racial equality, class and women's liberation do not always follow their liberal attitudes towards dress and music. Teenagers can be, and many of them are, extremely reactionary; we would be foolish to assume that a teenager is necessarily a radical. In fact, he or she (despite appearance) may have very conservative views on life.

It is interesting how many adults, as though caught in a time capsule, adore the music of their own teenage. The teens have become a peak experience time, rather than a rather boring apprenticeship for the adult world. In the forties all adolescents wished that they were grown-ups; in the eighties many adults wish that they were teenagers, and part of all the fun.

Teenagers seem to have found their way; adults seem to have lost theirs. Is it any wonder that adults, confused and harrassed by the strains of modern life, sometimes show jealousy of their teenage children?

That jealousy is ill-placed. Though teenagers can gain individuality and self-respect within their own culture, that same optimism and exuberance will not last long unless we can provide jobs for them, and some guide as to how they should set about living adult lives. Pop music is fun; despite appearances to the contrary it doesn't provide a philosophy of life, or pay the rent (except for promoters, performers and disc jockeys).

Thinking about it, I am not too concerned about the vibrancy, the noise, the colour and the vulgarity of the teenage pop culture. What worries me is the vacuum of standards, of fun and of convictions amongst the teenagers' parents. What sort of world are we making for these teenagers of tomorrow? When the music stop some of them face very bleak prospects indeed. Despite Dylan's fond wish to his fans, nobody stays forever young. How sad that older people have not managed to create a world that is more rewarding.

*Chapter Ten*

# The Education of Teenagers

It was Matthew Arnold who described education as 'the influence of one person on another.' For me, there's a lot of truth in that. When I look back on my secondary school days, I can remember people but hardly any facts: the faces and mannerisms of certain boys, certain teachers, are etched in my mind as though my schooldays were yesterday. The details of the Treaty of Utrecht, the Diet of Worms, and the South Sea Bubble are, alas, lost to me for ever.

When I was at my run-of-the-mill, northern grammar school I thought education was terribly important — and so it is. It gives us qualifications, and those 'bits of paper' enable us to get the jobs we want. What I caught a glimpse of, even then, was a tendency on the part of teachers to overvalue schools and schooling and those boys who had the same interests as themselves.

Life is long, and so is real education. It begins when we are born and ends when we die. We learn from our friends, and from our enemies. We learn lasting lessons in the hustle and bustle of life. Education is not only to do with schools: the educational research of the last thirty years has taught us, if it has taught us anything, that the child's home influences to a very large extent the child's school achievements. Parental interest and encouragement may determine, to a remarkable degree, the achievements of the child in school.

The home is there before the child ever goes to school, and after he has left it. Some famous people (like Winston Churchill) don't distinguish themselves in school and their talents emerge later. These are the late developers who succeed in the university of life rather than the classroom.

Teachers may overvalue schooling, and academic brightness: character, and ability to get on with other people, are equally important in the long journey through life. Many teachers go to school, then to college or university, and back to school — to teach what they have been taught. Their horizons *may* be narrow; they *may* find it hard to concede that a boy or girl may be poor academically but still have a substantial contribution to make within the community.

My own philosophy of education is: Every Child Is Worthwhile. We need doctors, and engineers and lawyers. We also need car mechanics, shop assistants, refuse collectors, factory workers and farm labourers. Headmasters and headmistresses should be careful at school speech days not to imply that those children with O-levels, or university and polytechnic admittance are to be valued a whole lot more than the academically less-bright. It is fine to be clever but not everybody can be and we also need the less able child to make a worthwhile contribution to the community.

In *The Prime of Miss Jean Brodie,* by Muriel Spark,* the heroine tells her pupils: 'Education means a leading out, from *e,* out and *duco,* I lead.' Miss Brodie has grasped that what schools should be doing is developing the innate potential of each and every child. Unfortunately, she is eccentric, and something of a snob. 'If only you small girls would listen to me,' she tells her class, 'I would make of you *la creme de la creme.*' Her understanding of the educational approach is not matched by her understanding of her pupils' needs, or the harsh reality of the world outside of the classroom. It is her reality which she wishes to impose on her young charges. 'Qualifying examinations or no qualifying examinations,' she tells them, 'you will have the benefit of my experiences in Italy.'

What I like about Miss Brodie is her passion to enthuse her pupils with knowledge. Education is more about lighting fires within hearts and minds, than about topping up the human mind with facts. We are curious, searching human beings rather than glass tumblers. 'Children are as wax,' says my uncle George (a teacher). 'We must write on them.' The trouble with this *tabula rasa* theory of education is that each child is different, with his or her own talents. If we treat all children of the same age in the same way, we forget that they are at different stages of intellectual, social and emotional development.

Also, we have to acknowledge that we live in a rapidly changing world. It is difficult to know what sort of knowledge, which facts, are going to be of most use to the adults of the twenty-first century. We can teach children to be resourceful, to be curious about life; we can give them confidence in themselves, so that they may face the future with optimism. How sad if, in teaching them 'the facts' we destroy the innate creativity and the optimism within them. The task is to build up their self-regarding sentiment, not to destroy it.

*Penguin Books Ltd 1965

Education is learning to live. It has three main aspects: a. individual b. social and c. vocational. We must, as Polonius in Shakespeare's Hamlet said to his son Laertes, teach children 'to thine own self be true'. We must build up the unique individuality of each child, and develop his or her talents. On the social side, we must teach (mainly through example) young people how to live alongside others in what we hope will be a caring, thriving, prosperous community.

These days, it is more important than ever to prepare youngsters for the world of work; to give them a chance of gaining employment within an increasingly competitive job market. The vocational aspects of education (together with the problem of what to do with unemployed youngsters) will be at the forefront of education over the next decade. Youngsters, when they leave school, want to work; it is their right (not their privilege) that society offers them an opportunity to find suitable employment.

There are those (and I count myself amongst them) who would argue that the education of the emotions, and of the spirit, are important too. Emotions (from the Latin *e*, from, and *movere,* to move) are the things which move us. The emotions, as the philosopher A N Whitehead has pointed out*, are the basis of all human experience; they can greatly influence our intellectual life. A young person who is emotionally disturbed, who is maladjusted, finds it much more difficult to succeed in school. Our emotional attitude to problems greatly affects our chances of solving them. It is through drama, creative art, music and dance that we express our emotions and these subjects, in school, have to jostle in the curriculum with maths, English, physics and geography and often lose out since they are regarded, in some schools as being 'less important'. My own view is that it is vital that we learn how to express our emotions in acceptable ways, learn how to live joyfully, how to be sad, how to be righteously angry, how to be happy. There is no point in being clever if we live lives of utter misery.

Some years ago, a young man came to me for help. Brian was twenty-five years old, and had had a distinguished academic career. He had won a scholarship from his grammar school to one of the best-known colleges at Oxbridge. He had a degree, a good job and, for the first time in his life, plenty of money. His problem was a loss of identity, feelings of loneliness and alienation. 'I don't know who I am any more,' he told me. 'I feel unhappy most of the time. I seem to have lost my self-respect, and my confidence.' It was possible to persuade Brian that he *was* a worthwhile person, that he existed in his own right, apart from his academic achievements.

*The Adventures of Ideas. Cambridge University Press 1933.

120

It is an appalling strain to feel that one is loved only for what one can achieve rather than who one is. Brian was able to persuade himself that he was a likeable person, and he stopped trying so hard to be first all the time. In his mind, to be clever equalled to be loved. He learned that we are still loveable whether we are clever or not.

What about the spiritual aspects of education? A headmaster of Eton once described education as 'a preparation for death'. At first glance, this seems macabre, morbid. Yet, how are we to live our lives fully unless we accept the gift of life, and the inevitability of death? All human beings are bound to ask: What is life about? If we have some working hypothesis as to why we are here, and what we intend to devote our lives to, it is more likely that we will succeed than if we drift aimlessly through a meaningless existence.

We are part of the life cycle. Like salmon we swim down stream in our youth to the open sea in which we live our lives. In later life, we must swim upstream, prepare ourselves for our demise, the fact that we are all going to die. Should not education tell us something about the meaning of life? There are, it is said, two great certainties: death and taxes. We should learn how to cope with both, and to realize that life is, indeed, a precious gift and that we must live each day to the full. Who wants to gain the whole world but lose one's own soul?

Krishnamurti, the Eastern mystic and teacher, asks some important questions about education in The Penguin *Krishnamurti Reader*.* He says:

Having a job and earning one's livelihood is necessary — but is that all? Are we being educated only for that? Surely, life is not merely a job, an occupation; life is something extraordinarily wide and profound, it is a great mystery, a vast realm in which we function as human beings. If we merely prepare ourselves to earn a livelihood, we shall miss the whole point of life; and to understand life is much more important than merely prepare for examinations and become very proficient in mathematics, physics or what you will.

Krishnamurti goes on to define education. It is meant, he says 'to help you from childhood not to imitate anybody, but to be yourself all the time . . . So freedom lies, not in trying to become something different, nor in doing what you feel like doing, nor in following the authority of tradition, of your parents, of your teacher, but in understanding what you are from moment to moment.'

*Edited by Mary Lutyens, Penguin Books Ltd, 1973

121

The job of teachers is to help us to make the best of ourselves, but always to respect our individuality, our innate potential. It is up to each of us to decide, with the help and advice of others, who we are and what direction we must take in life. Neither teachers, nor anybody else, can make those vital decisions for us. We must learn to know who we are in order that we may become ourselves more fully.

To get down to practicalities let us talk, first of all, about a subject that strikes terror into the heart of some youngsters — exams.

Common sense tells us that examinations are important in the lives of young people. The result of exams may determine a child's future: whether he or she is able to follow a chosen career. Exams are a good thing in that they are set under controlled conditions, they are subject to reasonably fair and co-ordinated marking and provide an opportunity to compare the achievements of one pupil (or school) with another. Most people accept them as a fact of life.

That's fine, providing that we remember that examinations are not the only way of assessing young people. America, and increasingly in this country, there is an emphasis on *continuous assessment*: marking the pupil as he or she goes along. The average marks can provide an individual profile of the youngster's work which is, perhaps a more accurate measure of ability and weakness rather than the 'sudden death' play-off that takes place in examination halls.

Too, we should remind ourselves that thousands of youngsters, as a result of the examination system, see themselves as 'failures' even before they have entered adult life. As a result of poor academic performances, they may be left with a lasting sense of inferiority. We parents add to this by stressing, and becoming anxious about, the result of exams. We push young people towards proving themselves in situations which most of us would, in private, admit to being highly artificial and often having little bearing on the realities of work and mixing with others.

Nevertheless, exams exist and the question must be faced by each parent: how can I help my child to do the very best he or she can at examination time? As with anything else, there is a technique to passing examinations. Youngsters preparing for them need to be systematic in their approach; they also need plenty of encouragement and practical support from parents. There are, in my view, certain rules that youngsters must follow, what may be termed the Ten Commandments of examination time. These are:

1  Don't leave revision until the last minute (or, just as bad, start panicking months in advance).

2   Don't attempt to revise in a noisy room (or whilst watching television). Working in a quiet, peaceful atmosphere does help. It does no harm to have a long-playing record as background music (providing it isn't too noisy).

3   Get enough sleep before examinations; to do well, you need to be relaxed, not over-tired.

4   Eat proper meals. My eldest daughter, at examination times, tends to disappear upstairs with a piece of toast, and refuses to speak to anybody. You *are* pushed for time, but you should have time enough to eat. You'll need, over the examination period, all the strength of mind and body you can muster.

5   *Plan* your revision. Do a definite amount of work each evening. Worrying about revision is possibly more painful than settling down and actually doing some.

6   Look up some old exam papers and have a go at some of the questions, using an alarm clock to time yourself. It is better to find out now that you are writing too slowly than to discover the fact in the examination itself.

7   Use a tape recorder to learn, particularly if you don't find it easy to read quickly or have a poor visual memory. Some people have good auditory memories and learn better by playing back relevant sections on a tape, rather than poring over a book.

8   Learn *main points* rather than try to revise everything. Write brief headings out on cards and use the headings as memory-joggers.

9   Use any memory aids you can think of. For example, you could use a mnemonic to remember the causes of the French Revolution. Jot down the word KNITTING. This reminds you that the King was corrupt; the Nobles were weak; the Intellectuals were stirring up trouble; there was a Terrible winter in 1788 and so forth. Making notes, working out memory aids, writing something down, is much better than sitting there reading a book (unless, of course, you happen to have a photographic memory).

10   Try to 'spot' questions that are likely to come up in the examination but *don't* rely on this method too much. If you do, and none of the questions come up, you are in for a very painful three hours and a disastrous mark.

Some children are better at exams than others; that is something that is patently obvious and that we must all accept. What worries me, and what I find hard to accept is that after eleven years of schooling so many children leave the school with very little to show for their efforts. These youngsters, without examination certificates, are not unintelligent: it is simply that the way in which we attempt to assess their intelligence (which may be of a practical sort) is totally unsuited to their needs. We have to have standards but do we have to impose academic standardization on young people who are, after all, very different in their abilities and potential? What we really need is a profile of the young person's achievements which would tell us, at each stage in the youngster's school career, what it is that he or she can or cannot do.

Be that as it may, parents must face up to the academic menu served up by schools, and part of that menu is yet another contentious item — homework. Homework is, like dying, something that everybody does but few people wish to talk about. One thirteen-year-old with whom I was chatting about homework told me, philosophically: 'It's just part of my life — like bee-stings, washing up or hitting my thumb with a hammer.'

The way in which some children set about doing their homework is truly amazing. My youngest daughter can sit on the living room carpet, eat biscuits, watch *Blue Peter and* do her homework, all at the same time (or so she claims). Since we've never had any complaints from the school about her standard of work I can only assume that she's right. The other two teenagers in the family start, in my opinion, too late in the evening and have a habit of emerging bleary-eyed at breakfast after a midnight vigil over the textbooks. Each child has his or her own individual manner of working and it's wrong to be too dogmatic over how the job should be done. I ask my two older children: 'Why not start earlier in the evening?' It has little effect: they insist on sticking to their own style of working*.

It is interesting to ask whether schools have, in fact, any legal right to set homework to their pupils. The only recorded legal case on this issue was in 1884, when a child was punished in school for not doing homework and the distressed parents sued the teacher for damages. The court found that the parents had a duty to send their child to school for the stipulated hours, but the ordering of the child to do lessons at home was *not* authorized in law. Before you pass to your child this good news I should warn you that a modern court of law would *probably* (and no-one I know has put it to the test) find that the setting of homework, in moderate amounts, *to children of secondary school age,* is legal.

Also, as many teachers will tell you, it is well nigh impossible for children to complete most examination syllabuses unless they do homework.

*A very useful book for teenagers is *Learn How to Study* by Derek Rowntree. Macdonald & Jane, 1976. Although it is aimed at sixth formers and university students it is very readable and capable of being understood by most youngsters due to go in for O-levels.

My own view is that a great many youngsters (and especially those approaching their O- and A-level examinations) work far too hard. Six hours per day at school is taxing enough; on top of this, many teenagers do as much as four hours homework in the evening. Few adults do ten hours hard work in a day, and yet we ask our children to cope with this enormous work load.

Homework is fine providing that it is given in moderate amounts and is interesting. But too often, it is a chronic burden and totally unstimulating.

The truth is that parents are, by and large, genuinely puzzled over homework. Some of it appears to be too easy and pointless; sometimes, it's too hard. At times, there is too little of it; at other times, too much. Some schools set a great deal of homework; others don't (and, for those that do, the age at which children are set homework seems to be getting younger). Parents become worried if their children are *not* set homework (does this mean that the child is less able than the others?)

The answer to this confusion is, of course, to go to the school and ask: 'What is your policy on homework?' Most teachers will be glad to explain how much homework is set, why it is set, and how long the child is expected to take to complete it.

What are the main arguments *for* homework? They are:

1 *It encourages children to work on their own.* This is an important preparation for adult life where we have to get on with tasks without constant supervision.

2 *Homework extends the time available for learning.* For example, it is better to learn French vocabulary, or to 'write up' notes, at home, rather than at school, because the teacher's skills can be used to tackle less mechanical tasks.

Most teachers of, say, French would claim that no child can effectively master the language without some work at home to supplement the all-too-brief (forty-minute) lessons in school.

3 *Some tasks are more appropriately done at home.* In this category might be placed reading a set book, 'writing up' a geography lesson, or copying out notes taken in the classroom.

4 *Many parents expect homework.* They become worried if a school does not set homework, and may suspect that the school which does has a higher academic standard.

An element of status, even snobbery, is attached to the setting of homework, particularly if brighter children are seen to be given more of it than their less able peers.

Near where I live is a school which regularly sets homework to eight-year-olds. It is reasonable to ask, I think: should not these children be doing 'their own thing' in the evening? Cannot what needs to be taught be taught during school hours?

The child who is obsessed with homework has little opportunity to talk, in a relaxed way, with parents. He or she has little opportunity to explore the world, follow individual reading interests, or just stand and stare.

Outside activities may have to be curtailed if a child is given too much homework. Yet it is in the street, at the scouts, guides, youth club and sports centre that the child or young person can meet with others of his or her own age and learn invaluable social skills, and learn to relax. Are we, by insisting that homework is an absolute number 1 priority, emphasizing the youngster's intellectual development at the expense of his personal, social and emotional growth?

The other major difficulty with homework lies in answering the question — what *is* a moderate amount? What takes a bright child (or bright parents?) half-an-hour may take the less able child far longer. Homework *does* affect youngsters' attitudes to school. I have met children who have developed a lasting dislike of French, or a permanent hatred of mathematics, simply because the homework set by the teacher was too hard or inadequately explained.

Nevertheless, we must face the fact that a certain amount of homework is inevitable in the face of the modern examination system. It has to be done. What can we, as parents, do to make sure that it is done properly and with the minimum of fuss?

All interested parents should:

1 *Discuss homework at Parent-Teacher Association meetings.* Make sure you know what the school is expecting to achieve by it, and take advice on the best way for your child to approach it.
2 Make allowances for an individual child's way of working but do *impose a limit on time spent watching telelvision.* Try to get the child into a routine, doing his or her homework at a certain time of the evening.
3 *Save time to be together and talk together* about things other than school. Homework should not dominate family life. You could, for example, ban any discussion about homework at weekends or during family meals, otherwise there is never any relaxed, open-ended conversation at meal-times.
4 If your child has a demanding hobby (e.g. music, gymnastics or some other activity) you must *ask the school what time is to be allocated to the child to follow his or her own interests.*
5 *Suggest that the school run evening classes (for parents) on particularly elusive subjects e.g. modern maths.* Some schools already do this. Others are less willing to demonstrate that the

homework set is something the child really needs to know and that it makes good educational sense.

6 *Go to the school and see the child's teacher* if the homework set is either too hard or causing the child chronic strain and worry. After all, it is your child that is under stress, your family that is disrupted, by ill-considered homework tasks.

Often, teachers tell me, homework can act as a bond between child and parent. It can also, I tell them, lead to tension, anxiety and argument in the home. Plenty of destructive passions are aroused if the question of homework is not kept in perspective. In some homes, where parents and children are baffled, frustrated and angry at the work which has been set for the child to do at home, tempers flare, insults fly, and a family version of World War III is enacted every evening of the working week.

I have a feeling that much of the homework that children do is irrelevant to life as it is lived, or will be lived, by the children concerned. I readily admit that I have long forgotten all the facts I ever learned during my own homework days, though I can remember the boredom of it. Homework could be made more exciting. It could be given in the form of projects to be handed in at the end of term. It could be set in such a way that it would make children look at their environment with enquiring eyes.

We parents must put up with homework, but it should not be as haphazard an activity as it usually is. Each school should have a sensible homework policy, and every parent should know what that policy is, what the homework is *for.* Ideally, such a policy would be developmental. An eleven-year-old would receive brief tasks to do at home. Lengthier projects would be given to older children, involving looking things up and finding things out for themselves.

By the time the youngster left school at sixteen or eighteen he or she would be capable of working conscientiously without supervision. Many of us are expected to do so in the adult world so it is as well to learn self-discipline at school. Until such time as homework becomes more meaningful, more imaginative, it will remain a burden and a chore to many thousands of children, and parents.

These days, many parents are worried about so-called progressive education. In a sense, this is inevitable since the way we think of schools is to recall our own education, and to gauge how different the school is from our own day. Many parents were taught formally and know little, if anything about modern maths and the more esoteric aspects of the modern curriculum such as environmental studies, home economics and sex education. Methods of teaching children have changed, though class sizes are often much larger than they ought to be if individual attention is to be given to pupils.

We tend to forget that some of the advocates of progressive methods taught in schools with very small classes. A S Neill, at Summerhill* was never faced with a class of thirty children. John Dewey's Experimental School in Chicago, an oft-quoted model of progressive education, had a staff-pupil ratio of one teacher to *six* children with ten part-time assistants thrown in. Maltings House, Susan Isaac's school, and another popular model of how to teach children, had no dull, or disadvantaged, children. It catered for the children of professional parents and the youngsters had IQ's ranging from 114 to 166 — the average was 131. The teachers at the school were extremely gifted.

If you take ordinary, devoted but human, teachers and put them in front of a mixed ability class of, say, thirty-six children it is quite clear that you are not going to get the same results as Neill, or Dewey or Susan Isaacs. Some succeed remarkably well, considering the circumstances. Others fail miserably to teach the children anything worthwhile. I think that traditional methods of education are still valid. It is not, or should not be, a question of progressive versus traditional approaches. Wherever possible the new (if it works) should be combined with the old to make the classroom a more effective learning environment for those youngsters concerned.

I am one of those people who believe that young children should know their tables and their basic number bonds. I believe both primary and secondary school children should be encouraged to write neatly. Why? It could be argued that, with pocket calculators and the telephone, young people don't need to be able to count or to write letters. I wish I could believe that, but I can't. The tables, and basic addition, subtraction, division and multiplication form a basis for subsequent learning. It is hard to have any understanding of maths if you cannot count, multiply, divide or subtract.

As for handwriting (and spelling) it should be remembered that young people have to apply for jobs, or for admittance to college or university. They are, in my opinion, less likely to be successful if their letters look as though they have been walked upon by a drunken, ink-stained spider. Employers might (rightly or wrongly) conclude that the appearance of a letter is important and that it may give some indication of the youngsters ability in general. I think that the appearance of school work is important — pupils take more pride in work which looks neat, and which can be read easily.

*Summerhill.* Pelican books 1968.

I had a phone call from a mother recently. 'My seventeen-year-old son's writing is awful,' she told me. Her son was in the sixth form at school and she was worried about the effect of his writing on his examination results. 'What can I do about it?' she asked me. Since the advice I gave her applies to a good many teenagers, it may be worth spelling it out. A youngster who wishes to write neatly should:

1 *Sit up properly,* with a straight back and both feet on the floor. The book, or paper, should be moved to suit the posture and not the other way around. Some teenagers, mysteriously, stoop over the writing book, eyes a couple of inches off the page, and sit on one leg. It is difficult, it not impossible, to write well in this contorted fashion.

2 *Hold the pen correctly,* i.e. not too tightly and about one inch from the nib. Elbows should be held slightly away from the book, not tucked in, and wrists and forearms supported by the desk or table.

3 *Have a decent pen* Platignum offer a wide range of pens and nibs. Mentmore (Platignum House, Six Hills Way, Stevenage, Herts SG1 2AY) sell writing instruction leaflets on the main styles of handwriting together with copy books.

4 *Be prepared to re-vamp a deteriorating style* All three of my teenage children, in turn, went through a stage when their writing became totally indecipherable (they were about thirteen at the time). Each of them was bought a Platignum fountain pen with an interchangeable nib unit. The nib each chose was an italic one. We then bought *Learn about Handwriting* by Tom Gourdie (Ladybird Books). The modified italic style advocated in the book suited the children and 'tidied up' their written work like a charm. They can now write quickly and neatly. They also enjoy writing, which is vital.

The best idea is to encourage youngsters to write *small amounts* with the emphasis on neatness. Writing exercises should never be overdone, especially when the young person concerned has become despondent and demoralized about the whole subject. A quarter of an hour, four times a day, is better than an hour all at once. Don't forget to make it enjoyable, to praise the youngster, and to stop before he or she gets bored. Writing can be fun, and parents can spoil the pleasure of it if they become too anxious.

With spelling, the main thing I can say to reassure parents is that, after years of writing, I still have to use a dictionary to look certain words up (e.g. accommodation; medicine; nursery). It's no use arguing that Queen Elizabeth I couldn't spell. Good Queen Bess didn't have to make a good impression on examiners or prospective employers. Many teachers don't teach spelling in school, which I think is a mistake. A teacher who enthuses about spelling (ten minutes a day keeps illiteracy, and the dole queue, away) will produce a classroom of children who love to spell.* Creative writing is important but so is spelling and spelling-bees, quizzes and team competitions in the classroom can all instil a love of spelling instead of a fear of the subject. A dictionary, too, is important — even for us adults!

Nowadays, a great many schools have Parent-Teacher Associations or 'Friends of the School' groups. Since the home has such a tremendous influence in the child's educational attitudes and achievements, the closer the liaison between home and school the better. There are schools which still display large signs which read: NO PARENTS BEYOND THIS POINT. I think this is wrong since parents should be encouraged to think of themselves as having a vital part to play in the education of their own children.

As the chairman of a local PTA for several years, it is my experience that parents are often eager to help the school in fund-raising, in working together with the teachers for the benefit of the pupils. Some schools are ambivalent about PTAs; they think that the parents will interfere too much in the running of the school; they fear that parents will become over-involved in educational issues. This has not been my experience. The PTA has an important part to play in stopping the propogation of the mistaken notion that the home and the school are two different worlds. They can become so, but only to the detriment of the child.

One of the problems we ran across in the PTA to which I belonged was that the keen and interested parents turned up regularly and tended to be a tower of strength. There was a large group of parents who would come along to PTA functions if somebody encouraged, or cajoled, them. There was a third group of parents who *never* turned up and, often, it was these parents whose children had problems in school or were doing badly in their lessons. It didn't matter whether the occasion was a jumble sale, bingo, square dancing or a cheese and wine party, it proved very difficult to persuade certain parents to attend.

This is very sad. It should be remembered that the teenager who behaves well in school sometimes has problems at home. Conversely, the child who presents no problems at home may be doing badly in school. It is only when school and home work closely together that the difficulties can be sorted out to the

*See *The Essential Spelling List,* Fred J Schonell, Macmillan educational 1932. Other useful books on writing are the *Nelson Handwriting* (Work books 3 and 4), Thomas Nelson & Sons, 1963, 1964.

benefit of the child. Some children are more introverted, or shy, than others. These children may need praise, prestige and a role in the classroom if they are to use their capabilities to the full. The parent can often give the teacher a good idea of the best way to approach the child, and vice versa. Many extravert children need a structured approach in the classroom so that they know what they are doing and are helped to become less erratic and anxious about their work. How can we understand the temperament, and the emotional feelings of children, if we know nothing of their parents and their home background? How can we sympathize with the demands made upon a child by the school if we don't visit the school and know nothing of his or her teacher and the approach of the school towards the education of our own child.

There are problems which stem, for example, from over-ambitious parents. Take Mark, for example. His father is an engineer, but badly wants his son to become a doctor. Mark, aged thirteen, has hardly been consulted in the matter; he rarely sees his father, anyway, since dad spends a great many evenings in the pub, where he boasts about his son's school achievements and adds that 'he's going to be a doctor, you know'. The strain is beginning to tell on Mark. The truth is he is a boy of just above average ability who would be better off following a career of his own choosing, and one more suited to his intellectual capacity.

The next thing that happens is, because of the burden of father's unrealistic hopes, Mark begins to underfunction in school; turning in work below his own potential. He is tired of being regarded as a non-person who's validity depends upon his achieving 'success'. To be something that a parent has dreamed up for you is a tall order for any child. It was only after having seen father on a number of occasions that I was able to persuade him to take a more realistic view of his son's capability, and to stop pressurizing the boy. The whole, distressing situation could have been avoided if school and home had been united in their efforts to help Mark. *His* parents, needless to say, were amongst the group I have mentioned who rarely visited the school because, as mother told me, they were 'too busy'.

A somewhat more bizarre case was that of Janet, aged thirteen. She had abdominal pains, and had had her appendix taken out. The pain persisted, and she was referred to the child guidance clinic for assessment. Janet was an extremely pretty and vivacious girl who conversed well. To my astonishment I found that her IQ was 86 — far below what I would have expected from her general appearance and demeanour. I tested her the following week — the IQ was still below 90. The parents were as misled as I was: *their* belief was that Janet was a very bright child and they gave her extra work at home in addition to her ordinary school work. The stress caused by the academic over-expectation was quite severe. When I diplomatically suggested to the parents that we were all expecting too much they took the pressure off. The result was that the pains disappeared. The girl was bright, happy and cheerful once more, her natural self. The alarming suggestion had been made that Janet should undergo explorative surgery for her abdominal pain. Again, a close understanding of a child's abilities, interests and needs, can ward off a lot of quite inappropriate and irrelevant conclusions being drawn!

School reports can give a clue to problems within the home, especially when a child who has attained high standards suddenly deteriorates in the quality of work produced. 'Doesn't concentrate,' says the report, or 'Lazy'. Investigation of the child's circumstances may show that there is disruption or disharmony at home, perhaps between the parents. There may be marital strife, or money problems, or a crisis in father's career, or mother's health may not be good. It is rather facile, in my view, for teachers to describe children as apathetic or inattentive without trying to find out why they should be like that. Are the lessons too easy/too hard/uninteresting? Is there an emotional problem which springs from the home? It is very hard for children to do well in school when they are faced with emotional turmoil, and even open aggression between parents, within the home. The answer, again, is that schools should know as much as possible (without being 'nosey' or spying) about the home circumstances of the children in their care. To try to educate a child whose parents are in process of being divorced, or (perhaps worse) who are constantly arguing or at odds with each other (whether they resort to physical violence or not) is rather like asking somebody to partake of a bowl of soup on a small boat in a Force 9 gale. Emotions affect the intellect; it is difficult for youngsters to make the most of their intelligence when their emotions are in a constant state of turmoil.

Children, these days, go to secondary school when they are eleven, twelve and thirteen. Some children go to primary school (usually from the age of seven until eleven, following infant school, from five to seven years); other children go to a first school (from five until eight, or nine, years) followed by attendance at middle school (from eight or nine, until twelve or thirteen). All this is very confusing to parents. I don't think it matters much which system is in operation providing there are good educational reasons for it, and those reasons are explained to the parents. Some people would argue that to change schools at thirteen is unfortunate since this is a time of rapid physiological and psychological change for adolescents and to ask them to get used to a totally new environment at this stage of their development may be ill-timed. Also, it leaves little time for the youngster to acclimatize himself to the more formal and academic patterns of teaching before the stresses and strains of O-levels and CSE examinations loom up on the horizon.

On the other hand, if a change is made at thirteen, the primary and middle schools could develop *their* curriculums and extend the range of subjects taught before children go on to secondary school. These schools could then concentrate on a more academic approach with a knowledge that they are teaching more mature children. Again, whatever the pattern of schooling there should be sound educational reasons behind any decisions made and, hopefully, parents will be consulted to make them aware of the why as well as the how.

There are two tendencies in secondary schools which I think are most unfortunate and regrettable. One is to force the child into early specialization; the other is to force children to follow an academic type of education whether they are suited to it or not. The child who is very bright is often asked to concentrate on a limited range of subjects from the age of fourteen years; certain subjects are dropped, others are taken at O-level, and then forgotten. The idea of the well-rounded, liberally educated person takes second place to the demands of competitive examinations. This is a pity because, as I have indicated, the function of schooling is to enable the person to earn a living and to enjoy his or her life. To specialize at an early age is to run the risk of turning out individuals who are narrow in outlook and who develop rigid attitudes of mind. In life, personal qualities (character) may be just as important as academic achievement.

The emphasis today is on qualifications, what is disparagingly called 'bits of paper'. Society needs practical young people, as well as academics. These days, it is hard to find a good plumber, or somebody to build a wall, or decorate a room. Even for the more menial jobs (which in the old days would have been prepared for by undergoing an apprenticeship) there is a growing demand that youngsters should be more and more qualified. I agree with this demand — if the training is largely technical or practical. I do not think young people should be forced into an academic mould if they are not particularly good at book learning. By all means let the old technical colleges be called 'colleges of further education' providing that the newly-styled establishments do not over-value the academic approach at the expense of the practical. We need people who have degrees in history, English literature and art; we also need more practically-minded young people who are not ashamed to work with their hands and who are not made to feel inferior as the result of an intellectually-biased school curriculum.

The whole question of the further education of young people needs very careful thought. I am not convinced that each and every child should be made to stay on at school until the age of sixteen. Some youngsters, perhaps, would be better off leaving school, finding a job, and then encouraged to attend evening classes, or day-release classes, to broaden their minds or to give them the chance of further qualifications. Is there any point in keeping young people of fifteen plus at school when their hearts and minds are dead-set against the whole notion of school and when they are itching to go out into 'the real world' and become 'more adult'? School is not synonymous with education — it is the width and variety of educational opportunity that we need to emphasize. The sixth form college takes its place alongside the sixth form, the colleges of further and higher education, the university, evening classes, day-release, the Open University and WEA classes. The aim should be to encourage *everybody* to regard school as only part of a life-time process of education and re-education. We are all different and there must be facilities to suit us all, dull or bright, practical or theoretical. We all have a contribution to make to society. We are all curious to find out more about the world, to enhance our skills and to scaffold our limited knowledge about ourselves and our potential. Life begins at forty, they say. Certainly, education does not end at sixteen, even for the non-academic. Most people can be attracted back to the classroom if the course being offered is suitable to their needs. We *must* get away from a narrow, intellectual view of education; we *must* see education as being available when needed for all ages and types of people.

Parents often ask me what I think about boarding schools, or mixed schools, or large comprehensive schools. The question I ask them is: 'Does the school suit *your* child?' What counts is the *quality* of the school and the excellence, or not, of the headmaster (or headmistress) and the staff. The parents should make it their business to find out what the school has to offer to *their* child.

Children differ enormously in temperament. Some sensitive children are unsuited to life at boarding school. In my opinion, there are very few children who benefit from the boarding school environment before the age of eleven or twelve years. Young children, of primary school age, need frequent contact with a caring and loving mother, and benefit enormously from a friendly, supportive relationship with father. I am surprised how many parents send young children away to school and thus deprive themselves of the fun and companionship of having them around the house. What point is there in having children if they are to be despatched away from the home for most of the year? The child becomes a visitor in his own home; his or her parents may become strangers; children and parents may have little in common, little to talk about. In the neighbourhood in which they live, the boarding school children may have few friends and may find themselves isolated and lonely during the school holidays.

Having said that (and my main objection is to sending very young and/or very sensitive children to boarding school) let me stress that there are children (of secondary school age) for whom boarding school is ideal. After all, the school can often offer a large variety of sport, hobbies and outside interests, far beyond the scope of the most inventive parents. The lively, active child who is an easy-mixer, and who needs plenty to do and lots of community life, is well placed in a school where many groups and activities are readily available. The child who is bored at home, or who does not get on with his or her parents is better off in the boarding situation. Let's face it, there are parents who don't particularly like children or, if they do, see them as less important than the pursuance of a career and adult interests. If that be the case, the child is better off catching the train to his school where he will be with his own friends and have teachers who will take an interest in him.

The majority of schools nowadays are co-educational. Most people agree that it is healthy for boys and girls to grow up together, and go to school together, so that they will see each other as real people and not have too many fantasies about the opposite sex. It is interesting that some parents very much like single-sex schools. 'The girls, or boys,' they tell me, 'can get on with their work better.' This may be so — there is time enough in the evening or at weekends to be attracted to, or distracted by, the other sex. My own view is that parents should, whenever possible, have the choice — the parents who strongly advocate single sex schools should have the opportunity to send their children to a school of this type.

What concerns me more than the single sex/co-education issue is the *size* of schools. In my opinion, many secondary schools are too big; they are by far the largest establishment that many of the children will attend in their lives. They contain so many people that it is impossible for the child to know all the teachers in the school, and for the teachers to know more than a small section of the pupils. Even where their school is divided into houses, and where counselling and tutor groups are very much in evidence, quite a few children feel lost and puzzled within the large comprehensive school. It is difficult for children to feel that they belong to the school, and that they have an important role to play in it. Many of the teachers they meet will not know who they are, what their home background is, what their hobbies and interests are. Is it surprising that some youngsters feel neglected and 'out of it' when the school is massive and reminds them of a factory rather than a family? It should be said, though, that some big, comprehensive schools (of say, 1500 to 2500 pupils) are very successful and seem to have a minimum of problems because of the dedication of the staff and the quality of the head. Nevertheless I would not like to see secondary schools get any bigger; I *would* like to see a greater number of smaller (500, or 600 pupils) and medium-sized (700-800) schools. As often as possible, parents should be given the choice of which sort of school they wish their children to attend.

What will the future be like for the youngsters of today? What will the world be like in the year 2000? It is anybody's guess. We must teach them to be flexible; some of them will change jobs in mid career. We must teach them to be resilient; the world is not getting easier. We must teach them to be curious and instil in them a love of learning. A N Whitehead wrote, in 1933:

> Our sociological theories, our political philosophies, our practical maxims of business, our political economy, and our traditions of education are derived from an unbroken tradition of great thinkers from the age of Plato . . . to the end of the last century. We assume, says Whitehead, that each generation will live amid the conditions governing the lives of its fathers and mothers and will transmit these conditions to mould with equal force the lives of its children. We are now living in the first period of human history for which this assumption is false.

There will be, socially and industrially, a new set of rules, a knew set of assumptions. Things will be vastly different in thirty years time, and we must not be arrogant about our knowledge but prepare our youngsters to face up to that difference. Whitehead wrote his warning in 1933. It is more meaningful and relevant in the eighties than it was fifty years ago. Education is education for change. We must hold fast to that which is good, and we must abandon that which no longer works.

## Chapter Eleven

# Teenagers With Special Needs

I first met John when he was seven-years-old. The headmistress of his infants' school had written to me about him. This is what she wrote:

Please can you tell us whether this little boy is a gifted child? He is seven and has recently done a piece of work for his teacher called: 'The Properties of the Nucleus'. She can't make head or tail of it and neither can I. Could you tell us how clever John really is and, more important, what we should do about him?

Signed . . .

Whatever else John was he was entirely normal in appearance for a seven-year-old boy. He had hazel-coloured eyes, freckles on his face, his nose was runny and he looked rather untidy. I lent him my handkerchief to wipe his nose, and took him out to the corridor to ask him a few questions from the intelligence test.

It was when I reached 'What is retroactive?' that I realized that John was unusual. 'Acting against,' he replied, 'as in retroactive rockets, you know.' I didn't, but I took his word for it.

John had no difficulty with words such as casuistry, sudorific, piscatorial and neologism; he defined the difference between contentment and happiness; he could tell me immediately why the words 'first' and 'last' were similar words. John was very good verbally, in fact, superb. But what was he like at other things?

I gave him some maths to do; he had the ability of a bright sixteen-year-old. His observation, reasoning, verbal and numerical memory were all absolutely first class. I worked out his IQ. The IQs on the test only went up to 170 and I calculated that John's was about 250. It was the highest IQ I had ever come across. I went back to see John's headmistress and his teacher. Over coffee, I told them both: 'He's gifted all right'.

What did we do about him?

I'm not very keen on special schools for gifted children — they already live in an isolated golden ghetto of the mind. They are different, and we should not exaggerate those differences. After all, they have to grow up to live in a world alongside people who are far less gifted than themselves.

On the other hand, in adjusting to the rest of us these children may lose their special glitter, their rare intellectual gifts, and end up frustrated and lost like silver sharks trapped inside a fisherman's boat.

We compromised. John had intelligent (but not gifted) parents who had already been in touch with the local library to provide suitable reading material for him. They had a scientist friend who chatted to John and gave him little tasks to do. (By the way, John's favourite reading material was the *Beano, Nature,* a highly intellectual scientific journal, and various aeronautical magazines!)

We supplemented this with a project on space travel (supervised by the senior science master at the local grammar school) and we arranged for John to purchase a cheap telescope and to write to certain experts and associations where he could keep in touch with people of the same interests and similar abilities to his own.

We kept him in the same class. After all, it is hard to see how you can have a runny-nosed, freckled boy learning alongside sixteen-year-olds. We arranged for John to join the cubs; we encouraged him to learn to swim, and to play football and cricket.

Despite the fact that the other children in his class all called John 'The Professor', they all liked him. Both the headmistress and myself were concerned that John's *emotional* and *social* development should not be ignored because of his outstanding intellectual gifts. He was different from the other children, much cleverer. Yet, as a human being, and as a child, he was in many ways the same.

John went on to grammar school. There, he joined various clubs and societies that offered him a chance to develop his gifts. He continued to correspond with experts in those fields in which he was particularly interested. I asked the senior science master what he thought of John. 'He's the most naturally gifted child I've ever come across' he told me. 'A top-drawer mind, an excellent all-round ability, and the nearest thing to genius I've seen in science subjects.'

I mention John for two reasons: (a) teachers do not always know what to do with children who are gifted and (b) parents are frequently puzzled when they suspect that one of their children may be in the gifted range, or shows exceptional ability in some area such as music, gymnastics, ballet, mathematics, drama or games.

Many gifted children, at present, stand a very good chance of being bored to tears in the ordinary classroom situation. Either their gifts go unrecognized or the child is under-stimulated, not given sufficient challenge. Indeed, it has been suggested (though there's no proof of it) that a proportion of the criminal population were, at school, unidentified, unstimulated and frustrated; later, as a consequence, they turned their talents to deviant pursuits.

Fortunately, there is more awareness these days of the problems which youngsters like John have to face. The National Association for Gifted Children, 1 South Audley Street, London W1Y 5DQ, offers advice to parents and, through their own newsletter, gifted children are kept in touch with each other and, in their spare time, explore all sorts of creative and intellectual subjects from mineralogy to chess.

More and more local authorities run Saturday Clubs where gifted children can meet each other, play and talk together, and where mothers can discuss mutual problems (having a gifted child asking questions all day can be a very tiring business, even for the most devoted mother!). Too, local authorities are willing, via the school psychological service, to assess gifted children and to advise on their needs. (The mother who suspects her child may be gifted may refer the child to the SPS via the family doctor, the school head teacher or, more informally, ask for an appointment by going along to the local child guidance clinic.)

My own advice to parents is: better to be sure than sorry. For the gifted child, boredom is a very real danger. If you think you have a gifted child in the family why not ask for an assessment by the educational psychologist, and for some practical advice? The earlier in the child's school life such an assessment takes place, the sooner appropriate steps to help the child can be taken.

We turn now from the problems of the gifted to the difficulties faced by a more unfortunate group of youngsters — the physically handicapped. In order to illustrate the courageous way in which these difficulties may be faced let us consider the case of Patricia, aged nineteen.

Patricia, or Trish, as she is more often called, is a very attractive, brown-eyed, dark-haired young woman. She is paraplegic (paralysed from the waist down) and confined to a wheel chair.

Trish was born physically handicapped but her mother was keen that she should attend ordinary school and not be singled out as 'different'. Trish therefore went to the local primary and secondary schools. It was not the severity of Trish's handicap that was the major factor in deciding not to send her to a special, boarding school; it was the simple fact that the local secondary school is built mostly on one level.

Trish could move quite happily about the place in her wheel chair and easily negotiate the two small ramps that were put at the

139

side of two (not too steep) staircases. Her friends and classmates were always willing to push her up the ramp, if she was in a hurry to get to lessons.

Even though the staff and pupils at Trish's school were helpful and understanding, and friendly without being patronizing, she nevertheless spent a great deal of time propelling herself around the school at speed simply to be in the right place at the right time. She wanted to be treated like the others. The teachers took her at her word. If she was late for a lesson she was asked, as she appeared at the doorway (in her chair): 'And where have you been?'

Trish's main criticism of the school was that the career's advice that she received was inadequate. On leaving school, Trish had no idea what to do so she signed on for a secretarial course at the town's Institute of Further Education. Whilst there, Trish decided to study for A-levels in psychology, sociology and English, and try to gain admittance to university.

It is interesting to note that the Institute of Higher Education which Trish attended had 'no lifts and stairs all over the place. Needless to say, the secretarial course was on the top floor.' It is lack of practical help, and attention to detail in planning such buildings, that severely limits the life-chances of physically handicapped young people.

There is still a patronizing attitude to these youngsters. One 'expert' has suggested that they should be ready to take up such work as cobbling (for young men) and basket weaving (for young women). Trish's attitude is that 'other people should not belittle our intellects or our emotions. We don't want to sublimate our emotional urges into making baskets, or shoes. We want what others want, including friends of the opposite sex.'

Now at university, Trish is studying for a degree in sociology. She wants to be a social worker and, with her personality and experience of fighting against handicap, would be ideal in the job.

Trish could travel, with help, to the office. She could live in a flat (if she had somebody about to help her) and be reasonably independent. She *couldn't*, with her degree of intelligence, bear being placed in a residential home and sit around all day, doing nothing.

In Sweden, by law, every new block of flats is required to have accommodation for at least one physically disabled person. A block of flats will have suitable lifts; the apartment in question will have easily movable furniture and electric points in accessible places.

Such foresight gives a disabled young man or woman a chance of the independence that they crave; it enables graduates, such as

Trish, to put their university education to effective use. Disabled young people don't want to play a helpless, parasitic role within the community; they want to do something useful, to contribute towards the community and it is up to us to help them.

When I see Trish wheeling herself (at great speed) about the university campus, and mixing quite unselfconsciously with the other students, I can't help thinking what a brave young woman she is although she would dismiss that thought as sheer sentiment.

What is needed, she maintains, are more universities with halls of residence (and not sick bays) specially designed for the physically handicapped. Perhaps *all* the Institutes of Further and Higher Education, Polytechnics and Universities within the United Kingdom should aim at an agreed policy towards the disabled.

There are problems. Should all profoundly deaf students go to the same university, study on the same campus? I doubt whether they would want that.

Do blind students have any problems getting suitable text books in braille? Can they get such books from the college library? Are there a variety of tape-recorded books on campus which they can use. Blind young undergraduates (who are often extremely adept in finding their way about) don't want tea and sympathy; they want practical help.

Young people in wheelchairs (like Trish) may not wish to follow arts courses. If they opt for science degrees are there places to which they can go where laboratories (and benches) are readily accessible? These are real difficulties which they face and it is up to us, the more fortunate, physically-able members of the community, to solve them.

Since the *Chronically Sick and Disabled Persons Act* (1970) there has been more awareness of the educational and social needs of physically handicapped youngsters. These days, we are beginning to see signs of more integrated forms of provision. The disabled want to be with ordinary people; they *don't* want to be segregated.

One thing is clear — where the handicapped youngster attends the ordinary school the quality of personal help and teaching (and vocational guidance) should not be inferior to that which he or she would receive in a special school. With more favourable teacher/pupil ratios, and with the help of medical and other specialist support services, there is no reason why we should not move towards the integration of disabled youngsters into the ordinary school.

What is required, if we are to learn from Trish's experience, are the following:

1   Adaptation of older school buildings, and colleges, to the

needs of the physically handicapped.

2   Special schools, where they are necessary, to be built within the vicinity of ordinary schools so that youngsters may intermingle whenever possible for their mutual benefit.

3   Integration of the disabled youngster into the ordinary school community wherever possible.

4   The training of teachers to include a mandatory course on youngsters with special needs, including practical guidance.

5   More advanced diploma courses for those teachers who wish to work with handicapped youngsters.

6   More effective co-ordination between health, social services and educational authorities to help the physically handicapped school leaver.

I am not starry-eyed. I know that blind youngsters, profoundly-deaf youngsters and many other handicapped young people will need special help in special day or residential schools. At the same time, I am optimistic about ordinary school placement. We must never be too namby-pamby in our approach to, and our expectations of, the disabled.

The Warnock Report* is a lucid and impassioned answer to the layperson's question: 'Why educate such youngsters at all?' The answer, the report says, is that the disabled are human beings and, as such, are entitled to the best education that we can give them. The Report adds: 'There are some children with disabilities who — through education — may be able to lead a life very little poorer in quality than that of the non-handicapped child . . . without this education, they might face a life of dependence or even institutionalization.'

That is true, and Trish, so modest and so very likeable and attractive, is the living proof of the argument. We must be aware of youngsters like her and, in thinking about them, plan not for the next few years but up until the end of the century and into the twenty-first century. These youngsters, like their able-bodied peers, deserve the best future that we can offer them.

'I want to be like everybody else, as ordinary as possible, and to lead the fullest life I can,' Trish told me recently. I'm quite sure she will reach her goal, such is her determination. I hope that the rest of us help rather than hinder her in her aims.

In talking about Trish, I may have given the impression that I am against special schools. This is not so. Many children receive an extremely good education within a special school setting and, at

*Special Educational Needs: Report of the Committee of Inquiry into the Education of Handicapped Children and Young People. HMSO 1978

present, it is difficult to see how certain youngsters could be given the attention they require in the ordinary school.

Angela is a case in point. She is fourteen, and attends a special day school for educationally subnormal youngsters. She is officially designated as an ESN (M) young person i.e. mildly educationally subnormal. However, this is merely a label, and tells us little about Angela as a real person, or about her educational needs, or the wishes of her parents concerning her schooling.

Angela attended the local primary school and was falling further and further behind in her school work when she was first seen by an educational psychologist. At the age of nine years, she had a reading age of six and was very poor at mathematics. Her general comprehension, the teacher reported, was 'extremely limited'.

The educational psychologist gave Angela an intelligence test and found that she had an IQ of 67. This placed her within the top end of the ESN (M) range. (The average IQ is 100.) More important, he considered Angela to be a shy girl, very immature for her age, and a child who was becoming increasingly less successful and more frustrated and depressed in the normal class.

The parents were consulted, and the local special school was considered. The advantages of such a placement were:

1   Smaller class (about fifteen children in each group) and, therefore, more individual attention for Angela.
2   Teachers on the staff specially trained to deal with children of Angela's ability.
3   A flourishing Friends of The School (parent-teacher) Association so that Angela's parents could feel involved with their daughter's progress at school.
4   The chance that Angela, in a smaller school of some 120 children, would be a 'large fish in a small pond' and would gain confidence from mixing with children of her own (and lower attainments) rather than being bottom of the class the whole time.
5   The social activities of the school (e.g. clubs, outings, art, sewing and Scottish dancing) would help to build up Angela's self-confidence and make her a little more outgoing.

The disadvantage of sending Angela to special school was that she might be made to feel different from other children. Considering the matter carefully, the head teacher, the parents and the educational psychologist decided that it was better for Angela to be in a smaller school, with smaller classes.

Angela is now fourteen, and is very happy at school. She can read at the twelve-year-old level, has a good understanding of basic number bonds, her handwriting is neat and she has acquired at school a number of useful social skills: she can cook, sew, wallpaper a room, do the laundrette and cope with simple household budgets.

The school has a flat, and a recreation room. Visitors to the school are served lunch (cooked by the girls) in the flat, and senior girls have an opportunity to converse with and show around the school various VIPs who visit regularly. Angela is a socially competent, outgoing, well-adjusted teenager who has benefited greatly from having an important role in the life of the school.

There is close liaison between the special school and local employers. The employers, both from large firms and small family businesses, have reported that they are extremely pleased with the children from the school to whom they have given jobs. 'Polite, courteous and dependable' is how local employers have described the youngsters. The school manages to find jobs for nearly all of its leavers; those who do not find employment are usually suffering from a physical handicap with entails their working in a sheltered workshop setting. In fact, the school's employment record is better than those of the neighbouring comprehensive schools.

It is for this reason (and the fact that the school has an 'old boys' and 'old girls' youth club for youngsters to keep in touch after leaving school) that Angela's parents want her to stay at the school until she is sixteen rather than return to the ordinary secondary school.

Walking around Angela's school recently, I noticed the high standard of art displayed on the classroom walls. I saw the magnificent woodwork done by both boys and girls and the first-rate job they had made of redecorating (and supplying simple furniture for) the flat. I was treated to a superb meal, cooked and served up in great style by the youngsters.

Here teenage youngsters were being given a very sound practically-based education which took into account their social and emotional needs. As I spoke to Angela, with her blue eyes, rust coloured hair and freckled face, I could see that she was happy at school and I had no doubt in my own mind that she was better off there than at one of the local, large comprehensives.

'I'm going to be a hairdresser,' Angela told me. She added that the older girls had lessons from a beauty expert from outside in personal grooming and care of face, figure and hair. The girls could wash and dry their hair in the flat; they could, if they wished (and if accommodation at home was cramped) have a bath. It was a hairdresser, one of the many visiting speakers from the community outside, who took Angela aside and told her that she appeared to have a talent in this particular direction.

Whether Angela becomes a hair-stylist or not, she will leave school with a good chance of a job, and plenty of social skills to help her through life. That is why we cannot say that, in all cases, children should attend ordinary schools. There are some superb special schools within the educational system and they do a great deal for their pupils.

I do not like to see youngsters labelled: labels are fine for bottles and tin cans but not for people. Nor do I like to see young people made to feel different. At the same time, there are youngsters like Angela who, where education is concerned, do need something special. They need individual help, and an opportunity to grow in confidence.

Our next handicap is one about which there is a great deal of controversy — dyslexia. Sometimes, the scepticism some people have towards this disability is expressed humorously as with the well-known graffiti 'Dyslexia rules, KO?'

Despite the humour nobody can say that being unable to read, or write, or spell, is anything but a severe embarrassment to the youngster concerned and a cause of anxiety to the parents of such a youngster.

Whether dyslexia exists or not the young person's feelings about his frustration in school, and his failure to reach an acceptable standard of work, are very real. Reading is a vital skill, and to be deficient in this skill in no joke.

What is dyslexia? The word comes from the Greek *dys* — bad, and *lexia* — words. A dyslexic youngster is somebody who has difficulty with words (and/or symbols). The signs of dyslexia are:

1  Clumsiness, and difficulty in such things as throwing and catching a ball
2  Left-handedness in writing or ambidexterity
3  Crossed-laterality (i.e. predominently right-handed, and right-footed but left eye dominant; or vice-versa)
4  Discrepancy between general ability and school attainments, particularly in reading and writing
5  Poor retention and recall of the written word
6  Mirror-writing, and confusion of the letters of the alphabet (*d* for *b*; *u* for *n*)
7  Reversal of words (*saw* for *was*; *god* for *dog*)
8  Reversal of numbers
0  Directional difficulties, and difficulty in reading maps
10  Low tolerance of frustration; accident proneness; lack of concentration
11  Difficulty in 'finding' words to express oneself
12  Slightly confused speech; stumbling over long words

13   Oddness; restlessness and hyperactivity
14   Very slow reading

This is not a comprehensive list, but it does detail most of the major signs. It is claimed that if a youngster shows three or more of these signs then he or she is dyslexic.

There is, however, a difficulty here. As a child, I was crossed lateral, had difficulty with direction, and was clumsy. Yet, I learned to read without any trouble.

Many children show signs of dyslexia and still learn to read. My son, who showed signs similar to my own, learned to read at the age of four. Why is this? Are those youngsters who fail to acquire this vital skill dyslexic or have they simply been badly taught? To answer these questions let us consider three youngsters, all diagnosed as dyslexic, who *did* learn to read.

CASE 1 Susan, an attractive and bright thirteen year-old, moved to a new school. She told her teacher 'I'm dyslexic', and mother confirmed that her daughter had been diagnosed by a medical expert as 'a severe dyslexic'. Susan was certainly behind in her reading: in spite of an IQ of 125, her reading age on the Holborn Reading Scale was roughly seven years.

The teacher was advised by the educational psychologist (myself). We found out that Susan, like many young teenage girls, loved animals and was particularly interested in ponies. A reading scheme was devised based on Susan's interests. It took into account Susan's strengths (good auditory memory and a high degree of motivation) and her weaknesses (abysmal visual memory; very poor perception of the written word).

The reading book was made up, and illustrated with pictures of animals cut out of magazines. A felt nib pen was used to write in the story (which Susan made up) in large, lower case (not *capital*) letters so that Susan could get a good visual picture of the words.

Any particularly useful, or frequently recurring words, were reinforced in her mind by being written on cards, two cards per word, in a red felt-tip pen. Susan was encouraged to jumble up the cards and pick out certain words, to play 'Snap' and to practise word matching (putting the same words next to each other).

Once these words were learned they were again reinforced by cutting the cards into two so that Susan could make up words by picking out the appropriate other half of a word from a selection of half-words in front of her. This synthesis of words is vital to youngsters with visual difficulties.

She was taught phonics — the sounds of words. A tape-recorder was used to develop her auditory skills. Susan was left to work, sometimes, with a work book and a tape recorder which told her what to do ('Turn to page 12. Put a line under a word on the first line beginning with the sound t . . .').

Susan loved these lessons, and particularly her book on animals which was her own book, based on *her* interests. At the end of six months of a structured programme and daily phonics she had a reading age of nearly ten. Even more important, her whole attitude to reading had changed: she now positively liked the subject.

Nobody in school, or the parents, were now concerned with the diagnosis of dyslexia. They were concerned that Susan was now receiving the help she needed and knew that the teacher was not pinning her faith on one reading scheme (since Susan has a history of failure on many reading schemes) but was willing to exploit Susan's interests getting on with the job of teaching her.

Susan is now fifteen, and reading at her own age level. By labelling her dyslexic did we run the risk of establishing a self-fulfilling prophecy? If we call children dyslexic are they less likely to read and are we merely using a scientific-sounding label to excuse our own failure to teach them properly? (By properly, I mean daily phonics and a systematic approach which still motivates the child.)

Let us consider another youngster.

CASE 2 Henry was a popular, good-looking boy who was captain of the school football team. He was fifteen and had an IQ of 120. He was outgoing, and conversed well on a wide range of subjects. Henry played the trumpet and was in the school orchestra. (Interestingly, he had no difficulty in reading music).

His spelling and reading were both appalling: his reading age was roughly twelve years, and his spelling at the eleven-year level. In talking to the parents it emerged that Henry's father had difficulty in school with reading and with written work. His spelling, as an adult, although he was a professional man (a surveyor) was littered with mistakes.

Was this evidence that dyslexia is hereditary? Or did it merely mean that Henry closely identified with his father? I assumed that there was a close bond between father and son.

The father, for recreation, liked golf and fishing. These two activities, therefore, formed the basis for a reading scheme. The materials were much the same as those used with Susan, though Henry required a great deal more motivation as he had become very much 'anti-reading'.

Father co-operated by taking the boy out fishing and for an occasional game of golf. I devised a remedial programme for the boy and trained his eyes (by the use of mazes, tracing, joining dotted lines and following arrows, to go from left to right) since he had a tendency to reverse words and to read from right to left.

During his remedial lessons I would say to Henry: 'Learn to read these words, and to spell them, and you'll be able to put dad right on a thing or two.' Henry started to read. The idea of building up words, or taking them to their constituent pieces, 'clicked'. He made tremendous progress.

After six months, he had gained two years in reading age and was beginning to spell correctly. He was intensely motivated; he wanted to learn to read.

Henry's success does *not* prove that dyslexia doesn't exist; it merely underlines the importance of doing something about reading failure rather than being drawn into fruitless arguments about definitions, labels and neurological diagnosis.

CASE 3 This third youngster showed all the major classic signs of dyslexia, including bizarre spelling, difficulty in scanning the written page, hopeless retention of the patterns of letters, and a good intelligence (IQ 119) linked with abysmal reading. On the intelligence test I gave him, his vocabulary and verbal understanding and reasoning were excellent. On the non-verbal scale (things like jig-saw puzzles, putting together various patterns of coloured blocks, spotting the missing parts in drawings of common, everyday objects) he was below average.

Paul made little progress in the first few weeks. Then I discovered that he was fascinated by television programmes in which there was a lot of action, and no small amount of violence. He was very interested in torture, and in war, and in gangsters.

I don't know how ethical this is but we made up a reading book together called 'Torture Down the Ages'. The word content was suitably graded (his reading age was a mere eight years) and an emphasis, as usual, was placed on phonics: learning the sounds of letters and of the various parts of the words.

Word building, word bingo, matching, sentence building all played a part in the approach. As Paul's reading improved, and his dyslexia began to disappear, so my knowledge of ancient tortures increased by leaps and bounds. I was very dubious about the nature of the reading materials but another child, initially thought to be dyslexic, was proved not to be.

It would be easy to be glib about dyslexia. I must repeat that, for youngsters who fail to learn to read, that failure is real enough and so is the associated frustration and pain.

Scepticism about dyslexia (including my own) remains. The Report of the Advisory Committee on Handicapped Children *Children with Specific Reading Difficulties* (HMSO, 1972) tells us: 'The term "dyslexia" has been very loosely used in educational contexts, and we do not consider it can usefully be employed for educational purposes. In particular, we cannot attach any scientific meaning to the term "acute dyslexia" and we are sceptical of the view that a "specific syndrome of developmental dyslexia" has been identified. We prefer the term "specific reading difficulties". . .'

So do I. If youngsters have specific reading difficulties (and some youngsters do) then we must find the appropriate, specific remedies to combat those difficulties. We must know what to do about crossed laterality, poor visual memory, bad spelling and all the other malfunctions which prevent youngsters from achieving their educational potential.

Reading (and spelling, and writing) are vital skills which must be taught, and taught systematically. It is silly to label children 'dyslexic' if they have not been given first-rate, systematic teaching.

At the same time, my sympathy is with the parents. As youngsters who cannot read grow older they, and their parents, become more and more despondent. The reading difficulties tend to increase rather than diminish and can affect the youngsters' whole attitude to school.

What can parents do? There are three important steps which parents may take:

1  Consult your local educational psychologist (an appointment can be arranged through the family doctor or via the headmaster or headmistress of the school). Ask that your child be assessed and provided with appropriate remedial, individual help. Correct diagnosis is vital, and the sooner, the better. Just as important, though, is that *something be done about the youngster's* problem.
2  If your child is entering for CSE or GCE (O- or A-level examinations) and suffers from specific reading difficulties — or has, despite being intelligent, severe problems with writing and/or spelling *ensure that you get a note from the educational psychologist explaining his or her difficulties to the examining board.* Special arrangements, such as the use of a tape recorder, or an extra time allowance, can be made in those cases where the youngster's chances of passing the examination are radically reduced by his disability.
3  Though it would be unfair, and impractical, to ask a local education authority to send each and every non-reader to a boarding school specializing in reading problems (and such private, fee-paying facilities exist) *you can ask the IEA to make appropriate educational provision for your youngster.* It is the authority's duty to make such provision — to educate the youngster in accordance with his or her age, aptitude and

ability, or disability — and parents should not hesitate to ensure that the IEA does provide remedial help for the youngster. The answer to the child who cannot read is, in my book, fairly simple — teach him (or her).

I have written about four types of youngsters — the gifted, the physically handicapped, the mildly educational subnormal, and the dyslexic. This is because these are the sorts of handicap we have all met, or are likely to meet. (Yes, I do think giftedness *is* a handicap: if we do not provide special help for the child or young person to cope with it.)

I have not mentioned other types of handicap which places the youngster in the special need category: the blind, and the visually impaired; the profoundly deaf, or those young people with marked hearing loss; the diabetic; the asthmatic; the delicate youngster; the autistic; the severely educationally subnormal child suffering, perhaps from Down's Syndrome (mongolism) or from brain damage. No mention has been made of young people who are deaf and dumb, or who suffer from cerebral palsy, or a multiple handicap (i.e. are deaf *and* blind; or ESN *and* visually impaired *and* diabetic).

Two things stand out from the many hundreds of youngsters I have seen who were handicapped in one way or another. One is their tremendous courage, and their ability to enjoy life, despite their disability. Often, such youngsters seem far more cheerful, optimistic and contented than non-handicapped young people (and adults).

The other is their need to be treated, within the bounds of caring and possibility, as ordinary human beings. They desire, above all else, to join in with, and contribute to, the rest of the community.

I will not be romantic and claim that they are all perfectly happy about the fact that they are handicapped. I once met a blind, teenage girl who was very resentful about the fact that she had never seen flowers, or trees, or another person's face, or water, or clouds, or a kettle. Who wouldn't be? I, too, would be slightly resentful at not having seen, not seeing, and not being able to see.

I described to her what punk rockers looked like and she laughed. 'Why do they wear safety pins?' she asked me. 'It's to add to the thrown-together, off-beat style,' I told her (I've no real idea whether that was the right answer). This blind teenager, aged seventeen, held down a job and travelled to work each day. After seeing her I found it rather difficult to ever feel sorry for myself again.

A teenage boy I used to see each week was a thalidomide victim.

His hands stuck out of his shoulders. He had no arms. 'Game of table tennis?' he'd ask me. It was his little joke, though I didn't feel it was very funny. 'You're too good for me,' I'd tell him. 'We'll play football instead.' That lad was one of the happiest, most cheerful people I have ever met.

When I say that we should educate more handicapped children in ordinary schools, or do our very best for them when they need to go to special school, I am thinking of the benefits to us as well as them. They have a great deal to teach us. Our attitude to the handicapped youngster is the litmus test of our humanity. By rejecting them, isolating them from the community, we rob other, normal youngsters of an opportunity to learn from those less fortunate than themselves.

I hope that the reader will forgive me if I become a little bit philosophical about handicap at this point. We are, in my opinion, all handicapped (mostly in minor ways), and many of us are full of self-pity. I know I used to be, grumbling about this, that or the other.

I had referred to me a boy with muscular dystrophy. I used to see him once a fortnight. Before he was confined to a wheel chair we would play cricket and 'rugby' together. Then, the calves of his legs grew fatty as his muscles deteriorated; the disease progressed and he could no longer walk and run.

When he was sixteen, he was hospitalized. I used to visit him there. One afternoon, he asked me what heaven was like. 'Golden pavements and free fish and chip shops,' I told him. I wasn't too sure what to say.

He smiled. 'Think of that,' he said. 'Free chips.' He paused for a moment. 'Do they have newspapers in heaven to wrap them in?' He had me there. That was the last time I saw him. He died later that week. He was a marvellous youngster, always cheerful. I never once, in all the years I knew him, heard him complain.

Let us work towards the integration of handicapped youngsters into the ordinary schools, and into the community. Let us give those with special needs the very best help we can. In caring for the disabled we learn many valuable lessons about courage, about optimism, and about life itself.

## Chapter Twelve

# The Problem Page

Before we look at a selection of problems presented to me over the years by teenagers of different ages I should like to make two points. They are:

1   Teenagers, many of them, look very sophisticated and grown up. Nevertheless, they still seem to have as many doubts, anxieties and hang-ups as their parents had.

2   *Some* of their problems are exactly the same as those that their parents spent many hours worrying about. In other words, certain fears and obsessions of the teenage years seem to be recurrent. They keep cropping up, like an old and well-loved song.

In answering each question I have, of course, tried to be as honest as possible. I have also made some general comments at the end of each reply. The queries start with specific issues (e.g. to do with physical appearance) and then move on to more general, emotional (but still very common) worries. I have shortened some of the questions but have left out nothing that would detract from the gist of the query.

*Q. Tomorrow, I am going for an interview for my very first job. I am terrified. What on earth shall I wear?*
A. Wear something that is reasonably formal, and which makes you look smart. It is a sad fact of life that others do judge us by our appearance, especially when they first meet us.

If you look like a slob, you won't get the job. A scruffy appearance means that you haven't taken much trouble to go along for interview; it's likely that you won't take too much trouble in the job. If your fingernails are dirty, your hair in 'rats' tails and your clothes creased, the interviewers might (rightly or wrongly) conclude that you don't take too much pride in your appearance, and you'd be unlikely to give your mind to the details of the work.

If we look good, it gives us more confidence; it also means that we respect the people we are with since we've looked as nice as we can for them.

I'm not saying you'll get the job; but you can say to yourself: 'I did my best'. Jobs, these days are scarce. To impress a prospective employer I suggest the following FIVE RULES FOR THE INTERVIEW:

1  *Dress smartly* (Make sure your shoes are clean). Girls can look very smart in a trouser suit or slacks, blouse and jacket. Neither girls or boys should go to an interview wearing jeans: the impression might be that you don't mind whether you get the job or not.

2  *Look up and Speak up* Look at the person who asks you a question and answer clearly (don't gabble). You have got to appear keen and enthusiastic, eager to get the job, *and* an interesting person, as well. You won't get the job if you look (and sound) half asleep.

3  Try to find out something about the job before you attend for interview. Don't forget to ask a few questions yourself. Don't just sit there saying 'yes' and 'no'.

4  If you don't hear or understand a question ask the interviewer to repeat it; answer the question honestly and directly; don't waffle.

5  Be yourself, and decide whether you really want the job. If you do, get that across to the person or people interviewing you.

COMMENT It's wrong, in my view, to judge people solely by appearance. Some of my best friends are terribly scruffy. Before you shout 'hurrah' and rush away to put on your Oxfam outfit I should point out that they don't have to attend interviews; they already have jobs; the time to relax, and let people get to know the 'real you' is when you have been successful in the interview and are well-established in the job.

*Q. I'm 5' 5" tall and I weigh 9 stones 10lbs. I'm only fourteen and my weight problem is really getting me down. What can I do?*
A.  You could certainly do with losing a stone in weight: perhaps a little more. Why not check with your family doctor or with the local branch of Weight Watchers? Either will tell you the amount of weight you should lose. (If you're fourteen and still growing, it's wise not to lose weight too quickly.)

By far the best way to lose weight is to go on a sensible diet (your GP would advise here). *Don't go* on a death-or-glory, starvation diet. These often don't last, you start eating again, and you're back to where you started from. To lose a few pounds per week is a really effective way to slim.

You may have heard of *anorexia.* This is the fear of putting on weight that becomes so strong that teenagers may end up in hospital, or die, as a result of their obsession with not touching food. This medical condition is becoming increasingly more common because of our sillyness over diet.

It cannot be said too strongly: (a) a sensible diet is a permanent thing; (b) the compensation for giving up such things as sugar in tea and coffee, potatoes and bread and cakes is to *feel* slim, look slim, and add to one's confidence rather than one's waist-line; (c) there is no short cut or easy road, to a good figure.

COMMENT Find yourself a good, sensible diet and *stick to it.*

*Q. I started my periods six months ago and have been having one or two headaches, and going hot and cold, and feeling rather awful. Is this normal?*
A. It is. What you describe is very common during the first few times one has a period. However, you could go to your family doctor who may recommend a simple, non-addictive pain killer. You should also discuss your discomfort with your mother. It is better to talk about these things than to keep them to ourselves.

COMMENT It makes it far worse to imagine that we are the only person in the whole wide world to suffer from such distress as period pains.

*Q. I have headaches after I have driven a car or watched television. Also my eyes ache quite often. I can't see such things as bus signs and posters very clearly, especially if they are in the distance.*
A. It sounds as though you need glasses. Do you read a lot? It may be that you are a little short-sighted. Your family doctor can advise you and, if necessary, refer you to an optician. However, you're quite entitled to find a good optician yourself and arrange to have an eyesight test, free of charge. Why not do so? It's better to be sure than put up with pain.

COMMENT The first time I wore my own glasses (prescribed for short-sightedness) I was astonished how clear and well-defined everything looked. (Before then, the whole world had a fuzzy look to it which I thought was how it was meant to be!)

*Q. I'm very constipated. What is the best laxative that I can take?*
A. There are a number of good laxatives on the market which you can buy at chemists. However, you should not take laxatives too often. You should rather try to cure your constipation by having more 'roughage' in your diet — brown bread, plenty of vegetables and lots of fruit. The best roughage is bran either in the form of

cereal or in packets from health food stores which can be eaten sprinkled on to your favourite cereal (or bowl of fruit, or soup). Also, you should drink plenty of water: it's good for you, and it's cheap.

COMMENT 'You are what you eat.' Though slightly exaggerated there is some truth in this saying. If we exist on a permanent diet of fish and chips, or cakes and white bread, we cannot expect to be healthy, or 'regular'!

*Q. My boyfriend is eighteen. He has this awful secret. He can't read. How can I help him?*
A. Quite easily. There are 'adult literacy' classes in most towns and cities throughout the country. You can find out the address of your local class at the public library. There is no shame associated with not learning to read. It is not your boyfriend's fault; rather it is the fault of his teachers for not teaching him properly. Do persuade him to avail himself of the splendid help which is now available to non-readers who have left school.

COMMENT Not to be able to read is a very great handicap. It is also excruciatingly embarrassing to the person concerned (who may have to pretend that he's 'forgotten his glasses' if somebody asks him to read something). Do seek help; it's there if you really want it.

*Q. My mother says that I should always wear knickers under, not over, my tights and I should never wear tights under my jeans. Why?*
A. The only thing I can think of is that tights are made out of nylon, a synthetic material, which doesn't allow the area of skin it covers to 'breathe'. If you wear tights under jeans, the skin gets very sweaty and very hot, and encourages germs to breed, besides giving rise to unpleasant odours.
Knickers, even when made of nylon, usually have a cotton-lined gusset which is more absorbent. Knickers, despite the demands of fashion, shouldn't really be so tight that no air is allowed to circulate around that part of the body.

COMMENT The most hygienic garments of all are good old fashioned bloomers (or underpants). Though very unfashionable, these do allow the crotch to breathe, and prevent sweatiness and personal odour. Sadly, these can hardly be worn with jeans so cellular knickers are the best substitute.

*Q. My daughter, aged fourteen, has been told by her dentist that she needs a complete set of false teeth as her own teeth are*

*'hopelessly bad'. What can I do about this?*
A. Nothing, I'm afraid, except take his advice. You're far too late. The time to start caring for youngsters' teeth is when they are at the pre-school stage. Let's hope that your daughter makes sure that *her* children have proper dental care, and from an early age.

COMMENT We all tend to put off visits to the dentist. The trouble is when we do eventually go we have more fillings (or worse) to face up to. Regular visits are the only way to cope with the necessity to look after our teeth.

*Q. I'm thirteen, nearly fourteen. I've noticed in the showers at school that my penis is smaller than boys of my own age. Does this mean I shan't be able to have proper sexual intercourse when I grow up?*
A. It does not. Penis size has nothing to do with satisfying one's partner. More important are psychological factors, especially how much you care for the person with whom you are making love.

It is men, not women, who are obsessed by penis size. Women will tell you that some of the best lovers have small penises. What good lovers do have is plenty of affection for the person they are with.

COMMENT This is one of the most common fears amongst young men. It's a shame that they cannot get the truth fairly and squarely into their heads: *penis size is irrelevant; it's how you make your partner feel emotionally that counts.*

*Q. I have an awful problem. I keep breaking wind at school, in the classroom. My popularity is going down fast. I can't seem to stop myself. Can you help me? It's not a joke, please believe me.*
A. I believe you. Involuntary 'farting' (as it is usually called) is quite common though, I admit, embarrassing. Everybody farts, though most people try to avoid doing so in public for obvious reasons.

I recommend that you avoid those foods which are likely to produce wind in the intestines e.g. cakes, sweets, curries, chewing gum, fizzy drinks and highly-flavoured, spicy foods. If you stay to school meals be sure that you go to the toilet during the lunch hour. You must go to the lavatory regularly and not 'leave it till later'.

Check your diet and ensure that you're not constipated or eating all the wrong things. Regular exercise also helps.

COMMENT I once saw a gymnast do a beautiful floor exercise. She finished. The music stopped. Then she broke wind and the

156

noise resounded throughout the hall. I have never since then thought that involuntary farting was anything other than highly embarrassing for the person concerned.

*Q. I am eighteen years old and intend to live in 'digs' and lead a reasonably independent life. I am thinking of going on the Pill in case I meet a nice boy. I don't intend to sleep around. Do you think it's a good idea (to go on the Pill I mean)?*
A. Why not wait until you meet that nice boy you mention? Living by yourself is going to take a lot of courage and flexibility. Why complicate things? When you do decide to go on the Pill you will need advice from your doctor or from one of the advisory agencies (such as Brook, or Family Planning) to make certain that it is safe, from a health point of view, to do so. Don't rush it.

COMMENT You don't have to sleep with a boy unless you really want to and until you're well and truly ready to. The Pill should be considered if you're really serious about somebody, and not before. Even then, no boy should want you just for your body. Never be persuaded into doing something you don't want to do. The Pill should be a background to love and affection rather than a passport to sex.

*Q. I'm terribly moody. One minute I'm as happy as a lark, the next minute I get terribly anxious and depressed and think that everything in my life is going wrong. I'm fifteen. Is it normal to be so 'up and down' like this?*
A. Quite normal and very, very common with most of the teenagers I know.

When you get into a mood try not to let it drag you down. The best cure is action of some sort, perhaps going for a walk for doing something like baking a cake or knitting a jersey, or something else that you especially enjoy.

I know one teenager who helps in a home for mentally handicapped children. This is good for her moods since it makes her stop feeling so sorry for herself. If you find yourself brooding either get up and do something active or switch your mind on to some constructive thoughts i.e. work out plans for the weekend or for your holidays.

COMMENT Who is happy all the time? Nobody that I know. Moods (and a little unhappiness) are part of life. The sentiment to be avoided at all costs is self pity. There are always people worse off than ourselves who need our help and attention. By helping them, we put our own problems in proper perspective.

157

*Q. I have never had a 'jab' for German measles. I'm eighteen and I'd like to have children when I'm married. Should I be immunized?*

A. Yes. Go along to your doctor and he will give you an injection against Rubella (to give German measles its medical name). The injection is painless but catching Rubella during early pregnancy does represent a very real danger to the unborn child. Why put it off now and take the risk later?

COMMENT Non-immunized mothers who are in the first sixteen weeks of pregnancy and who suffer an attack run little risk to themselves (since it is not a very serious illness). The risk to the foetus, the baby in the womb, is serious and babies have been born, as a result of infection *in utero,* physically and/or mentally handicapped.

Too, a mother who contacts this illness in the early stages of pregnancy faces the agonizing decision as to whether she will opt for an abortion or go ahead and have the child. The simplest thing is to make sure that one catches German measles as a child (I know one mother who gave a German measles party — deliberately exposing the children of the neighbourhood to the illness) or, as I have advised, go to your GP and ask to be immunized against infection.

*Q. I'm sixteen, and my left breast is bigger than my right. What can I do about it?*

A. Very little. Lots of girls have exactly the same problem as you, since the breast tissue (especially at puberty) may grow at varying rates for each breast.

Does it really matter? Very few of us are totally bi-symmetrical (i.e. one side of the body the same as the other). You could, I suppose, buy a padded bra if you're worried about it but I suggest you leave well alone and hope that your breasts will even themselves out as you grow older.

COMMENT Looking at my own face in the mirror, one side of it is slightly different from the other. I'm told that it is this slight assymetry in human beings which makes us beautiful (though this doesn't apply in my own case). Certainly, if you look closely at the Mona Lisa and other paintings or photos of beautiful women (or handsome men) you will not find that their features are completely regular, or that one side of the face is the 'mirror image' of the other. This, like oddly-matched breasts matters only if *we* think it does; it causes harm only if we worry about it. The advice is — *don't.*

*Q. My best friend has bad breath. We go out together and I'm sure it puts boys off us. What can I do about it?*
A. You can tell her, and be quite straightforward (but gentle) about it. That's what friends are for: to be honest with each other.

I'm sure, too, that it puts boys off, but who are you really concerned with — your friend or yourself? Don't prevaricate, beat around the bush, or drop hints about cleaning her teeth more often. Tell her the truth — she needs to know, and soon.

If she's a real friend she won't resent your being frank with her. Open up with: 'Would you mind if I tell you something personal?' Go on from there. She'll respect you more for telling her than not mentioning it, and being resentful.

COMMENT It never does any harm to be told honestly about such things as BO or bad breath — especially when we know the person really cares about us. We owe a duty to our friends to be honest and straight with them.

*Q. I'm fourteen, but I have to go with my mother when I buy new clothes and it always ends up with her choosing some ghastly old-fashioned outfits for me. What can I do?*
A. You can compromise. I suggest that you have a clothes allowance each month and make yourself responsible for choosing what you wear. Don't overdo it. If you wear ear-rings without consulting her, or go out and buy the most outlandish dresses in sight, she is not going to trust you.

For the first time or two, go out with your mother but emphasize that it is your allowance and that you'd like to do the choosing. If she sees that you do pick clothes which are smart as well as fashionable, then she will be more ready to let you go out with friends and choose your own clothes.

COMMENT Teenagers, I've said, need some responsibility. This extends, in my view to as much responsibility as possible in such matters as dress, and grooming. If we trust them, guide them rather than foist our choices upon them, most of them will respond to that trust.

Spending an allowance also gives them an opportunity to learn to budget and to save up for an item that they really want.

*Q. I met this marvellous Spanish boy whilst on holiday on the Costa Brava last summer. I love him deeply. He promised to write to me but never did. I really do love him so don't tell me I don't. Please help.*
A. I wouldn't dream of telling you that you don't love him. You know your own mind and that is your decision. I can only point out

that holiday romances are often doomed to end when the holiday is over.

It's easier to fall in love whilst on holiday: we're more relaxed, more friendly. The sun-lit beaches and the moon-lit nights, the freedom, all the nice things, may be associated in our minds with one particular person — in your case, this Spanish boy.

I don't blame you for not wanting it to come to an end but it does, and it has. If he'd liked, or loved, you enough he would have kept in touch.

If it's any consolation I know a girl who married a Spaniard. During their courtship he was *very* romantic: he bought flowers for her whenever they met, and was extremely affectionate. Now that they're wed she spends all her time at home cooking and doing the housework. She is not expected to go out by herself, or to talk to other men. Her erstwhile romantic boyfriend is now, as a husband, extremely strict and not at all romantic.

Why not count it your good fortune that you had a wonderful holiday and leave it at that? You'll have other holiday romances. Enjoy them, but don't turn them into something they were never meant to be. If a boy *is* serious he'll write. If he doesn't do your very best to forget him and get on with living your life.

COMMENT There is nothing unusual about the glamour of courtships abroad going to our heads. It *is* romantic, it *is* extremely exciting (just as it is when we go out with any boy or girl for the first time). Nevertheless, time is the test of friendship just as marriage is the test of love. When the romantic encounter comes with the holiday, don't expect one to last when the other is over.

*Q. My Mother is very attractive. My boyfriends seem to talk to her a lot. I'm sure they like her more than me (and think she's better looking). What can I do? I'm getting an inferiority complex about it all. I like my mum but I'm starting to think I'm plain and unattractive compared with her.*

A. Poor you. This situation must make you feel very fed-up.

I think you're worrying needlessly, though. My son's girlfriends talk to me but they're definitely not attracted by me; in fact, they think that I possibly date from the ice age and that I'm certainly eccentric. They like me, but think of me quite rightly as belonging to another generation I'm sure that's the case with your boyfriends and your mum.

Even if they do fancy her, it would be very much as you would fancy a teacher at school, or an older pop-star: all very useful from a distance but not much to do with the reality of your life or your friendships.

Count yourself lucky that you have such an attractive and interesting mum! Many young women I know would swap with you since their mothers are very straightlaced and frumpish. Make a pal of her and take her advice on making the most of your looks — she obviously knows how to make the best of herself. Count her as a good friend, rather than a rival. Still let your boyfriends talk to her: she needs as much reassurance as you do.

COMMENT As a teenager I went out with a girl who had the most attractive mother. I was struck by how pretty and interesting the mum was, but I certainly didn't want to take her out instead: I simply envied my girlfriend for having such a super mother. If you happen to be one of the lucky ones my advice is — make the most of it.

*Q. I'm sixteen. I get £1 each week as pocket money. I don't think it's enough, and it's less than most of my friends. What do you think is the correct amount?*
A. There is no 'correct amount'. It's a difficult question to answer. Some twelve-year-olds receive £5 a week pocket money but £3 of this is from grandparents and is invested, or put into a savings bank. Some of them, with the remaining £2, have to help towards buying clothes for themselves. After this, there's very little left.

One thing we can say for certain about pocket money — nobody seems to get enough. Perhaps, when you think of all the discos you'd like to go to, records you'd like to buy, evenings-out you'd like to have, it's not surprising.

To answer your query: £1 per week is sufficient if you are at school, don't go out a lot, and your clothes and other essentials are bought for you. What about working for all the other things you want? This might give you a better idea of the value for money.

You could take a holiday job, or be paid for doing jobs at home such as wallpapering a room, digging the garden, or any heavy jobs about the house. The advantage of *earning* money (as opposed to being given pocket money) are that you get more of it, appreciate it more and you can spend it on what you like.

Washing the car, cleaning windows, keeping your room tidy could be paid for. Better, in my view, is to take a job in the school holidays and learn something of the world, about work and about earning.

The danger of being paid for doing jobs at home is that it descends into bribery and corruption: youngsters may feel unwilling to work in the house unless there is the prospect of payment. Make your responsible for yourself. By all means ask your parents for an extra 50p per week but, at the same time, find a job whenever you can and gain some freedom from the restrictions of the weekly dole-out. Whilst you're working, think of all those marvellous LPs you'll be able to buy!

COMMENT Some people say that a five-year-old should receive 30p a week, a seventeen-year-old £2. I cannot see that we can have a definite age-related scale of pocket money: it all depends on a child's situation and what the child or young person is expected to do with it. I am sure that if you want to encourage thrift, and a real appreciation of money, having to earn it works on most youngsters like a charm.

*Q. I am eighteen and have recently been receiving obscene telephone calls. What should I do about them?*
A. Inform the police. There are people who talk to obscene callers, try to counsel them. Others blow a whistle down the telephone to give them a nasty shock. I advocate neither approach. If the caller persists tell him that you intend to inform the police, put the telephone down, and keep to your word.

COMMENT Obscene telephone calls, heavy breathing, offensive remarks, can be very upsetting for most people but especially for those who live alone. Don't try to act the Good Samaritan, unless you live within a large family or in digs with lots of friends, and you have bags of confidence. The best, and safest thing to do is to let the police know what is happening and they will advise you.

*Q. I am seventeen. My boyfriend is nineteen. I like him a lot and we have always got on very well together. Lately, though, he has become very possessive. He wants to know what I am doing, where I am going, and who I am meeting. He doesn't like me to talk to other boys. I resent this. He doesn't own me and I object to him telling me what I should do or shouldn't do. Am I right to be annoyed about his attitude? It's come to the stage where I am going to finish with him if he doesn't show less jealousy and morbid interest in my life. I've dropped one or two hints but he's taken no notice.*
A. Firstly, you're right to be angry. He *doesn't* own you; you are not a piece of furniture, or an item of clothing, or a doll — you are a human being. What you must do is *tell him* what you want: to have him as a friend, as part of your life, but not to have him as your lord and master who says how you should be leading your life. If he doesn't like it when you tell him and doesn't see your point of view, you would be wiser to finish with him.

162

COMMENT There is no need to divide our loyalties between boyfriends and our other friends — there should be time in our lives for both.

When a boy becomes too serious, too possessive, he must be told, and the sooner the better. Then, there will be the chance of a good relationship.

No boy should be able to tell a girl what she should be doing each and every day. If the girl accepts this she runs the danger of becoming a puppet, with her boyfriend pulling the strings.

The THREE NEVERS should help: NEVER be bossed about; NEVER forget that you're a person too and NEVER hesitate to make it clear what it is that *you* want. You'll be respected more if you stick up for yourself, and define the relationship so that there are no misunderstandings either way.

*Q. I'm fifteen and I'm very, very lonely. I have felt like this — alone and without any real friendships — for two years now and it seems to be getting worse. I have nobody to talk to. Both of my parents are old (both in their fifties) and my older sister has left home and has a family of her own. I'm desperate. Please help me. I hope you won't think that I'm wasting your valuable time but I have no friend and I'm so lonely.*

A. I don't think you're wasting my time. Loneliness is very real — and it hurts. Everybody needs at least one friend to talk to and confide in.

What you must do is stop thinking, and start doing something about your isolation. You are, I can tell, a sensitive person but you must bring yourself to join a youth club, a sports centre or join an association where you can go youth hostelling or rambling and meet other people.

We form many friendships through mutual interest. That interest may be an after-school activity, or it may be a passion for table-tennis or bird-watching. It doesn't matter what it is so long as it helps to break the ice when it comes to meeting strangers.

You could do the Duke of Edinburgh Award Scheme (which will help you to get out of the house) or volunteer to help at a children's home or a home for mentally or physically handicapped youngsters. There is always something useful we can do and it's far better to help others than to sit at home moping.

Don't worry whether people will like you. Join in, be yourself, and they will — people are not as heartless or cruel as you may sometimes think they are. You have to give them the opportunity to get to know you.

Your parents are rather old, but that is not your real problem. I would guess that you are very shy. You must learn to be courageous

163

and join in those activities around you which interest you. Smile at people — the chances are they'll smile back. If you don't people will think you are snobby and stand-offish instead of desperately lonely.

Make the first move. Most friendships are built up from a casual relationship so, I repeat, *go out and* meet people. It's agony at first but it's worth it.

COMMENT Loneliness, like friendliness, is a habit. Once we get into the habit of being by ourselves, being alone, it's very hard to get out of it. Yet, we have to try. The best way to do it is to find out what clubs and associations meet locally, and join one. Many people are shy and lonely and they are usually very pleased to help somebody else in the same boat.

*Q. I keep all my letters from my boyfriend in a draw in my bedroom. Last week I caught my father reading through them. When I asked him what he was doing he just blushed but didn't apologize. In the past I've caught my mother reading my diary. Why do they sneak into my room like this and pry into my private things? What can I do about it? It's so unfair. I'm seventeen and I think I'm entitled to have secrets of my own. Do you agree with me?*

A. I do agree with you and it is unfair. I can understand your sense of disgust and shock, which shows through in your letter. It is not a nice feeling to have one's private possessions rifled through, or one's highly personal diary looked at — even by parents. (Or especially by parents?)

Both your father and mother seem to be over-curious, and to have forgotten that you are not a child any more. In fact, soon you will be an adult and they seem to be singularly ill-prepared for the fact since they trust you so little.

You can do one of two things. You could buy a diary that locks or put all your personal, private belongings which you wish to keep secret in a drawer (or a box) with a lock on it and keep the key yourself. Or, you could have the whole thing out with your parents and put your point of view to them — that you expect, and deserve, some privacy.

I advise the second course of action. Bring the subject up with them in a reasonably relaxed, not too emotional way. Tell them that you will open up a bit more and talk to your parents more (if you're terribly secretive, they may suspect that you are doing the most awful things — hence the anxiety and nosiness).

Don't shut your parents out from your life. Tell them some of the things you do; try to create a nice, easy, honest atmosphere at home. Don't leave your diary lying about. That is *Private* and make sure your privacy is respected.

Ask yourself, am I forcing my parents into being nosey snoopers by not telling them anything about myself? If the answer is yes, try to draw them into your confidence more, include them, rather than exclude them. Especially, have little chats with your mother about make-up, or clothes or even boyfriends. When she sees that you are being open and friendly her snooping should stop.

Keep your diary, and your letters, to yourself. They are your business, and nobody else's. All human beings including teenagers, are entitled to one or two areas of their lives which are strictly private, especially as far as close relatives are concerned. Meet them half-way, though; be more forthcoming with them. It always helps.

COMMENT Every teenager needs to put a bit of space between himself or herself and parents. It is up to parents to respect that space.

*Q. Since my girlfriend and I split up (we're both eighteen) I have been drinking a lot in the pub, sometimes eight pints in the evening, sometimes nine or ten. Now I have started drinking at lunch-time too. I attend a college of further education and am going into catering. Can you say whether you think my drinking is excessive?*
A. It sounds excessive to me, and dangerous. I have seen several youngsters who were confirmed alcoholics at the age of eighteen and it is a very depressing experience to witness such a tragic waste of a young life.

You're lucky. You are training for an interesting job, you have good prospects. Stop feeling sorry for yourself. Go out and find yourself another girl, and stop drinking so much. There are far more interesting things to do than sitting in pubs seeing how many pints of beer you can manage to swallow.

COMMENT Drinking, like any other pleasure, does us no harm in moderation. Taken to excess it can, like other over-indulgences or addictions, do us grave harm physically and (especially) psychologically. It is certainly not manly to drink too much. Most of the time it is both boring for the drinker and less than edifying for those that have to look at him. Life can be beautiful. Why go through it in an alcoholic haze?

*Q. My parents were divorced last year. Since then, I've been living with my mother who I love, but I also love my father who I see once a fortnight. I'm really unhappy and miserable. Can you help* me? What is happening to me? I'm so sad inside. I wish all the time that they were still together, even though they quarrelled a lot when they were. P.S. I am an only child, aged thirteen.

A. I have deep sympathy for you. Every year there are more than 120,000 divorces. Though not all of these involve tragedy and suffering many of them do, and it's usually the children who suffer the most. The pain is no easier for teenagers than it is for young children — in a way it may be far worse. I realize how puzzled, and wounded, you are at your parents decision to live apart.

What can I do to help you? I can only say that you must be the one who is grown-up, and the one who continues to love. See it from your parents' point of view: they may well be happier apart; it *is* better than suffering (and making you suffer) by constant quarrelling.

It may seem to you that your world has crashed in ruins but you are still in touch with both your parents and still love both of them. Wouldn't it be better, now, to think of each one as an individual rather than to try to do the impossible i.e. mend a marriage which is over and done with? Try to treat your father as a friend, a pal, somebody you dearly love. You can love your mother too: loving one does not exclude loving the other.

You are 'Piggy in the Middle', and it hurts. You have to be as mature, and as brave, as you can. Ask yourself, honestly: 'Are my parents better off apart?' If the answer is yes, if your parents are happier going their separate ways, you must accept the fact, stop worrying about *them,* and start to live your life to the very best of your ability. From your letter, I know you will succeed.

Q. *I am seventeen and I have been going steady with a boy for the last six months. I have decided that I don't like him very much. My mother and father don't like him very much either. He's twenty, and too old for me really, though he's very immature. Anyway, I don't like him. How do I end our relationship?*

A. You tell him — not that you don't like him, merely that you don't wish to go out with him again. *Don't* write a letter. *Don't* tell him through a friend. *Do it yourself,* and tell him straight, to his face. After all, it's your life and if you don't like him you're wasting his time and yours. Tell him.

COMMENT Why beat about the bush in a situation like this? The more you delay it, the kinder you try to be, the worse it is. It's far better to be totally frank and honest.

Q. *I'm fourteen and have been going out with a boy for ten weeks. I like him a lot but he never shows me any affection. When we sit*

*together in the cinema, or at home watching television he never
puts his arm around me. If we're out walking he never holds my
hand. He does kiss me but only when I want him to. Why doesn't
he show me more affection? (Not just when we're kissing goodnight,
I mean.) P.S. I think he's great except for this one thing.*
A. Your boyfriend may (mistakenly) believe that to show affection
means he isn't tough, or manly. Many boys think this: it is all part
of the taboo on tenderness, or fear of being gentle and loving,
which is so prevalent in our society. On the other hand, he may
simply be shy.

You don't say whether there are other people present when you
are watching television. If there are, I can understand his
reluctance. If there aren't, all you have to do is take his hand.
Similarly, when you are at the cinema, or out walking, take hold of
his hand yourself. He'll soon get the idea.

COMMENT Snuggling up, linking arms, holding hands, putting
one's arms around each other, are all good for the health and
cost nothing. How I wish we were all more affectionate towards
each other. How boring to have a manly, stiff-upper-lip boyfriend!

*Q. I am nineteen. I have been doing out with the same boy for a
year. Lately, I have started to fancy his best friend. I was sure I was
in love with Henry (my steady boyfriend) until this happened. To
be honest, I do look at other boys at work and some of them I
fancy too. Am I in love? I'm not sure if I am or not. Please help.*
A. When you're in love you'll know! It's not a feeling that you can
be mistaken about. It's like being hit in the eye by a large custard
pie, or tapped on the head with a big wooden mallet. When you're
in love, you don't fancy other people, or start to wonder if you
should have chosen your boy's best friend.

I suggest you give up Henry, or cool off the relationship, so that
you can look around a little more for the person you really want.
You are at the moment tied to a relationship that doesn't satisfy
you, and (judging from your letter) certainly isn't true love.

COMMENT One of the signs of being in love is that we want to be
with the loved one more than anybody else in the world and we
*don't* fancy (or envy) others. If it's true love, when it hits you,
you know!

I started this chapter with two comments, and I want to end it by
pointing out that *everybody has problems* (when you have no more
problems, you're dead). However, it *does* help to talk over our

problems with another person, or with other people, rather than keep them all 'bottled up' inside us. One of the greatest advantages of bringing our problem or problems out into the open is that we suddenly realize we have company, that we are not the only person in the world with that problem. We are not alone. It is true that a problem kept to ourself is a problem doubled. A problem shared is a problem halved.

*Chapter Thirteen*

# Where's Father?

I can understand the resentment that some women have about the dominant position that men hold in society. Men, by and large, earn more, have more power — in medicine, in law, in industry and on the factory bench. Women have been relatively powerless for thousands of years and Women's Lib, a recent phenomenon, has sprung out of a very real, and longstanding, sense of grievance.

As recently as the Victorian era, women had little power within the family. Their job was to bear children and to look after them. It was men who held the purse strings, who owned the property, and who ruled the roost. They could, if they so desired, throw their wives out on to the streets homeless and penniless.

In *The Forsyte Sage* by John Galsworthy, Old Jolyon Forsyte, an authoritarian father-figure of the late nineteenth century, embodies the paternalistic role of that era: he orders people about and keeps a tight rein over his possessions (and women are part of those possessions). Forsyte rejects his son, Young Jolyon, for going against the prevailing moral code concerning divorce. Old Jolyon, you say, was wealthy, middleclass and had power but, in those times, the same power over the life of the family was accorded to a skilled craftsman, a tradesman, even a labourer. The father was the figure of authority within the home and the sole bread winner. He was the family money-box. If anything untoward happened to *him,* if an accident befell *him,* the whole family would fall on hard times. During Queen Victoria's long reign, because of this complete dependence upon the man of the house, many families did become destitute and many children were brought up in workhouses.

If we move on just a few generations to today, we notice a dramatic change. It is possible, today, for a wife to earn as much as her husband. More than a half of all women with children of school age have some type of employment and are not totally dependent on their husbands financially. Today, the father's authority within the home is often challenged, or ignored. I am lucky to be told that my daughter is planning a trip to Paris; when I am told it is usually to be asked to finance the excursion rather than my permission being sought for my daughter to go. If my son decides to devote his affection to girlfriend X rather than Y, I am not consulted — he makes his own decisions in the area of personal relationships and I only offer advice when asked. The family, in my case, exists as a responsible democracy — father rarely lays down the law.

Old Jolyon would have wept at the way modern families carry on. He was autocratic, and supremely confident, in his role. Modern fathers, often anxious, harrassed and over-worked do not have the time to be autocratic. They have to cope with getting to work (often in heavy traffic) and the pressures of today's technological society. When they come home, many of them are tired out and want only to have a meal and to collapse in front of the television. The man in the factory, these days, works as hard as a professional man and, in order to earn enough for the family to live on, may have to spend long hours at his job. The result is that, at all levels of society, many fathers spend very little time with their own children.

The toll of two world wars, the decline of religion (and of the 'Heavenly Father'), the loosening of family bonds, have left us without authoritive father-figures. In the West, young people respect (and identify with) older brother and sister figures — hence the popularity of 'pop stars'. In the eighties it may not be a coincidence that the Conservative Party have as their leader a woman, Mrs Thatcher. There has been, over the last thirty years, a tremendous decline in the authority of the father. (Curiously, this does not apply to those countries behind the Iron Curtain. Paternalism is, at least at present, part and parcel of Communism. Russia has had, and still has, a stern array of authoritarian father-figures, so does Czechoslovakia. In East Germany (or the German Democratic Republic, as they prefer to be called) there are the same sort of strict (male) political leaders. Yugoslavia had, for years, President Tito — an archetypal father-figure. To the east, in China, discipline and inspiration comes from the internalized thoughts of ex-Chairman Mao, another father. What, here, happened to mother?)

It is my contention that there are, in Britain, thousands upon thousands of paternally deprived children and young people. I am not referring, here, to children who do not have a father. I am referring to those children who have 'ghost fathers' whose presence in the home is either very intermittent or whose absence is a form of concealed desertion. On paper, these children have fathers; in reality the fathers have little influence in their lives.

We would, I think, expect that long-distance lorry drivers, men serving in the armed forces (particularly in the Royal Navy) and, say, men working on oil-rigs or travelling salesmen would have children who are at risk when it comes to being paternally deprived. However, it is not as simple (or as limited) as this. What seems to count, as well as the amount of time that father spends with his children, is the *quality* of his relationship when he is there. It is possible, providing that father contributes emotionally to family life when he is home, for the children to show few adverse effects when he is away.

One example of a good, but intermittent, father was a captain of a merchant vessel who was a personal acquaintance of mine. The father was extremely loving and supportive of his wife who 'ruled the roost' during his absence at sea. The wife in the family was a competent, intelligent and out-going mother who played both the mother and father roles to perfection. She could be extremely strict; she was very loving. I could not honestly say that any of her children showed any symptoms whatsoever of emotional or social maladjustment. They had a mother who was a good mother, and a good father, into the bargain. *She* could cope.

Paternal deprivation is subtle, and it exists at all levels in society. The paternally deprived children I have seen had fathers who included a doctor, a teacher, a film executive, a farm labourer, a policeman, and a brick-layer. They were a mixed bunch of fathers but had something in common: they saw very little of their children, and had very little impact on their children's lives when they were at home.

One of the boys I remember as suffering from paternal deprivation had a father who was a milkman and who, in the evenings 'made up his money' by working in a pub. Andrew, aged nine, was a pugnacious-looking boy with carrot-red hair cut very short. He looked, with his freckled face and large brown eyes, the sort of friendly, outgoing boy who is constantly in trouble, and constantly laughing his way out of it. Yet, when interviewed in the clinic, he smiled rather sadly at me and said very little. It was hard to establish contact with him. He had been referred to me, by the educational psychologist, because he was 'a solitary and lonely child who has no friends at school, and talks to no-one.'

Andrew's mother was interviewed and she mentioned immediately that she saw very little of her husband. The family lived in one of a row of terraced houses on the outskirts of the town, about four miles from the High Street (where the shops are) and mother did not like her neighbours very much. She had built up her life around her daughter, Karen, aged three, who 'follows me everywhere'. Mother was brought up in a family of girls and described herself as being 'better with girls. I don't really understand boys. I'm not used to them.' Both mother and father lived a long way away from their respective parents.

Andrew turned out to be a boy of above average intelligence but his reading was poor and his school work erratic and well-below his own ability level. He missed his father because, as he says: 'I get on fine with my dad, but he doesn't have time to do things with me.' The issue here was quite simple — more money or more family life? Father was interviewed and it was suggested to him that he work in the pub only on three nights per week; also, that he should consider keeping Saturday to take his wife out shopping, and devote Sunday to his son. Father was very cooperative. 'I'm working,' he said, 'to buy my wife a new fridge-freezer.' He was genuinely puzzled when I suggested to him, diplomatically, that they might prefer his company, his presence in the home, to the freezer. He agreed to spend more time with Andrew and the two of them arranged to go to the football match on Saturday afternoons and to go swimming together on Sunday. Father also said that he would arrange a baby-sitter so that he could take his wife out occasionally. The mother, on my advice, took Karen along to a playgroup in the town and got a part-time job in a shop. Nothing more was done.

Six months later, the change in Andrew was remarkable. He was lively and out-going, his school work was improving week by week, and he had become a happy, cheerful boy with plenty of friends at school. Mother was much happier, too. 'Thank you,' she said when I saw her. The father didn't say too much, either. 'I was a fool,' he told me. 'I was missing out on relaxing a bit and enjoying myself, and my family.' He added: 'I was doing it for them, you know.' This is often the case; few of these fathers are anti-social, anti-family. They are the victims of an increasingly money-orientated and competitive society.

Fathers are important. A boy needs a satisfactory father-figure to identify with if he is to grow up into a rounded, well-balanced adult. The boy needs a model upon which to base his idea of maleness. Boys cannot identify by proxy; they need the father to be there, to take an interest in them. The father's character, the extent to which he has made a success of his life, and his ability to pass on his ideas to his son in a close relationship, will form the basis of a boy's concept of masculinity. To many children the touch, smell, tone and talk of maleness are denied and they have little idea of what men are, or do.

For girls, too, a good relationship with father is terribly important. A girl first learns, through her father, how to relate to men and how to live in a world that is half-male. Since father is the initial model of masculinity, the girl's ability to relate to him may affect her ability to make relationships, when she is older, with other men. If she has had a close and rewarding relationship with her father she is more likely to choose a suitable male when it comes to courtship and marriage. A relationship between a father and daughter can be a beautiful thing and can have a lasting influence in a girl's life; after all, the father is the first man a girl ever loves and her first example of what men are like. Girls are left with a huge gap in their lives if their relationships with their fathers is unsatisfactory.

Take Joanna. She was a slim fifteen-year-old with jet-black hair and watery dark eyes. In conversation, she seemed intelligent, sensitive and shy. Joanna was intelligent, with an IQ of 123, but socially and emotionally immature. She was doing very badly in school and, according to her headmistress, was 'depressed and unhappy. Most of the time she looks the picture of misery.' Joanna's mother was worried about her daughter's depression, about her school work, and about the fact that Joanna refused to play with, or talk to, her two younger sisters. It was interesting that, when mother was telling me about the two young children playing 'house', she mentioned that neither of them ever made any reference to father. 'They don't mention father when they play,' she said.

I asked Joanna's mother about her husband. He was a highly-paid sales manager and his job took him abroad very frequently. The pressure in the office was such that he was rarely home (when working in this country) to see the children before they went to bed. Mother thought of her husband as a kind and considerate man, but her pride in his rapid promotion was tinged with regret. 'We don't see a great deal of him,' she told me. 'At week-ends, when he is home, he is so exhausted that all he wants to do is to catch up on his sleep, or read a novel.' She also told me that Joanna was very like her father — intelligent and sensitive. 'She is closer to him, really than she is to me,' added mother. 'Myself and my other two daughters are far more noisy and talkative.'

I interviewed father and explained to him what I saw as the truth of the matter: his eldest daughter missed him, and he would have to address himself to a major question. Was making money more important than spending time with, talking to, or just listening to, his children and, in particular, his eldest child? (I didn't put it quite as bluntly as that, but *that* is what it boiled down to.) This father, like Andrew's, was an intelligent man and he saw immediately what I was getting at. He promised to try to spend more time with Joanna.

Again, the father was as good as his word and, again, there was a remarkable effect on the child. Three months later I saw Joanna and she had 'perked up' considerably. 'I go out bowling with dad on Thursday evenings,' she told me, 'and we go fishing together on Sunday.' Father and mother have revived an old interest in ballroom dancing and *they* go out together once a week. More essential than these outings, the father had decided to put at risk his chance of promotion and said to his firm that he intended to spend more time with his family. The change in father was apparent too — he looked more relaxed and appeared to be enjoying life. 'I didn't realize,' he said, 'I was missing out on a lot of fun.' He and Joanna talked together now, of this and that; their relationship was revitalized; Joanna's school work was described as having 'improved out of all recognition'.

I am not naive. I am not suggesting that every father *can* make adjustments to his working life in order to give more time to his children. I am saying that when income takes precedence over family life it is often the children, or young people, within the family who take the consequences. Ironically, it is also society itself that pays a high price for the current emphasis on more money and a 'higher' standard of living. The *quantity* of goods we may purchase for the home is not to be equated with the *quality* of life that we lead. It is not true to suggest, also, that intervention always ends as happily as it did for Andrew and Joanna. There are cases, and plenty of them, where advice and intervention is a total (or almost a total) failure.

David, aged fourteen, was referred to the clinic because, according to his headmaster, 'he is extremely aggressive and, on several occasions, has viciously attacked other boys on the way home from school.' David turned out to be a huge, well-built boy with black, curly hair and blue eyes. He looked tough, and it was easy to imagine other boys being frightened of him. He was interested in motor-cars and motor-cycle speedway, and football. He was not unintelligent (IQ 108) but took little interest in school work. His ambition, he told me, was to become 'a racing-car driver'.

I interviewed David's mother. She was a large woman dressed in a vivid red crimplene dress and with purple fingernails. Her hair was dyed blonde and she was wearing a lot of make up. She worked for a funeral director, washing the dead bodies, and told me: 'They're dead, so they can't hurt you, can they?' If anything she struck me as being just as formidable, in her own way, as her son. I met David's father on one of his visits home; he was an enormous man who drove a bulldozer for a living. He worked away from home, on one of the new motorways. He was a friendly, gentle giant and it was clear that David could do with some of his influence.

When I suggested to mother that David was, perhaps, a little rough she laughed. 'Rough?' she said. 'You should see his older brother.' I declined her offer, since Ted (the older sibling, aged eighteen) had just come out of borstal; my job was to help David. Father was not willing to, or could not, spend any more time with his sons; he was happy working away from home, living in digs, and seeing his family from time to time. All suggestions, advice and blunt confrontation failed. In desperation, I turned to a more immediate, and practical, solution to the problem.

At home, I had an old bicycle. It was kept in the garden shed. I told David he could have the bike, and he called round to the house and took it away. Two weeks later the headmaster phoned me up at the clinic. 'David has stopped being vicious,' he informed me. 'How did you do it?' I told him, truthfully, that I had no idea. A few days later I saw David cycling through the town; he had bought a bell for the bicycle and generally smartened it up.

'How are you?' I shouted across to David. 'No more aggro?'

'Too much trouble to get off the bike,' he replied, laconically. I never did find out whether the cure was temporary or permanent. What I did discover, however, was that David was getting a great deal of his aggression from his mother, and his brother. He did miss his father. A strong father can keep a boy like David in check, and provide a steadying, calming influence in the home. David, though, is only one of many youngsters who live in a paternal wilderness. The security and optimism that spring from having an authoritive (*not* authoritarian) and caring father are denied to boys like David. Can we expect youngsters like David to behave well when they have very little emotional support, very little *fathering,* in their lives?

There has been little emphasis, in the past, on the role of the father, and very little research into paternal deprivation. John Bowlby, in his book *Child Care and the Growth of Love** stresses the importance of mother-love but has far less to say about father-love. The word 'father' is missing from many text-books of child development. At child guidance clinics, it is usually mother who attends with the child and who receives the advice of professionals as to how to look after the child, and how to make adjustments for the child's sake. What, we might ask, is the role of father in all this? Where's father? If children need love, should not that love come from father as well as from mother?

Nowadays, the child does not have as many substitute father-figures available to him as he had, say, thirty years ago. The uncles within the family may, for example, live a long way away rather than in the same town or the same street. Today, it is rare for a

*Pelican Books, 1953

child to strike up a friendship with the postman, the village blacksmith (villages, and blacksmiths, are in short supply as far as city children are concerned), the baker or the milk roundsman. Milkmen do their rounds in the manner of Brands Hatch and their own children may, like Andrew, be paternally deprived. Most men are too busy working to have time to devote to children, even their own. Time is money, earning money takes time; it is time spent with satisfactory father-surrogates that paternally deprived children need.

Father figures may be available within the school context. Certainly, children at boarding school have a better chance than those at day school to make a lasting relationship with a father substitute. There are youth club leaders, scout and cub masters, football team organizers and a myriad collection of both professional and voluntary workers for many children but my own impression is that there are *not* enough father figures to go round. We have plenty of human resources within the community to solve the problem. The available fathers, however, are too busy, too tired, or too uncaring to contribute to the welfare of the youngsters who live in their neighbourhood. It is often the case that those children who most need father substitutes live in areas where fathers (their own or somebody else's) are least available.

Has the problem been adequately recognized and acknowledged? It is significant that there are very few male teachers in infant, or first, schools although, to be fair, the number is growing. Many of the young children in these schools are paternally deprived and it would be emotionally beneficial to them to have some father figures within the school. If their own father is a tough, blunt man, it may help them to see, and to relate to in the classroom, other types of men from the tweed-suited, elderly, male teacher to the boyish, sports-jacketed younger man. The child's emotional development has a crucial part to play in education. Should not more attention be paid to the balance of the two sexes on the staff of each school (including first schools)?

Having etched in the problems of children with intermittently absent fathers ('ghost' fathers, flittering in and out of the home) let us now turn our attention to that large number of children with no father at all. The Finer Report estimated (in 1971) that two thirds of one million parents in Great Britain were looking after 1 million children single handed.

Some 400,000 mothers, then, were coping with 720,000 children whose fathers were alive but not living with the family. 190,000 of these women were deserted or separated, 120,000 divorced and 120,000 widowed. One sixth of the lone parents were fathers. The effects on the mothers, the Finer Report tells us, included grief, a sense of loss and resentment at having to face material and emotional difficulties alone. Many of the children concerned said that they felt different from other children.

Now, in the eighties, there are still over 1 million children who (whether because of bereavement, separation of parents, desertion or divorce) do not have a father; for these children there is no man in the house. Naturally, some of the divorced women will remarry. Some women cope very well alone. Where a father has been brutal, a drunkard, shiftless and thoughtless it may be that the family will be better off without him. At the same time, it is a massive deprivation that these children of the new millenium have to face; it *is* more difficult for them to face life without a father.

I want to reiterate my belief that some families are better off without a father if that father is destructive or totally inadequate. Most children would rather live in peace and quiet with one parent than be in the middle of continuous guerrilla warfare between two adults. If the father has done nothing to contribute to the lives of his wife or children, few tears will be shed for him if he goes elsewhere. I asked one teenage girl, whose father had deserted the family, whether she missed him. 'Yes,' she replied. 'There's a really nice atmosphere now he's gone.' A family unit *can* become more energetic, more viable, without the presence of a negative father.

On the other hand, it would be silly to argue that all families without fathers are better off without them. Margaret Wynn, at the beginning of her book *Fatherless Families** says: 'Many of the consequences of fatherlessness discussed in this study are primarily the consequence of poverty.' There is no doubt that, from a material point of view, father's income is sorely missed in homes without a man in them. In some cases, there may be the threat of homelessness hanging over the family and a woman alone with young children may have to place herself in the hands of the State in her search for somewhere to live.

I would say, judging from the fatherless families that I know, that *on average* they are poorer, worse housed, worse fed and not so well dressed as those families with two parents. There are always exceptions: the mother who manages, without a husband, to take an unflagging interest in the children's lives and to send them out into the world well-fed, well-clothed and happy. There are fathers too, without wives, who make a magnificent, heroic job of being a single parent. It is, nevertheless, not easy, and often extremely difficult.

Some children do miss the companionship of a father a great deal, especially when they have enjoyed a close relationship with

*Fatherless Families,* Margaret Wynn. Michael Joseph, 1964.

177

him, and he suddenly disappears from their lives.

Simon is a case in point. His father deserted the family and left mother with two young children to look after — Simon aged eight, and Beverly, his sister, aged six. Simon came to the child guidance clinic because he started to wet the bed and to withdraw from the friendship of other children in school. Simon played with the puppets in the playroom. He would always choose a father-figure, usually 'the King' and the other puppets would try to get up to mischief at court to damage the King. At the end of each play the King would make a speech. 'I am going to war now,' he would declare, 'and you may not see me again for a very long time. But I shall think of you and when I return we shall have lots of gold and be very rich.' The boy blamed himself (as some children do) for father's desertion of the family. It took Simon some time to get rid of his own guilt concerning the reasons why father went and realize that he, Simon, must not blame himself for father's action.

When Simon did realize, deep down, that his father's desertion was more to do with the quarrels between the parents than anything to do with him, he was able to take a role as 'the little father' in the family, help his mother, pay more interest in his sister. The family worked together, towards survival, and Simon's bed-wetting ceased, as did his withdrawn behaviour in school.

The Finer Committee on One-Parent Families made 230 recommendations. Some of these related to the ways in which schools could help these families. Norman Murchison, a psychiatrist member of the Finer Committee, made an analysis of the research into one-parent families and he concluded that the children in such settings, compared with the children of two-parent families (a) show more signs of delinquent behaviour (b) are less likely to do well in school (c) tend to leave school earlier (d) truant more often and (e) tend to achieve a lower level of attainment. This is hardly surprising, since the home looms very large in the life of the child, and the situation at home may be one of survival rather than comfort. As the Finer report put it:

The child may have to cope with a mother who is constantly worried with the effort of making the money go round, who has nothing to spare for extras which most other children take for granted, and who is lonely and depressed. Such a child may have to fend for himself because the mother is working, carry a share of domestic responsibilities beyond his years and capacity: and so be compelled to frequent absences from school.

Some children suffer lasting depression on the death of a parent and may suffer from bitterness or divided loyalties when their parents have parted. Such children may feel different from the others at school, or in the community at large . . .

Teachers may, through insensitivity or ignorance, make things worse rather than better for the child. Young children can be told to write on Christmas cards: 'With love to mummy and daddy.' The whole class may be told to address envelopes to the home 'Mr and Mrs'. A teacher may ask a child: 'What does your daddy do?' unaware that father is dead, or no longer living at home. A child will be told to ask mother to make a cake, or contribute to the school jumble sale, when there is no mother in the family. These sort of incidents are excruciatingly embarrassing to the children concerned. It is the responsibility of the class teacher to know, and to sympathize with, those children in the class who come from one-parent families. Lone parents may find it difficult to come along to school in the day to talk to the teacher, and arrangements may have to be made to see the parent in the evenings. Where home and school do work together it is easier to solve a child's educational difficulties and to be better aware of the child's problems.

Of course, not all children of one-parent families do have problems. As Finer says, on a more optimistic note:

Many lone parents and their children are successful in their own relationships, form rewarding relationships with others, attain a measure of personal and social competence and success, and enjoy a level of happiness which in no way differentiates them from other families or groupings of families in the community.

There remains a recurrent issue for single-parent families. What should lone parents tell the school? A large majority of parents feel that the teacher should be told when there has been a bereavement or marital breakdown. A few parents are reluctant to provide this information for fear that their children will be singled out and made to feel different. It isn't easy to tell the school about such matters but it *should* be done; class teachers, and the teachers responsible for pastoral care must be told if the school is to work closely with parents to ensure that no damaging verbal or written remarks are made about the child.

It has to be faced, squarely and honestly, that fatherlessness can be a cause of delinquency. The Gluecks* in America, studied five hundred delinquent boys and compared them with the same number of non-delinquents in terms of IQ, sub-cultural (neighbourhood) factors, ethnic and socio-economic influences. The Gluecks

*Unravelling Juvenile Delinquency, Glueck, S. & Glueck, R. New York: The Commonwealth Fund 1950.

concluded that there were five major factors in delinquency:

1  Discipline (or non-discipline) of the boy by the father.
2  Supervision (or non-supervision) of the boy by the mother.
3  Affection held (or not held) by the father for the boy.
4  Affection (or not) of the mother for the boy.
5  Cohesion (or lack of cohesion) of the family group.

We could speculate about these delinquent boys and say that one reason for their behaviour is the difficulty they have in coming to terms with the Oedipus Complex. This was the name given by Freud to the desire a boy has, when still an infant, to get father out of the way and to keep mother for himself (this desire, tinged with incestuous thoughts regarding the mother, is entirely unconscious). The only way out of the Oedipal dilemma is for the boy to identify with father, to be like father (and, in his own fantasy, to *be* the father). In this way, the child is the man in the house and the mother belongs to *him*. When the child reaches teenage it has to learn to direct its sexual drives outside the family. The boy who has not identified with a father (or father-figure) will be unable to do this. He will still be 'in love' with mother and unable to relate to teenage girls of his own age. He will be caught in the Oedipal situation, as a butterfly may be caught in a net. He will try to relate to his own age group, try to make friends with the opposite sex, but his 'heart belongs to mother'. There is no father with whom to identify; his road forward to maturity is closed; he finds it difficult to break the symbiotic bond with mother and to make satisfactory relationships away from her.

Looking around, one cannot help but be dismayed at the extent of paternal deprivation in our society. At the very least, a father gives the child another adult to relate to. When mother is tired, depressed, out at work the child can turn to father. What the child receives from father depends upon their feelings for him, his feelings for them, his capacity to relate to them and his ability to play a convincing role within the family. This will vary from father to father but fathers do have a role to play. Fathering is important.

From what the critic Cyril Connolly called 'the great frieze of father figures' in *The Forsyte Saga* we have moved to a situation where father is absent from, or ignored in, many families. Is it without significance that, on television (in shows such as *Some Mothers Do 'ave 'em, Dad's Army, George and Mildred, Father, Dear Father* and *The Good Life*) father is often depicted as a buffoon? It is women who act sensibly, make decisions, rule the roost. Many fathers, who might be able to play the role of autocratic paterfamilias, if such roles were still available, are now uncertain as to what their role within the family is. Many solve the problem by contributing financially but letting the responsibility for the emotional and moral development of the children fall upon mother.

Maureen Green, in her book *Goodbye Father*\*, claims that 'the decline of the father may well be the best thing that has ever happened to girls.' Many feminist writers, she says, have found their voice because authoritarian fathers haven't been around to tell them that it is unladylike to shout. A strong father, she points out, can keep a son in necessary check; he can also easily squash a daughter and make her timid and lifeless. At the same time, Maureen Green stresses that an open-minded and loving relationship with father can lay the foundations for many of a girl's later sexual attitudes, and consequently for her success with men for the rest of their lives. Girls who get on well with their fathers, claims Ms Green, find marriage easier because they have had successful practice in dealing with a man.

With boys, the father's own character, the extent to which he has made a success of his own personal life, plus his ability to pass on the intangibles of happiness and optimism through an affectionate relationship with his son, make it easier for the boy to play a positive and adaptive male role in life. It is the quality of the relationship that counts. The father who does things with his son (whether it be fishing, walking, reading, talking or just listening to his offspring) is a better model of masculinity than the father who sits slumped in an armchair or who lies on a couch during his time in the house, watching television.

To my mind we are still, all of us, uncertain as to what fathering consists of — apart from begetting the child and paying the family bills. This uncertainty about, and neglect of, father is reflected in the literature on child development. In many well-known text books the word 'father' is missing from the index. This is not, in my opinion, to be the pattern for the future. I expect the father to play a much more active part in the upbringing of his children. The old simple, black and white roles have gone; sexual stereotypes are disappearing; the new roles within the family *will* be more confusing but they will allow more freedom to both mothers and fathers. They will allow of more choice to sons and daughters when they grow up. 'I'm going to be a really good cook when I grow up,' girls will say, 'like my daddy.' Why should we teach children in the home sexual stereotypes and roles that are out of date and unadaptive? Why should we prepare them for rigid, sex-based parts in the family drama that certainly will not be available when they are adult and try to make a family of their own?

\**Goodbye Father*, Maureen Green. Routledge & Kegan Paul, 1976.

The incidence of paternal deprivation in our society is striking, and so is the disrespect of many young people for their elders, for the church, the law, the government and other authoritarian institutions. Are the two linked? Has the decline of the father led to a decline in respect for any person, or institution, which may smack of authority? Do those young people who complain of feelings of rootlessness, alienation, isolation and loss suffer from the lack of emotional support which springs from not having, or not identifying with, a father-figure? How much of the delinquency of young people stems from the relentless diminution of paternal authority?

Whatever the answers, I would like to see a more varied and productive role for fathers within the home; a greater contribution from fathers in the neighbourhood to the lives of the young people in that neighbourhood (where not everybody has a father, we must learn to share and utilize more effectively the stable fathers that are around); father reinstated as an important part of family life. Nobody wants Old Jolyon Forsyte to make a comeback. At the same time, it would be useful if we all agreed that fathers are crucial to the emotional stability of young people. They don't have to be autocratic dictators. They should be themselves, contribute and care.

The decline of a paternal contribution (an emotional contribution, as well as a practical one) has led to a decline in family life. Fathers are puzzled, lost. We cannot do without them. We need to consider their contribution to family life most carefully, to consider the detrimental effects of paternal deprivation upon children and young adults. As one of my confused clinic children wrote to his absent father: 'Come back, dad. We need you.' How true. Fathers are necessary and, for those children who do not have a father, there must be help and support and a lively contribution from those families who are lucky enough to have both parents. 'When did you last see your father?' That is a question that would be unkindly asked of many children. It is a question that society ignores at its peril.

*Chapter Fourteen*

# Conversations With Teenagers

'The youth of this country is going to the dogs. They are selfish and think only of themselves.' We've all heard this kind of statement often enough. It's a generalization, and it's far too simple.

Below, I let ten teenagers speak for themselves. They show, in what they have to say, that today's teenagers are individuals, each with his or her own views on life. Their comments prove too, that teenagers are concerned with moral values and how people should behave towards one another.

Adults may be going to the dogs. I doubt whether teenagers are. They want something better. Here are their own observations:

HIGH IDEALS

Diane, seventeen, is an attractive brunette dressed in a white blouse, blue skirt, socks and sandals. When I interviewed her she had just finished her A-levels and hoped to go to university to study for a degree in agricultural botany.

Q. *'Tell me about yourself, and your ambitions.'*
A. 'Well, the main thing in my life is my belief in God. I am a Christian, a follower of Jesus Christ. What I'd really like to do is missionary work — to help people less fortunate than myself.

'I mean, this country's supposed to be Christian but it isn't, is it? Most of the adults I know are into material things, like getting a bigger freezer or a new dishwasher, but I want something different from that.

'You know, things are getting worse. Unless we all learn to respect each other more, and to respect the earth and it's resources, we're going to end up in a terrible mess. There seems to be a running down of society. People don't believe in anything any more, except getting bigger houses and bigger cars.

'I hope, like a lot of other young people, to marry and have kids, but only if it's God's plan. I believe in God as a person, as well as a spiritual force. I believe in the Devil too. Just like God, he's everywhere. You can see the works of the Devil all around you.

'Mind you, God will come out on top in the long run — he's already proved that by raising Jesus Christ from the dead.'

*Q. How long have you had your religious convictions?*

A. 'Since about the age of eight. When I was thirteen I began to think about it all more carefully and to read the bible regularly. I'm Church of England, Anglican Evangelical I think you'd call it, but I'm not completely happy with the Church of England. I sometimes think I might become a Methodist. The less fuss made about the trimmings — incense and chanting — the better. The Church has to get out and help people rather than be so respectably middle class.

'I didn't get any of my views from my parents. I worked them out for myself. The school didn't help. For example, our sex education was a farce: a few lessons on biology and that was all. Flowers, bird and bees. Then we had a talk on contraception. Nothing about ideals, loving people, relationships.

'A lot of blokes I meet expect me to go to bed with them but I won't. Some of them say: 'That's it, then'. Fine with me. God is the matchmaker and I hope he will lead me to somebody with the same beliefs as myself. I don't think I would let myself fall in love with somebody who did not have faith in God. I'm not intellectual, I don't want anybody clever, but somebody who is keen, like me, to follow God's purpose for the world. In my life I hope to be of use to people and to pass on something of what I believe to those around me, but only if they want to believe it too. I mean, if you don't believe in a God, in a power greater than yourself, what point is there to life?'

UNEMPLOYMENT

Len, eighteen, lives on Merseyside. He is six feet tall, and wears blue denim jeans, black shirt and a black leather jacket. Since leaving school at the age of sixteen he has never worked, except for one job in a glass fibre factory, which he had to leave since he is allergic to glass fibre and broke out into a skin rash which covered his entire body.

*Q. 'What's it like being unemployed?'*

A. 'You try it — it's terrible. I have to live on fourteen quid a week supplementary benefit. I give my mam six quid a week for my board and lodgings and, out of the rest, I buy clothes and everything else. I'm skint, flat broke, most of the time.

'I don't know if you've ever been to sign on at the dole. They're really nasty places — you queue up and nobody wants to know. There just aren't any jobs round here. People say: 'You could find work if you wanted to.' Believe me, I've tried and there's nothing going.

'My dad's been out of work for the last six months and we get on each other's nerves. I try and get out of the house as much as possible. Hang around outside the bookies or in the pub. It's rotten when you can't buy your mates a drink. You should see our pub at lunch-time, crowded out, just like a Saturday afternoon. Everyone's watching the racing on television. Daft, because nobody's got any money to bet.

'In school we had a careers master. He used to tell us about the different kinds of jobs — vocational guidance, like. The thing was he knew, and we knew, there were no jobs.

'It gets you down. You get this dole sickness — never wanting to do anything. I've got mates who stay in the house all day, doing nothing. How can you keep your self-respect like that?

'The worst thing is my sister and my girlfriend have both got jobs It's easier for women to find work. My girlfriend wants us to get engaged but what sort of a life would it be if we got married, and me on the dole and her working?

'I'll tell you, it was bad in the glass fibre factory and I wasn't sorry I had to leave but I'd rather do that then do nothing. It really gets you down, hanging about. I'm getting depressed at the moment and my dad and mam both get on to me at home. What am I supposed to do?

'There's thousands of young people like myself around here. They'd work all right, if they had jobs to go to. Try getting up in the morning, about ten to eleven o'clock, no money, nothing to do, nowhere to go except the pub, just hanging about. It's murder.

'The government should do something about it. I'm not clever but I'm good with my hands. My dad was an apprentice ship-wright when he left school. At least he had a chance to work. I've never had a chance. I want a proper job — a trade — like him. I'd like to get married and buy a house and have a family. What chance have I got?

'My girlfriend gets forty-odd pounds a week. She's got a good job. The whole thing gets me down. I'm not lazy. I'm willing to work. There just aren't any jobs going.

'What kind of a country is it that can't find work for the people who live in it? It's terrible. People who've got jobs, who go out to work every day, have no idea what it's like. I'm dying of boredom, honestly, I am.'

Q. 'What do you want most of all?'
A. 'I want a job and a decent life, like everybody else.'

ON BEING BLACK

Debbie, sixteen, is married to Ewan, twenty-one. They live in London. Debbie was born in this country, Ewan came at the age of seven, but the parents of both were born in the West Indies. Debbie has just left secondary school and has started work as an accountancy trainee.

Q. *'Debbie, how do you get on with your parents?'*
A. 'I'm lucky. We get on quite well. My parents are Muslim but they haven't insisted that I should be a Muslim. Some Muslim parents, you probably know, are very strict. They insist that their daughters are Muslim and they want a say in who the daughter marries — a big say.

'My father says: "If you can't hear, you have to feel." That means that you can only learn by your own experience. I respect him for his views. He tried hard to get his two daughters to become Muslim like himself but when we wouldn't he accepted it.

'I was taught Christianity at school and I suppose I'm half-Christian, half-atheist. I don't go to church or anything like that.'

Q. *'How did you get on at school?'*
A. 'Very well. I enjoyed it, and I got my O-levels. When I first went to secondary school there were some people who called me 'nigger'. I was shocked, and very upset, about that but you soon learn to ignore it.

I still have some white friends who I met at school. Most of my friends are black but there's a small circle of white people I'm friends with and I hope to meet a few more nice, white people now I'm at work.

'It's not easy being black in this country. There is prejudice against young black people. I think it's wrong that, when you're just waiting for a friend on the corner of the street or at a bus stop, a policeman, anyway in London, can come up to you and arrest you on a 'sus' charge.*

'That certainly doesn't do anything to improve racial relationships. There's good and bad people, black and white, but the sooner people realize that most black people are decent, law-abiding citizens, the better.

'Ewan is a teacher of Kung Fu. In London, there are a lot of aggressive people about, white and black. He teaches Kung Fu as self-defence. In some places he goes to, he only has to look at somebody and he'll be attacked. Everybody's competing, everybody's aggressive. It's awful really.

'Young black people have problems with unemployment. A lot of them haven't got jobs. They have problems with racial prejudice, and they have problems with their own parents.

'Usually, the parents' values are different from ours. Some of

*Suspicion of loitering with intent to commit a crime.

186

them were maybe brought up in Jamaica, and maybe very poor. They had to scrape around for a living. A child would be beaten, hard, for not eating all his food at the table.

'We can't take their advice any more. Things are different for us. When black parents say to their teenage kids things like "when I was young" the kids shut their ears. The world has changed. We have our own problems and we have to solve them ourselves.

'Take Ewan. When he came to this country from Jamaica at the age of seven he had never seen snow before. The first time he saw snow he was terrified. He had to adapt to a completely different way of life. The gap between him and his parents grows bigger as the years go by. He's learned to be hard because, in this country, you have to be hard, use your wits.

'Don't get me wrong. I'm an optimist as far as I am concerned but there are a lot of young black people with no real future. A lot haven't got jobs. Some of them become pick-pockets, 'sticks boys', and fight back that way. Others keep trying to get a job but without success.'

Q. *'What happens to them?'*
A. 'They become depressed and fed up, then angry. Then, the next thing is they become aggressive, or steal, and end up on the wrong side of the law. Being young, and black, in this country, the odds are stacked up against you'.

THE WORLD OF WORK (1)

Sean, nineteen, lives in a large, industrial town in the north of England. He works in a factory, on shift work. He is a pleasant, friendly youngster dressed in a flowered shirt and grey trousers.

Q. *'Sean, tell me about your job.'*
A. 'Well, I don't know what to say. It's a bit pathetic. I work in a canning factory. We can vegetables — peas, mostly. My job is to cook the peas in these big vats. When they're cooked you open the bottom of the vat and the peas pour into the cans, so many at a time. It's all automatic. Dead boring.

'There's women in our place and their job is to pick out the stones and bits of pea-pods as the peas go along this conveyor belt. Fancy doing that all day. It'd drive you mad. They seem to enjoy it though, always yattering to each other. Some of them, mind you, are as thick as two short planks.

'Working in a factory is no joke. There's a bloke here and he's been here twenty years. He pinches something from the factory every night before he goes home, even if it's only a bolt or a screw. It's a wonder the bloody place hasn't fallen down. Theft of the Day, we call him.

'Believe me, I never eat peas. I can't stand the sight of them. When there's no peas, it's something else. We can meat as well, in the other factory. That's even worse.

'Still, it's a job isn't it? £70 a week, plus overtime. I'm not grumbling. Work isn't my life anyway. At the weekend, I go to see my team, scarf over my wrist, and have a bit of fun. I go away to see them if I'm not working. The away games are best. Sometimes, there's bother but I don't mind. I can look after myself.

'In the job, if you're on early shift it means that you finish about two o'clock in the afternoon and you've got the rest of the day to yourself. I've got a loft, and six pigeons — racers and I spend most of the time with them. You ask me about pigeons, I'll tell you anything you want to know.

'Or, football; I'm daft about football. I've been following my team since I was seven so I'm one of their best supporters.'

Q. *'Do you get any satisfaction from your work?'*
A. 'You must be joking. With steam in your face all day, and the smell of peas, or something worse, what satisfaction is there in that? It's just a job. The blokes are OK and some of the women are a good laugh. I'd rather do it than be on the dole. When you've worked in a factory for three years you come to hate the sight of it.

'I can't wait to clock off, get back to the loft. Then, there's weekends. It's not a bad life. What more is there?'

THE WORLD OF WORK (2)

Paula, eighteen, is a smartly-dressed blonde. She is wearing a peach-coloured blouse, fawn skirt and fashionable shoes with stiletto heels. She has worked for two years as a cashier in a bank in a town on the south coast.

Q. *'Paula, what did you think of school?'*
A. 'I always wanted to go to the grammar school but I failed the eleven plus mainly because I was so nervous. Then, at secondary school, they put me in a B stream when all my friends were in the A stream, so I never really did my best in school.

'Anyway, school is a bit peculiar. I want to get married and have a family but, at school, you had to choose between Housecraft and Childcare. I chose Housecraft. I didn't learn anything about children.

'Also, there was no advice about choosing a career. The choice of a job, how to look after children — those were the two most important things as far as I was concerned. We had no advice on either of them.

'It's much better when you've left school. In the bank where I work there are people of all ages. You can make friends with people of the same age and with people older than yourself. Everybody's very friendly. The main thing is they treat you as an adult, not a child.

'The manager gives you responsibility and, because people treat you as an adult, you respect them and you act responsibly. The customers are interesting, too. We get all sorts of people coming into the bank, some nice, some not. It gives you a lot of experience with different types of person.

'I was glad to get out of school. The job has made me more confident in myself and less dependent on my parents. I mean, I give my mother £10 a week for my keep but the rest is mine to do what I like with.

'I spend too much on clothes — about £40 a month — but I can't resist them. And (laughs) I spend too much time drinking in pubs. All my friends eat and drink too much. It's very bad for you really but I like going out — I can't bear to stay in at night — and if you go out you tend either to eat or drink, don't you?

'Don't get the wrong impression. I do save some money. This year I saved up and myself and a girlfriend went to America. It was terrific. I love meeting people and seeing different places.

'I'm having a good time really but I want, eventually, to settle down and have a family. Two children. I've got it all worked out. Nice house. Kind considerate husband. One boy. One girl. The man I marry must be someone who doesn't spend money carelessly and a man who shows me respect. And he mustn't be tattooed. I can't stand men who have tattoos over them.

'I think you should have sexual experience before you settle down, as much as you can, but I don't believe in sleeping with every Tom, Dick or Harry. I don't think many girls now are virgins by the time that they get married. I don't think it's necessary to be one.

'You were asking about work. I love my job. I like getting dressed up to go to work in the morning — everybody's fairly smart in our place and I love the job itself. I don't find it boring serving the customers. You get to know them and it's very interesting really.

'The happiest day of my life was when I left school. I never did justice to myself the whole time I was there. I'm really doing well in the bank, because people treat me like a grown-up person, not an idiot.

'Mind you, I have expensive tastes. My favourite drink is a Martini, or a Cinzano. My father says I have champagne tastes on a beer income, but I manage. When you're at work, you decide who you want to be. When I was at school, other people decided what I had to be. What right have they got to do that?'

*Q. 'As a matter of interest, do you believe in God?'*
A. 'No. You can have a reasonable society without God, and without religion. It's just common sense. People have to treat each other with courtesy and respect.

'Take the Bible. It's like a fairy-tale. It isn't really true, is it? Mind you, with my own children I shan't stop them from going to church if they want to but I won't be pushing religion down their throats like they did to us at school.'
*Q. 'So you really like your job?'*
A. 'I love it. At the week-ends we go to discos. I'm into all sorts of music; I like Fleetwood Mac, Genesis, New Wave, Rock, David Bowie, soul, Diana Ross (that's soul) and even reggae. We have a great time at weekends. Some people don't like it when Monday morning comes around but I don't mind a bit, because I like my work and I like the people I work with. They appreciate me, I do my job well and I appreciate them.'

PRIVILEGE

Alastair is eighteen. He lives on the outskirts of a small town in the West Country. He is a smartly dressed boy, in blue blazer and grey flannels. We chat on the patio, facing a large and very beautiful garden. The house is enormous and set in about six acres of land.

*Q. 'Alastair, can you tell me a little about yourself?'*
A. 'Well, I went to a prep school, not a famous one but a local one and did quite well, I suppose. I liked it there — they made you work, and I'm a fairly scholastic type really. Then, I passed my Common Entrance exam to public school and enjoyed that too. I got nine As at O-level and three As at A-level which is pretty reasonable I suppose. After the holidays I shall be going up to University which I'm looking forward to enormously.

'I'm lucky in that I'm quite good at exams and, in fact, quite enjoy them. I've always known what I want to do.'
*Q. 'What are you aiming to do?'*
A. 'Well, I shall be reading for a law degree and then I hope to specialize in company law and try to get a job with a large international firm where there's a chance of getting on the board. I like the idea of being in business, and I like travel very much. As you know, my father's a doctor and I should hate to work in the same place, day-in, day-out, as he does.

'I suppose I'm pretty selfish, really. I don't think that any individuals can solve this country's problems so the best thing that any of us can do is to try to make the best of the gifts we have and try to make as much money as possible. There is no moral law, as

190

far as I know, about wanting to be wealthy.

'We're pretty well-off, I suppose, two cars and that sort of thing, but we pay a great deal of taxes and we contribute to the nation's wealth. I think that this country is heading for disaster if it spreads the notion that it's wrong to make money.

'The trouble is human motivation. When people work for themselves they work harder. The notion of the welfare state is based on a misreading of human nature − if you give people something for nothing they get the idea that the world owes them a living, they become lazy, and refuse to take responsibility for themselves.

'Take dad. He has a private practice besides his hospital work. He takes far more interest in his private patients but, then, he's bound to. He knows them personally, there aren't so many of them. How can you take an interest in hundreds of people who come to hospital, every year, who he doesn't know from Adam?

'Don't mistake what I'm saying. I'm not completely selfish − I've done my Duke of Edinburgh Award and that sort of thing. I do believe in helping others. I simply don't believe you can institutionalize kindness. I mean, these days they have paid, salaried, social workers. That's absolute nonsense. People who live in the same place should help each other, rather than pay others to be kind on their behalf.

'I'm not ashamed of living in a big house and having gone to boarding school. My father earned it, he studied hard and it's up to me to work as hard as he did and to forge out a career for myself. What's wrong with that? We are a great nation, or we were, and individual enterprise really mustn't be derided if we're going to keep our place in the world.

'I'm in the local youth club, at least when I'm home. I have a motor bike and I know most of the young people around here with bikes. I get on well with everybody. There's no snobbery around here and no comparison of who is rich and who is poor. We all get on well together. Perhaps it's because we don't have trade unions in the village − everything that the trade unions say is based on greed and envy.

'I'm just like any other teenager. I like rock music and soul. I wear jeans. I like discos. The only thing is that my family is a bit more wealthy than most of the young people in this area. I don't see that that's a crime. I just think I'm very lucky to have such good parents.'

PHYSICAL HANDICAP

Tracey, sixteen, is visually handicapped. She suffers from congenital cataracts and nystagmus (or, as Tracey put it: 'My eyes wobble about'. She is an attractive, slim girl with a lively personality, wearing a long flowered dress, and smart shoes.

*Q. 'Can you tell me something about yourself and about your handicap?'*
A. 'I went to an ordinary school when I was five, and liked it there. In those days, my parents didn't know there were special schools for partially sighted children and, anyway, I'd be very young to go away to special school.

'When I was eleven I was in hospital for a year which was very lonely. I had some sort of blood disease and they had to give me a lumbar puncture and to take my spleen out. It was horrible.

'When I got out, I went to middle school which I liked but when I went to secondary school the children used to bully me, or some of them. One day, I got knocked out in the corridor by a gang of boys.

'Some people at the school didn't like anybody who was different so they decided to pick on me which wasn't very nice. At the age of thirteen I went away to a special boarding school for blind and partially-sighted children.

'I loved it there. Everybody was very kind and they understood about people without much sight. They let us go out and tried to make us as independent as possible, but they did a lot for us; the teachers were like parents.

'The other children there were very friendly and I got to know everybody very quickly. I think boarding schools like that are much better for people like me.'
*Q. 'What are you going to do with your life?'*
A. 'At school I got five CSEs and I left last July so, in September, I'm going to the local College of Further Education to do a child care course. It's called the Preliminary Certificate in Residential Child Care. My ambition is to work with mentally handicapped children. I've always loved children. At one time I was going to be a nurse but my sight isn't good enough for that. Working with the mentally handicapped you have to have lots of patience and I've got plenty of that. I've spent the summer holidays working in a unit for mentally handicapped youngsters and I enjoyed it a lot.

'I want to live as normal a life as possible. I've got a boyfriend — he's not handicapped, and I'd like to marry and have three children. At least, if they're visually handicapped like me I'll know what to do to help them.'
*Q. 'How does your handicap affect you?'*
A. 'Well, I can't see in the dark and, too, when I go into shops it can be difficult. If you put things up to your face they sometimes think you are shoplifting and I have to explain that I'm partially-

sighted and have to put things near my eyes to see them properly.

'If I go out with my white cane people — old people especially — come up and help but they don't know what I really want. 'I'm going to the High Street,' I tell them. They cross me over the road. 'I'm all right now,' I tell them. But then they follow me, make too much fuss, and grab me if they think I'm going to walk into the nearest lamp-post.

'I'd love to learn to drive but I can't because of my sight. Another thing. When I'm watching television nobody else can see because I have to get so near to the tele. I can read all right, though. We have low visual aids (shows me one). There is a magnifying glass here, for the right eye and the left eye is blocked out. I can't see out of my left eye.

'I like to knit — blankets and things — and I like to read — those are my two main hobbies. I do the shopping for mum now that I'm home and I'll get the bus to the college. I've been having some sessions with the blind mobility officer so I shan't have any difficulty in getting about.

'The main thing for visually handicapped children is for their parents to know of the facilities that exist for them. At my boarding school there was an assessment unit for visually handicapped three-year-olds. Things are getting better. There is more knowledge of the handicap now, and more help.

'I like the idea of special schools. When I was little I could hardly see at all and I had to try to cope in an ordinary school where the teachers were nice but didn't know anything about being partially-sighted. In some of the secondary schools the older boys have got the wrong idea about being handicapped. They tease you and keep on at you.

'I'm very normal really. What I want to do is a satisfying job and I think work with mentally handicapped children will be a useful thing to do, and personally satisfying. Then, I'd like to get married and have a family of my own. I adore children and I'm looking forward to learning a lot about them when I go to college.

'I'm grateful to the school I went to. I got my qualifications. Also, they taught us independence. The only thing I'm at all self-conscious about is when I go out with the blind mobility officer in the daytime and they're just coming out of school and some of the older ones shout: 'Look at her. She's definitely blind now.' You have to do it, though, learn to cross roads and traffic lights, I mean.'

MOTOR BIKES

Eddy, nineteen, is an impressive, somewhat fierce-looking youngster. He is six feet tall and wears a black leather jacket, crimson sweat scarf, old denim trousers and motor-cycle boots. His leather jacket is covered in metal badges — on the right, the names of various motor bikes; on the left, the motor bike rallies which he has attended. We talk in a pub — the local 'bikers' meeting place. On the back of his jacket is painted, in bright blue, the single word: REBEL.

*Q. 'Can you tell me something about yourself and about your philosophy of life — what you think about things in general?'*
A. 'Philosophy of life? I can tell you that all right. Tomorrow, you could be dead, right? So you've got to live for today. At thirty, I reckon you're past it, well, most people are, so you've got to enjoy yourself while you're young. Mind you, there's a bloke who comes to bike rallies and he's well over sixty and he's really into bikes, he can tell you all about the old days, about bikes in the First World War, an' that. He's a good bloke, but he's an exception. Most people who are past thirty are straights* and past it.'
*Q. 'Can you tell me something about motor bikes?'*
A. 'I live for bikes. I spend about twenty quid a week on mine. It's an old Norton and it's worth a lot of money. See, what you do is read the *Motor Cycle News* to find out if there's a rally on somewhere and you get there — sometimes it's on the south coast, sometimes up in Scotland — wherever it is we're there.

'On the way there we meet in a pub and on the way back we meet in a different pub. They have to be pubs where they like bikers. Some pubs you go in, they throw you out or call the police before you've got over the door. Just because we wear leathers people think we're Hell's Angels, or out for bother, but most bikers are polite and friendly. Even the Hell's Angels don't look for bother. It's only when people come around looking for trouble that they turn nasty.

'I've been interested in bikes since I was seven. I'm a motor mechanic but I don't like cars — waste of time they are, and expensive. With bikes, you get to know people, we all stick together, and they're a good crowd. Once you know someone is interested in bikes it gives you something to talk about. Most of us repair our own bikes and we know a lot about them.

'At the rally, it's great. We have a beer tent. If it's a big rally, there's a group and a disco. I take my girlfriend. She's into bikes too. She's eighteen, and she's got a Yamaha 250. You look in the car park outside any college and see all the bikes — young people are into bikes more than cars. I'll bet you, when petrol gets short, everybody'll be into bikes.

*i.e. living in a conventional way, in ways approved of by the majority of the community.

194

'I'm in a local club. We meet on Wednesdays. It's great down there. A really good crowd. What people don't understand is that, when you're on a bike, you're in the fresh air, out in the open. You can get away every weekend, go anywhere. I hate television. I never watch it. I'm either on the bike or mending it.

'My old man and my mum are straights. They don't like bikes, and they don't like the way I dress but it's got nothing to do with them, has it? You get to the rally, get a few vodkas inside you, see the different kinds of bikes there and you really feel life's worth living. We have an enjoyable time, don't we, instead of sitting round watching the goggle box?

'You go along a road, you pass someone on a Harley, or an old bike, or any other bike. They wave to you. Sometimes, you get off the bike and have a yatter. It's friendship, see? That's what it's all about. Maybe the police, in some places, cause hassle. Older people look at you in your leathers as though you were crap. We're not crap.

'Bikes are the greatest things going. People that ride bikes have got their values straight. They enjoy themselves, have a good time, and they don't cause any harm to anybody else. You should come to a rally sometime. See how people can get together without any hastle, and enjoy themselves. Until you've tried, you don't know.'

DISCIPLINE

Ian is eighteen. He is at a police training college and intends to make his career in the police force. He is a tall and well-built young man with ginger hair, a freckled face and a ready smile.

Q. *'What made you join the police?'*
A. 'Well, I've always liked an outdoor life. I'd hate to be cooped up in an office all day, and in the force there's plenty of variety — different jobs, you get posted to different parts of the country — and that suits me fine. Also, you get a good cross section of people in the police. I suppose you get the odd creep, just like anywhere else, but I haven't met any so far.

'I got five O-levels at school — three Os and two CSE grade 1s — and, with the police you get plenty of opportunity for further study.'
Q. *'Can you tell me a little bit about yourself personally and how you see things at the present time in Britain?'*
A 'I'll tell you one thing: I believe in discipline. If you let everybody do just as they like nobody gets anything done.

'I mean, you take this country. When you go out anywhere, or go on a train, there's litter everywhere. Rubbish all over the place. Drunks staggering about in broad daylight. I don't believe in that.

'When I was at school I had friends whose parents couldn't care less what they did. All they — their parents — wanted to do was to come home, collapse, and watch the tele. There were girls in our village, thirteen and fourteen, who used to get smashed out of their minds on booze. That can't be right.

'It's not only, say, in the family. There's no discipline in industry either. You've got trade unions and bosses cutting each others' throats and firms going bust. If they worked together, they'd both have more money.

'Look at criminals. I'd build work camps for them, not just put them in prison. If somebody does wrong he has to be punished, and he has to pay back society for his crime. These days, we're too soft. It just encourages people to go wrong.

'Look at the hippies. They went down the drain, didn't they? They had no rules, no discipline. You can't run a country, a family, or anything else, without rules that everybody sticks to. Otherwise, everybody goes a bit barmy.

'I mean, when these football hooligans have a go at each other, or when you get marches, the National Front and that, the police have to keep order. They're in the middle, and people soon shout if it affects them. Most policemen are just ordinary people like myself, doing a job. Say what you like about them, they're necessary. People criticize the police until they've been burgled, or beaten up, or mugged, then they change their tune.

'This country needs more discipline. Things have to be stricter. It's only common sense. You can't let people do as they like, especially kids.

'Anyway, with the police training I'll get, I can go elsewhere if things get really bad. I wouldn't mind going to Hong Kong or Bermuda, or New Zealand. I like sport. I'm not into pop, rock and all that. I'd rather have a good game of rugby than go to a pop concert. Everybody's gone soft, young people especially. It's the fault of the parents. They're supposed to set a good example.

'Things would be all right if everybody knuckled down, worked hard and pulled together. I don't expect they will though. I don't honestly give much for this country's chances.

'Not that I mind. I expect, in ten years time, I'll be in New Zealand, or somewhere, out of it. Over there I'd have a better chance of building a better life for myself. Look at this lot [we are sitting in a bus station which is littered with empty cigarette packets, cigarette ends, ice-cream cartons and other detrius of living]. Don't you think people would have a bit more self-respect than make this place look like a dump?

'As I said, nobody cares. Nobody bothers. You can't get anywhere like that. The country seems to be going down the Swannee. You can't expect the police to do anything with that lot

196

[he points to a crowd of young, scruffily-dressed young people at a bus stop]. They don't know the meaning of the word discipline. They've never had any.'

MAKING ONE'S MARK

Litsa is sixteen. She is a very attractive girl with huge brown eyes, black curly hair and high cheekbones. She is casually dressed in a wide-shouldered fawn jacket, denims and sandals. She has just left school (a large, mixed comprehensive) and is due to go, after the summer holidays, to a college of further education to study drama.

A. 'Can you tell me something about school?'
A. 'Well, I'm not brainy at all and I can't say I liked school very much. I liked some of the other kids and some of the men teachers. I didn't seem to get on with the women teachers at all [laughs]. What I didn't take to was the way they treated you all the same. You were an object. In that place, it was so big, you weren't anyone really.

'There were exceptions. I used to sing in the school choir and the music teacher said I had a good voice and he was very interested in jazz so I got interested in jazz singing. I've sung on television, and in local pubs. I love singing and I love jazz.

'The music teacher was great. He took an interest in me as a person but most of the teachers didn't care about us and there were loads of lessons when the teacher didn't even turn up.

'I liked the drama teacher, too. I was in the plays and the musicals at school. Everyone says I'm a theatrical type, always acting, and I suppose I am. I love acting even more than singing. That's really what I want to do. When I've done two years at the college here I want to go to drama school in London and work on the stage — in plays and musicals, I hope.

'I'd like to act and to sing. To do both would be magic. School wasn't a complete waste of time. I got my CSEs to go to college. Now I have to get four O-levels so that I can get a grant to go to London when I've finished at college. My parents can't afford to pay for me.'
Q. 'Did you learn anything apart from drama and music at school?'
A. 'Not a lot [laughs]. We had RE lessons which were supposed to be about human relationships but the only thing I can remember they said was that you had to be a virgin until you married. We had sex education from the biology teacher but that was mainly personal hygiene and diseases and how important it was to be a virgin [laughs], I think they're a bit behind the times.

'I think parents influence you more than teachers. I go with my mum to the Quakers Meeting House and I do believe in God — I need somebody to talk to — but I don't believe all that stuff about it being a sin to swear or to have sex with someone you love. All that's adults trying to put you off, make you frightened. It's a load of codswallop.

'The main thing in life is for parents to put their children first and look after them properly. But I believe that parents have to share — the man has to do his bit in the house or it just doesn't work. I do believe in divorce. I don't think two people should stay together if they don't love each other. People should promise, when they get married to love, honour and cherish each other until they stop liking each other. Then they should split up and go their own way.

'The adults I don't like are people who put me down. If they expect a lot from you, they get a lot. If they're always criticizing you just stop trying. I can't stand adults who make their homes immaculate and are always tidying up. Houses are to live in, not to keep polishing.'

Q. 'What is your ambition?'

A. 'I just want to act. I don't want to be a star or anything like that. If I could act somewhere, with a small rep theatre, I'd think of that as success. I really do think you have to find something that you're good at, something that you can do and other people praise you for. Otherwise you just drop out. Everybody needs to be good at something, don't they? Everybody needs a bit of success.'

Good luck to them, today's teenagers. They really are, when you get to know them, a marvellous group of young people. Let's hope that we, as adults, don't fail them. They deserve the best that we are capable of. After all, they are the next generation of parents and they are depending on us for a good example.

Don't let them down. They deserve better than that.